The Wrath of the Lamb!

Stanley O.Lotegeluaki

authorHOUSE®

AuthorHouse™
1663 Liberty Drive
Bloomington, IN 47403
www.authorhouse.com
Phone: 1-800-839-8640

Published by AuthorHouse   05/02/12.

ISBN: 9781468594621 (sc)
ISBN: 9781468594638 (e)

Contents

INTRODUCTION

1. The king shall joy in thy strength, O Lord; and in thy salvation how greatly shall he rejoice!
2. Thou hast given him his heart's desire, and hast not withholden the request of his lips. Selah.
3. For thou preventest him with the blessings of goodness: thou settest a crown of pure gold on his head.
4. He asked life of thee, and thou gavest it him, even length of days for ever and ever.
5. His glory is great in thy salvation: honour and majesty hast thou laid upon him.
6. For thou hast made him most blessed for ever: thou hast made him exceeding glad with thy countenance.
7. For the king trusteth in the Lord, and through the mercy of the most High he shall not be moved.
8. Thine hand shall find out all thine enemies: thy right hand shall find out those that hate thee.
9. Thou shalt make them as a fiery oven in the time of thine anger: the Lord shall swallow them up in his wrath, and the fire shall devour them.
10. Their fruit shalt thou destroy from the earth, and their seed from among the children of men.

This next verse says much about the Invisible war between Satan and his demons.

Psalm 21:11-13.

11. For they intended evil against thee: <u>they imagined a mischievous device, which they are not able to perform.</u>
12. Therefore shalt thou make them turn their back, when thou shalt make ready thine arrows upon thy strings against the face of them.
13. Be thou exalted, Lord, in thine own strength: so will we sing and praise thy power.

Psalms 37

1. Fret not thyself because of evildoers, neither be thou envious against the workers of iniquity.
2. For they shall soon be cut down like the grass, and wither as the green herb.
3. Trust in the Lord, and do good; so shalt thou dwell in the land, and verily thou shalt be fed.
4. Delight thyself also in the Lord: and he shall give thee the desires of thine heart.
5. Commit thy way unto the Lord; trust also in him; and he shall bring it to pass.
6. And he shall bring forth thy righteousness as the light, and thy judgment as the noonday.

7. Rest in the Lord, and wait patiently for him: fret not thyself because of him who prospereth in his way, because of the man who bringeth wicked devices to pass.

8. Cease from anger, and forsake wrath: fret not thyself in any wise to do evil.

9. For evildoers shall be cut off: but those that wait upon the Lord, they shall inherit the earth.

10. For yet a little while, and the wicked shall not be: yea, thou shalt diligently consider his place, and it shall not be.

11. But the meek shall inherit the earth; and shall delight themselves in the abundance of peace.

12. The wicked plotteth against the just, and gnasheth upon him with his teeth.

13. The Lord shall laugh at him: for he seeth that his day is coming.

14. The wicked have drawn out the sword, and have bent their bow, to cast down the poor and needy, and to slay such as be of upright conversation.

15. Their sword shall enter into their own heart, and their bows shall be broken.

16. A little that a righteous man hath is better than the riches of many wicked.

17. For the arms of the wicked shall be broken: but the Lord upholdeth the righteous.

18. The Lord knoweth the days of the upright: and their inheritance shall be for ever.

19. They shall not be ashamed in the evil time: and in the days of famine they shall be satisfied.

20. But the wicked shall perish, and the enemies of the Lord shall be as the fat of lambs: they shall consume; into smoke shall they consume away.

21. The wicked borroweth, and payeth not again: but the righteous sheweth mercy, and giveth.

22. For such as be blessed of him shall inherit the earth; and they that be cursed of him shall be cut off.

23. The steps of a good man are ordered by the Lord: and he delighteth in his way.

24. Though he fall, he shall not be utterly cast down: for the Lord upholdeth him with his hand.

25. I have been young, and now am old; yet have I not seen the righteous forsaken, nor his seed begging bread.

26. He is ever merciful, and lendeth; and his seed is blessed.

27. Depart from evil, and do good; and dwell for evermore.

28. For the Lord loveth judgment, and forsaketh not his saints; they are preserved for ever: but the seed of the wicked shall be cut off.

29. The righteous shall inherit the land, and dwell therein for ever.

30. The mouth of the righteous speaketh wisdom, and his tongue talketh of judgment.

31. The law of his God is in his heart; none of his steps shall slide.

32. The wicked watcheth the righteous, and seeketh to slay him.

33. The Lord will not leave him in his hand, nor condemn him when he is judged.

34. Wait on the Lord, and keep his way, and he shall exalt thee to inherit the land: when the wicked are cut off, thou shalt see it.

35. I have seen the wicked in great power, and spreading himself like a green bay tree.

36. Yet he passed away, and, lo, he was not: yea, I sought him, but he could not be found.

37. Mark the perfect man, and behold the upright: for the end of that man is peace.

38. But the transgressors shall be destroyed together: the end of the wicked shall be cut off.

39. But the salvation of the righteous is of the Lord: he is their strength in the time of trouble.
40. And the Lord shall help them, and deliver them: he shall deliver them from the wicked, and save them, because they trust in him.

The great tribulation is over. Satan's camp has been attacked by Jesus Christ with His army the Church. The Catholic's were the first wave to surround and swarm into Satan's camp. They went over the fence first. They got stopped by the layers of wires over the ages, by mines, "foo" gas (burn't at the stake) and machine gun fire from the enemy. They were stopped by the worship of Mary, the belief of purgatory, the inquisition, the selling of indulgences and wars etc.

Then Jesus sent in the second wave- the Protestants. They attacked and assaulted violently Satans camp further in. They destroyed Satan's supplies and took most of Satan's camp. But they were stopped by enemy fire with conformity- the acceptance of homosexuals, abortion, adultery and fornication etc.

Now Jesus is sending in the Third Wave who will completely wipe out Satans command post. The Third Wave are Christians who ate the "Refreshing" and believe in the Bibles version of the collapse of the universe and life before the big bang. They entered Satan's command post and killed the enemy. Now the war is over. Jesus is coming. The Return of the King.

Thats how the Tribulation was fought. The earth is ours. Jerusalem will be the Capital city of Jesus.

THE BANNER - THE DOCTRINE OF THE SECOND COMING.

THE THIRD WAVE.

THE NEW CHRISTIANITY. THE LEADING EDGE OF CHRISTIAN DEVELOPMENT. WE ARE GOING INTO SPACE- TO CONQUER THE STARS WITH JESUS WHEN HE COMES BACK AT THE SECOND COMING.

Christians existed before the Big Bang. We lived with Jesus in peace in a kingdom called the Kingdom of the King of Glory. (before the Big bang, before the goats and Satan were created). Then we Christians all volunteered for the Invisible War to be fought in this universe on a planet called earth. That is why we are here. That war has been fought and the Bible is the history of it. At the Second Coming which is in my lifetime, Jesus will come back. Then Jesus is going to lead the human race into space, to conquer the stars with Christ Technology and Angel Technology. Satan and his goats, the Beast angel and demons will be thrown into the Bottomless Pit while the goat people will be "taken" to comfortable hell for 40 billion years +/- or the 1000 Christ years. 40 billion years from now, or in 1000 Christ years, WWIII will be fought in spaceships against the Beast 666, Satan, demons and goats when they are rereleased into Christ's perfect 1000 year reign or spacekingdom. That is when Armageddon is fought, not now before the Second Coming. Armageddon is after the 1000 years of Christ's reign, it will be fought when the universe is in Blueshift, when the core of the collapsing universe exists or as Christians call it the "Lake of fire" (II Peter 3:7).

After the war the goats and Satan will be thrown into the Lake of fire and we Christians will live in peace until the universe finishes imploding. We Christians will be given a New Heaven and a New earth or universe to live in. Actually the nations will be given billions of universes to live in.

3

Read all of my books to see the entire scenario of the Life before the Big Bang, the Invisible War and the collapse of the universe and the New Christianity. We are the Third Wave. The Catholics were the first wave Jesus sent in, and they discomfited Satans camp. Then Jesus sent in the Second Wave, the Protestants and they tormented Satans camp and now Jesus is sending in the Third Wave, StarChildren who believe in Life before the Big Bang, the Invisible War and the Collapse of the universe doctrine and they will wipe out Satan's command post completely. Jesus will soon return to give the First, Second and Third Wave medals at the Second Coming. Thus the end of the Invisible War for a 1000 years.

Matthew 24:28:

"For wheresoever the Carcase is, there will the eagles be gathered together"

The Eagles are Jesus and satan. They hover over a Carcase- a born again Christian who has died or crucified his flesh in the cross of Jesus (Gospel of Paul in Romans). Every born again Christian is a Carcase, but this special individual was to welcome Christ. And the happenings of Mt 24 depended on his decisions and Christs decisions. Jesus deleted the war of the Second Coming and the Carcase agreed. Thats why there is no war before the Second Coming- it will be in 40 billion years. The sand of the sea in Revelation chpt thirteen is time. Each grain is a year. How many grains on the seashore? Billions- so WWIII is 40 billions years away- also the Lake of fire existed during that time for the false prophet to be thrown in it. They co-existed. That can only happen in Blueshift- when this finite universe of ours is collapsing. They co-existed. False prophet and Lake of fire. So WWIII is 40 billion +/- years from now. So there will be no war in our times. Thats why Jesus inserted Mt 24:28. but some bibles say vultures and other strange stuff. Dont tamper with the Bible.

- Encyclopedia World Book 1988
- The Invisible War. By Dr. D. Grey Barnhouse, Martyr and hero of the Lord.
- Sit, Walk, Stand. By Watchman Nee, Martyr and hero of Christianity.
- Pastor Gong Shengliang. Martyr and hero of Chrisitanity.
- CINDY SONGHER MARTYR KILLED BY SATAN, ANTICHRIST AND FROGS.
- PEOPLE KILLED IN RWANDA, BURUNDI, SUDAN, CONGO, CAMBODIA.
- WWII, ARMENIAN MASSACRE, VIETNAM, WWI -ALL WARS ARE
- CREDITED AS PARTCIPANTS IN THE INVISIBLE WAR AND ARE
- THE REASON FOR BURNING SATAN, AND THE WRATH OF THE LAMB!

"VENGEANCE IS MINE SAYS THE LORD"

Isaiah 31:

4. For thus hath the Lord spoken unto me, Like as the lion and the young lion roaring on his prey, when a multitude of shepherds is called forth against him, he will not be afraid of their voice, nor abase himself for the noise of them: so shall the Lord of hosts come down to fight for mount Zion, and for the hill thereof.
5. As birds flying, so will the Lord of hosts defend Jerusalem; defending also he will deliver it; and passing over he will preserve it.

Isaiah 30: 30.

And the Lord shall cause his glorious voice to be heard, and shall shew the lighting down of his arm, with the indignation of his anger, and with the flame of a devouring fire, with scattering, and tempest, and hailstones.

CHAPTER ONE
40 BILLION YEARS OF PAIN

Satan is a liar and he lied to his demons. This book is written for his demons to see through Satan's lies- so they the demons can be better prepared or steel themselves to spend 40 billion 800 million years being burned in the Bottomless pit. After the Bottomless pit ordeal they shall be visited and they will perform WWIII for God- then after being used, they will spend eternity in the Lake of fire forever. The Lake of fire is the core of the collapsed universe- hot stars and fiery galaxies smashed together. Very hot!

One of the lies Satan told his demons is - "that which does not kill you, will make you stronger"- that term or idea came from Satan to help his demons. They thought they only had to spend a 1000 years in hell. Actually Satan was supposed to go into the Bottomless pit alone while his angels went to hell to torture the poor humans. Also as a safety measure, if the time came to be burned, Satan and his demons could just surrender to God and no one would be burned. But surrender is not an option. God promised to burn them and God does not lie.

Actually lets start with the Second Coming. Satan had told his demons that there would be a war where the antiChrist would take over the world for them and they would build an army to fight Jesus as He returned for the Second Coming. That is a lie even the Church believed.

I explained in detail in other books how WWIII was deleted and postponed by the Carcase for 40 billion +/- years. Everything hinged on II Peter 3:7

II Peter 3:7

II Peter 3:7- *as the lake of fire the universe will burn men and not rexplode.*

"7. But the heavens and the earth, which are now, by the same word are kept in store, reserved unto fire against the day of judgment and perdition of ungodly men."

Peter said that the whole universe will be used to burn the wicked.

We can also deduce from the Bible that the universe is going to collapse. That there is enough dark matter- just enough to collapse the universe but not enough for a " bounce". It will permanently lay in a state of collapse forever as the lake of fire just as Einstien predicted.

Isaiah 51:6

6. Lift up your eyes to the heavens, and look upon the earth beneath: for the heavens shall vanish away like smoke, and the earth shall wax old like a garment, and they that dwell therein shall die in like manner: but my salvation shall be for ever, and my righteousness shall not be abolished.

Psalm 102:25-27.

"Of old hast thou laid the foundation of the earth: and the heavens are the work of thy hands. 26 They shall perish, but thou shalt endure: yea, all of them shall wax old like a garment; as a vesture shalt thou change them, and they shall be changed. 27: But thou art the same, and thy years shall have no end.

Mathew 24:35

35. Heaven and earth <u>shall pass away,</u> but my words shall not pass away.

Luke 21:33

"Heaven and earth shall pass away..."

II Peter 3:7

- as the lake of fire the universe will burn men and not rexplode.
7. But the heavens and the earth, which are now, by the same word are kept in store, reserved unto fire against the day of judgment and perdition of ungodly men.

II Peter 3:10

10. But the day of the Lord will come as a thief in the night; in the which the heavens shall pass away with a great noise, and the elements shall melt with fervent heat, the earth also and the works that are therein shall be burned up.

II Peter 3:12

12. Looking for and hasting unto the coming of the day of God, wherein the heavens being on fire shall be dissolved, and the elements shall melt with fervent heat?

Hebrews 1:10-11.

"..., AND THE HEAVENS ARE THE WORKS OF THINE HANDS: 11: THEY SHALL PERISH, BUT THOU REMAINEST; AND THEY SHALL WAX OLD AS DOTH A GARMENT."
Just as Einstein guessed there wii be no bounce for our present particular universe. This verse in Revelation says no place was found for our universe so it was used to burn the wicked as II Peter 3:7 notes.

Revelation 20:11

"And I saw a great white throne, and Him that sat on it, from whose face the earth and the heaven fled away; and there was found no place for them."

Concerning WWIII

WWIII is in 40 billion AD.

Christianity is superior to Islam, Buddhism , Hinduism, Communism and the religion of Science for the Bible spoke of the collapse of the universe and that the universe is closed thousands of years ago in king David's time, Isaiah's time, Matthew, Mark, Luke, II Peter, I Corinthians and Revelation all say the universe is going to collapse, but science is just finding out today by sending inquiring satellites into space. Most astronomers believe the universe is closed and will collapse into itself (World Book Encyclopedia 1988). Science and the Bible agree for once proving the Bible is Truth. But then the Bible spoke of the collapse of the universe first thousands of years ago before science.

Before we start on the next book I must tell you how I found out that WWIII is 40 billion years from now. It took a little physics and our knowledge that the universe is now expanding and that one day it will contract. Its contraction phase is called blue shift. Well we know the passages in the Bible that say the universe will contract and collapse. But did you know there is a verse that says this universe's burning core once it collapses will be used to burn the wicked ? Well II Peter 3:7 says so.

II Peter 3:7

> 7. But the heavens and the earth, which are now, by the same word are kept in store, reserved unto fire against the day of judgment and perdition of ungodly men.

Ungodly men will be burned in the Lake of fire. Now when will the Lake of fire exist ? A physicist will tell you it will come to exist in blue shift or once blue shift starts. That's in about 30-50 billion years from now. So the Lake of fire will definitely exist in 40 billion AD.

Now for the deduction. The false prophet was a man and he only could have only lived for 60 to 100 years, and he was thrown into the Lake of fire. So the Lake of fire existed in his days and the false prophet existed in the days when the universe was collapsing and had a fiery core- the Lake of fire. The only time that could happen is between 30-50 billion AD. So WWIII must have been 40 billion AD+/-. The false prophet and the lake of fire co-existed. They existed in the same time frame. That will happen in about 40 billion years from now- in Blueshift. That means all the chapters where the falseprophet is mentioned in the book of Revelation is 40 billion years from now. Chapters 13-20 Revelations. That whole war is not in our times, but Jesus will be back in my lifetime and our generation. WWIII is after the 1000 year reign of Christ. 1000 Christ years = 40 billion human years.

Read my books.

Book I. Christians existed before the big bang and will exist after the collapse of this universe.

Boo II. What the Bible says about the collapse of the universe.

Book III. Jesus Christ is Lord and is worshipped in infinte multiple universes- throughout infinity.

Book IV. The Holy Bible. " The Refreshing".

Book V. The Second Coming of Jesus Christ. The Return of the King.

Book VI. Intergalactic Jesus Christ Superstar.

Book VII. Africa: The Intergalactic Federation of African Tribes.

By Stanley O Lotegeluaki. Amazon.com, Barnes & Noble.com, Authorhouse.com

So that explains when WWIII will be, so that means the 1000 years will last until the universe is in blueshift, probably between 30 billion AD to 50 billion AD+/-.

Now why is God going to burn Satan and his demons ? It started with Abraham, actually it started with Eve, but Abraham's near sacrifice of Isaac got Satan thinking. What if people could sacrifice their children to him. So Satan tempted the nations to sacrifice their children to him- the Canaanites did it and Israel did it in the valley of Tophet. In Isaiah God says Satan is fighting the Church as it whips Satan with the praises of God. And God starts the fires of the Bottomless pit with the breath of His mouth. "Tophet" is remembered.

Isaiah 30:31-33.

31. For through the voice of the Lord shall the Assyrian be beaten down, which smote with a rod.
32. And in every place where the grounded staff shall pass, which the Lord shall lay upon him, it shall be with tabrets and harps: and in battles of shaking will he fight with it
33 For Tophet is ordained of old; yea, for the king it is prepared; he hath made it deep and large: the pile thereof is fire and much wood; the breath of the Lord, like a stream of brimstone, doth kindle it.

So the reason why God chose this particular punishment- burning alive forever- is because Satan tempted people to burn their children to him. If Satan had done something different- that particular form of punishment would not have been instituted. Also Satan's demons participated. Now the Bottomless Pit fires will cleanse Satan and his demons of all their sins, from the killing in Cambodia, Rwanda, Burundi, Ethiopia, Sudan, Congo, Bosnia, Kosovo, Armenia, Stalins 20 million, Mao's 70 million, Hitlers 56 million, the killing of the Jews in WWII, killing of the Jews throughout history, killing Christians throughout history etc- all that will be cleansed as God takes vengeance (Isaiah 34:8) in the fires of the Bottomless Pit except for one sin, the blasphemy of the Holy Spirit.

What is Blaspheming the Holy Spirit? It is not the wicked cursing that we people do against God, and Jesus.But It is to tell people to worship you as God when you know that your not God. That is unforgivable forever . Jesus said so . So after Satan and his demons left the Bottomless Pit they had that one sin and committed that sin again, where they had people worship the Beast and Satan in WWIII.

How do I know that you demons will spend time in the Bottomless Pit? Isaiah 24 says so.

Isaiah 24:21-22

21. And it shall come to pass in that day, that the Lord shall punish the host of the high ones that are on high, and the kings of the earth upon the earth.
22. And they shall be gathered together, as prisoners are gathered in the pit, and shall be shut up in the prison, and after many days shall they be visited.

You will be visited billions of years from now when the universe is in Blueshift. Now why do I believe you are not going to hell? Well Satan and his demons did go to hell, but they were kicked out of hell by the inhabitants thereof.

Isaiah 14:18-20

18. All the kings of the nations, even all of them, lie in glory, every one in his own house.
19. But thou art cast out of thy grave like an abominable branch, and as the raiment of those

that are slain, thrust through with a sword, that go down to the stones of the pit; as a carcase trodden under feet.

20. Thou shalt not be joined with them in burial, because thou hast destroyed thy land, and slain thy people: the seed of evildoers shall never be renowned.

Satan and his demons did not go to hell to rule it, but they were kicked out by the humans and Satan and his demons were thrown into the Bottomless Pit.

Jesus says "Satan" is a house.

Revelation 20:1-3.

1. And I saw an angel come down from heaven, having the key of the bottomless pit and a great chain in his hand.
2. And he laid hold on the dragon, that old serpent, which is the Devil, and Satan, and bound him a thousand years,
3. And cast him into the bottomless pit, and shut him up, and set a seal upon him, that he should deceive the nations no more, till the thousand years should be fulfilled: and after that he must be loosed a little season.

What will happen to you in the Bottomless Pit ? Well your skin will be burned in a furnace, as you fall through space. Then the Angels of St. Abaddon- the King of Terror (Job 18:14) will torture you with exotic tools.Junipers.

Psalm 120:2-4

2. Deliver my soul, O Lord, from lying lips, and from a deceitful tongue.
3. What shall be given unto thee? or what shall be done unto thee, thou false tongue?
4. Sharp arrows of the mighty, with coals of juniper.

Your skin will not fall off but it will be fresh always to feel the pain of the fire. Also maggots and death will feed on your body for 40 billion years. St. Abaddon is a sadist, God's most terrible sadist- the King of Terrors- and his Angels are all sadists. They dont even cut their hair as a sign of dedication and devotion to sadism. They are Monks- Nazerites of torture. And they have exotic tools to get the most of your screams. You will be burned for 40 billion 800 million years +/-

FURTHER PROOF OF BEING BURNED.

Psalm 11:5-6

eyelids try, the children of men.

5. The Lord trieth the righteous: but the wicked and him that loveth violence his soul hateth.
6. Upon the wicked he shall rain snares, fire and brimstone, and an horrible tempest: this shall be the portion of their cup.

11

Psalm 21:8-12

8. Thine hand shall find out all thine enemies: thy right hand shall find out those that hate thee.
9. Thou shalt make them as a fiery oven in the time of thine anger: the Lord shall swallow them up in his wrath, and the fire shall devour them.
10. Their fruit shalt thou destroy from the earth, and their seed from among the children of men.

This next verse says much about the Invisible war between Satan and his demons.

Psalm 21:11-13.

11. For they intended evil against thee: they imagined a mischievous device, which they are not able to perform.
12. Therefore shalt thou make them turn their back, when thou shalt make ready thine arrows upon thy strings against the face of them.

Psalm 140:9-11

9. As for the head of those that compass me about, let the mischief of their own lips cover them.
10. Let burning coals fall upon them: let them be cast into the fire; into deep pits, that they rise not up again.
11. Let not an evil speaker be established in the earth: evil shall hunt the violent man to overthrow him.

Isaiah 14:4-24

4. That thou shalt take up this proverb against the king of Babylon, and say, How hath the oppressor ceased! the golden city ceased!
5. The Lord hath broken the staff of the wicked, and the sceptre of the rulers.
6. He who smote the people in wrath with a continual stroke, he that ruled the nations in anger, is persecuted, and none hindereth.
7. The whole earth is at rest, and is quiet: they break forth into singing.
8. Yea, the fir trees rejoice at thee, and the cedars of Lebanon, saying, Since thou art laid down, no feller is come up against us.
9. Hell from beneath is moved for thee to meet thee at thy coming: it stirreth up the dead for thee, even all the chief ones of the earth; it hath raised up from their thrones all the kings of the nations.
10. All they shall speak and say unto thee, Art thou also become weak as we? art thou become like unto us?

11. Thy pomp is brought down to the grave, and the noise of thy viols: the worm is spread under thee, and the worms cover thee.

12. How art thou fallen from heaven, O Lucifer, son of the morning! how art thou cut down to the ground, which didst weaken the nations!

13. For thou hast said in thine heart, I will ascend into heaven, I will exalt my throne above the stars of God: I will sit also upon the mount of the congregation, in the sides of the north:

14. I will ascend above the heights of the clouds; I will be like the most High.

15. Yet thou shalt be brought down to hell, to the sides of the pit.

16. They that see thee shall narrowly look upon thee, and consider thee, saying, Is this the man that made the earth to tremble, that did shake kingdoms;

17. That made the world as a wilderness, and destroyed the cities thereof; that opened not the house of his prisoners?

18. All the kings of the nations, even all of them, lie in glory, every one in his own house.

19. But thou art cast out of thy grave like an abominable branch, and as the raiment of those that are slain, thrust through with a sword, that go down to the stones of the pit; as a carcase trodden under feet.

20. Thou shalt not be joined with them in burial, because thou hast destroyed thy land, and slain thy people: the seed of evildoers shall never be renowned.

21. Prepare slaughter for his children for the iniquity of their fathers; that they do not rise, nor possess the land, nor fill the face of the world with cities.

22. For I will rise up against them, saith the Lord of hosts, and cut off from Babylon the name, and remnant, and son, and nephew, saith the Lord.

23. I will also make it a possession for the bittern, and pools of water: and I will sweep it with the Besom of destruction, saith the Lord of hosts.

24. The Lord of hosts hath sworn, saying, Surely as I have thought, so shall it come to pass; and as I have purposed, so shall it stand:

Isaiah 66:23-24

23. And it shall come to pass, that from one new moon to another, and from one sabbath to another, shall all flesh come to worship before me, saith the Lord.

24. And they shall go forth, and look upon the carcases of the men that have transgressed against me: for their worm shall not die, neither shall their fire be quenched; and they shall be an abhorring unto all flesh.

Ezekiel 28:18-19

18. Thou hast defiled thy sanctuaries by the multitude of thine iniquities, by the iniquity of thy traffick; therefore will I bring forth a fire from the midst of thee, it shall devour thee, and I will bring thee to ashes upon the earth in the sight of all them that behold thee.

19: All they that know thee among the people shall be astonished at thee: thou shalt be a terror, and never shalt thou be any more.

Mathew 25:41

41. Then shall he say also unto them on the left hand, Depart from me, ye cursed, into everlasting fire, prepared for the devil and his angels:

St. Abaddon will yank out Satan's and the Beast's tongues out of their mouth's in the Bottomless Pit

Psalm 52:2-6

2. Thy tongue deviseth mischiefs; like a sharp rasor, working deceitfully.
3. Thou lovest evil more than good; and lying rather than to speak righteousness. Selah.
4. Thou lovest all devouring words, O thou deceitful tongue.
5. God shall likewise destroy thee for ever, he shall take thee away, and pluck thee out of thy dwelling place, and root thee out of the land of the living. Selah.
6. The righteous also shall see, and fear, and shall laugh at him:

What will happen to the people who went to hell, not the Bottomless Pit which is reserved for Satan and his angels? The people in hell had a good sleepy time after they kicked Satan out of hell. Isaiah 14:15-20

Isaiah 14:

15. **Yet thou shalt be brought down to hell, to the sides of the pit.**
16. They that see thee shall narrowly look upon thee, and consider thee, saying, Is this the man that made the earth to tremble, that did shake kingdoms;
17. That made the world as a wilderness, and destroyed the cities thereof; that opened not the house of his prisoners?
18. All the kings of the nations, even all of them, lie in glory, every one in his own house.
19. But thou art cast out of thy grave like an abominable branch, and as the raiment of those that are slain, thrust through with a sword, that go down to the stones of the pit; as a carcase trodden under feet.
20. Thou shalt not be joined with them in burial, because thou hast destroyed thy land, and slain thy people: the seed of evildoers shall never be renowned.

Isaiah 14:18 says people in hell slept in their glory for 40 billion years. You see the Church felt sorry- Mother Church felt sorry for the people who looked like humans in every way. So she was squemish, and Jesus gave them a second chance in 40 Billion AD+/-.

Isaiah 14:18.

18. All the kings of the nations, even all of them, lie in glory, every one in his own house.

After that, they were released and they entered Christ's kingdom and contaminated it. WWIII happened for Satan and his angels were also released into Christ's kingdom or 1000 yr Reign.

Now Satan and his demons did not just lay around and wait for their medicine - the Bottomless Pit. They tried to fight, they were dragged kicking and screaming into the Bottomless Pit. They tried to stop the Carcase, or the person who was supposed to welcome Christ at the Second Coming. The kingdom of heaven suffereth violence again, but I made it through with all of my books.

Isaiah 14:31-32

31. Howl, O gate; cry, O city; thou, whole Palestina, art dissolved: for there shall come from the north a smoke, and none shall be alone in his appointed times.

24. What shall one then answer the messengers of the nation? That the Lord hath founded Zion, and the poor of his people shall trust in it.

Jesus defeated Satan. Jesus is Mighty in Battle.

Psalm 24

1. The earth is the Lord's, and the fulness thereof; the world, and they that dwell therein.
2. For he hath founded it upon the seas, and established it upon the floods.
3. Who shall ascend into the hill of the Lord? or who shall stand in his holy place?
4. He that hath clean hands, and a pure heart; who hath not lifted up his soul unto vanity, nor sworn deceitfully.
5. He shall receive the blessing from the Lord, and righteousness from the God of his salvation.
6. This is the generation of them that seek him, that seek thy face, O Jacob. Selah.
7. Lift up your heads, O ye gates; and be ye lift up, ye everlasting doors; and the King of glory shall come in.
8. Who is this King of glory? The Lord strong and mighty, the Lord mighty in battle.
9. Lift up your heads, O ye gates; even lift them up, ye everlasting doors; and the King of glory shall come in.
10. Who is this King of glory? The Lord of hosts, he is the King of glory. Selah.

CHAPTER TWO
SATAN: THE HIGHPRIEST OF EVIL

Isaiah 28:12 " To whom He said, This is the rest wherewith ye may cause the weary to rest; and this is the refreshing: yet they would not hear"

This book is new material for Christians and the Church.

SATAN :THE HIGHPRIEST OF EVIL

A CHRONOLOGICAL HISTORY FOR SERIOUS STUDENTS.

INFORMATION ABOUT SATAN NEVER REVEALED BEFORE.

Isaiah 27

1. In that day the Lord with his sore and great and strong sword shall punish leviathan the piercing serpent, even leviathan that crooked serpent; and he shall slay the dragon that is in the sea.

Isaiah 74:13,14

13. Thou didst divide the sea by thy strength: thou brakest the heads of the dragons in the waters.
14. Thou brakest the heads of leviathan in pieces, and gavest him to be meat to the people inhabiting the wilderness.

Stanley O Lotegeluaki.

A sheep of Jesus Christ. The Standard Bearer of the Lords Army.

Striking fear and terror into the forces of Satan.

Leviathan and the Dragon is Satans names and he lives in the political sea. God has broken his head and fed us information about him.

Isaiah 74:13,14

13. Thou didst divide the sea by thy strength: thou brakest the heads of the dragons in the waters.

14. Thou brakest the heads of leviathan in pieces, and gavest him to be meat to the people inhabiting the wilderness.

Jesus said in Mt. 18: 6,7 that the highpriest of evil Satan was responsible for the pedophile scandal. Jesus knew beforehand 2000 years ago that it would happen before the Second coming. Also Islam, Mormonism, Buddhism, New Age, Hinduism, Wicca, Communist Athiesm, Taoism etc all are from the highpriest of evil and will be destroyed at the Second Coming. Satan used to be a highpriest of God, but since he was removed from his position he has created rebel religions on earth to fight God- The God of Israel and Christ. Christianity. This book has information about the Chronological history of Satan. Also a recommended book to read as a companion is " The Invisible War" by Dr. Donald Grey Barnhouse my mentor whom Satan killed in a car accident for writing his book.

Isaiah 31:

4. For thus hath the Lord spoken unto me, Like as the lion and the young lion roaring on his prey, when a multitude of shepherds is called forth against him, he will not be afraid of their voice, nor abase himself for the noise of them: so shall the Lord of hosts come down to fight for mount Zion, and for the hill thereof.
5. As birds flying, so will the Lord of hosts defend Jerusalem; defending also he will deliver it; and passing over he will preserve it.

Isaiah 30: 30.

And the Lord shall cause his glorious voice to be heard, and shall shew the lighting down of his arm, with the indignation of his anger, and with the flame of a devouring fire, with scattering, and tempest, and hailstones.

ISAIAH 29: 6.

Thou shalt be visited of the Lord of hosts with thunder, and with earthquake, and great noise, with storm and tempest, and the flame of devouring fire.

SATAN

There are some people who don't believe in Satan and they believe that Satan and demons are just bad thoughts and evil intentions in our minds. But Iam here to tell you that Satan is a creature created by God and that his demons are fallen angels who control and bring harm to this small planet of ours.

The history of Satan actually starts before the big bang when God determined that He was going to create him. This was the worst thing that happened to Satan and his demons. God's decision to create them.

He creates evil as He says in Isaiah.

Isaiah 45:7

7. I form the light, and create darkness: I make peace, and create evil: I the Lord do all these things.

I will show the chronological history of Satan, just the highlights in the Bible for it would take volumes just to write a rudimentry history of Satan. The only thing you have to understand is that Satan's greatest weapon is his incognito. If you don't believe in him you cant defend yourself against him and that's the way he wants it in this world. To fully understand this small book you must have first read a book written by Dr. Grey Barnhouse called "The invisible war" This book Ive written will only show some of the things that he missed in his excellent history of Satan. So I hope you have read his book or will read it if you are really a good student of the Bible . This book is a supplementary, an attempt to fill in the blanks of Dr. Grey Barnhouse "The invisible war".

Dr. Grey Barnhouse did not understand the preistory of Satan. He didn't talk about what happened before creation and he missed the tellatale history of Satan in creation in Genesis 1:1-7 in which I will explain in detail. In the garden of Eden Dr. Grey Barnhouse explained what happened so well that I will skip it. After Satan and his visible angels had sex with humans and caused the flood, I will skip to St. Job. Again Dr. Grey Barnhouse showed the battle of St. Job so well that I will skip most of it, but he missed the biggest part of it all when he left out Chpt 41 Job which is dedicated to Satan. Leviathan is Satan. Leviathan throughout the Bible as well as dragon is Satan. The sea is not H2O but the political sea and waters in the Bible means political waters, or political circles or just simply politics. Water of life means the politics of life or the gospel of Jesus.

After that I will jump to Isaiah and explain God's dictation to Satan at the Second Coming. Ezekiel 28 is a gold mine of information on Satan. Then we jump to the New Testament and finally Revelation where Satan is called the devil. I could write this book with pictures and it could be 2000 pages long, but I'll leave that task to Christ's Angels when they come back at the Second Coming. I'll reduce the history of Satan to just a few pages. Read "The invisible war or what the Bible says about the Collapse of the universe" my first book-not Third Wave Christianity but my other book to understand and have a clear picture of Satan and what the Bible says. Satan martyed Dr. Grey Barnhouse in a car accident. So this information was given to you by the blood of a Christian.

SATAN   40 BILLION BC+/-

BEFORE THE BIG BANG SATAN'S FATE IS DETERMINED.

40 billion B.C years ago was the day of the Great Volunteering where Christians volunteered to come to earth to fight for Jesus against Satan. The forces of Light against the forces of darkness. You see Jesus created all Christians 100 billion years ago and after spending billions of years in peace in a kingdom called The King of Glory Kingdom, He decided to spice up our lives with a war. We did not know what war was but He explained it to us in so many ways. Evil against us, the good, Christians against non Christians, Love versus hate, Light versus darkness, Truth versus lies, etc.

So Jesus wrote the Bible and we read it from Genesis to Revelation and when we found out He was going to burn the wicked forever we were affrighted. So St. Job says.

Job 18:5

5. Yea, the light of the wicked shall be put out, and the spark of his fire shall not shine.

Job 18:20

20. They that come after him shall be astonied at his day, as they that went before were affrighted.

Verse 20 also says that we were astonished after the wicked disappeared in the Lake of fire 100 billion A.D. after the collapse of the universe and the end of Judgment day.

I found out we existed with Jesus 100 billion years ago with John 17:24 and Job 18:20. For Jesus said He existed before the big bang 20 billion B.C.. And since Jesus has always been a King, He must have always have had subjects. And who were His subjects? Christians were His subjects. Also God goes on to give us a hint of our existence when He asked St. Job " Where was thou before I created the foundations of the earth"

Job 38:4

4. Where wast thou when I laid the foundations of the earth? declare, if thou hast understanding.

The foundation of the earth was the big bang. We had to exist before Satan and his angels to be affrighted at their fate. What Iam trying to say is that we Christians existed before Satan and his demons were created.

John 17:5

5. And now, O Father, glorify thou me with thine own self with the glory which I had with thee before the world was.

Think of the Great Volunteering. Meditation. The fool hath said in his heart, There is no God. They are corrupt, they have done abominable works, there is none that doeth good.

SATAN   20 BILLION B.C.+/-

THE BIG BANG.

20 billion years ago Genesis 1:1 came true with the big bang of the universe. God created a perfect heaven and earth .

Genesis 1:1

1. In the beginning God created the heaven and the earth.

Think of the big bang. Meditation. The Lord looked down from heaven upon the children of men, to see if there were any that did understand, and seek God.

SATAN   20 BILLIION BC+/-

LUCIFER CREATED.

God created Lucifer and his angels.

Ezekiel 28:12-14

12. Son of man, take up a lamentation upon the king of Tyrus, and say unto him, thus saith the Lord God; Thou sealest up the sum, full of wisdom, and perfect in beauty.
13. Thou hast been in Eden the garden of God; every precious stone was thy covering, the sardius, topaz, and the diamond, the Beryl, the onyx, and the jasper, the sapphire, the emerald, and the carbuncle, and gold: the workmanship of thy tabrets and of thy pipes was prepared in thee in the day that thou wast created.
14. Thou art the anointed cherub that covereth; and I have set thee so: thou wast upon the holy mountain of God; thou hast walked up and down in the midst of the stones of fire.

Lucifer means "Light bearer". The Word of God is the Light, so Lucifer was the prophet of God for he bore the Word of God.

Think of the creation of Lucifer. Meditation. They are all gone aside, they are all together become filthy: there is none that doeth good, no, not one.

SATAN   20 BILLION BC+/-

THE MIXING.

After Jesus created Lucifer, He mixed our good Angels from above the heavens (Psalm 148:4) with Lucifer's angels in the heavens.

Think of the mixing of sheep and goats. Meditation. Have all the workers of iniquity no knowledge? Who eat up My people as they ear bread, and call not upon the Lord.

SATAN   20 BILLION BC+/- - 7000 BC+/-

SANCTUARIES.

Lucifer was the highpriest, prophet and governor of God over all the Angels and he had Sanctuaries or church's in heaven to worship God.

Think of the Church's of Satan. Meditation. Ye have shamed the counsel of the poor, because the Lord is his refuge.

SATAN   20 BILLION B.C +/- -7000 BC+/-

STRONG ARMING.

Then Lucifer started to strong arm the other Angels for their stuff. God calls it merchandise or violent dealings in merchandising- wheeling and dealing- that went through Lucifer's hands.

Ezekiel 28:15-18

15. Thou wast perfect in thy ways from the day that thou wast created, till iniquity was found in thee.
16. By the multitude of thy merchandise they have filled the midst of thee with violence, and thou hast sinned: therefore I will cast thee as profane out of the mountain of God: and I will destroy thee, O covering cherub, from the midst of the stones of fire.
17. Thine heart was lifted up because of thy beauty, thou hast corrupted thy wisdom by

reason of thy brightness: I will cast thee to the ground, I will lay thee before kings, that they may behold thee.

18. Thou hast defiled thy sanctuaries by the multitude of thine iniquities, by the iniquity of thy traffick; therefore will I bring forth a fire from the midst of thee, it shall devour thee, and I will bring thee to ashes upon the earth in the sight of all them that behold thee.

Think of Satan strong arming the other Angels for their stuff. Meditation. Hear the right, O Lord, attend unto my cry, give ear unto my prayer, that goeth not out of feigned lips

SATAN   20 BILLION BC+/- -7000 BC+/-

THE FIRING.

So Jesus fired Lucifer from being highpriest and prophet of God. Remember Jesus is God, but He hadnt used that terrible name Jesus yet. The name Jesus is an arrow designed to destroy Lucifer. Lucifer means Light bearer and the Word of God was the Light that Lucifer bore.

Ezekiel 28:16

16. By the multitude of thy merchandise they have filled the midst of thee with violence, and thou hast sinned: therefore I will cast thee as profane out of the mountain of God: and I will destroy thee, O covering cherub, from the midst of the stones of fire.

"O Covering Cherub" means that Lucifer was the highpriest of God and was God's clothing. The rock group "Stain" is named after that verse. After Lucifer was fired God made him fall to Serpent, Satan, Devil to Dragon and the good Angels observed his fall and Ezekiel records it.

Ezekiel 28:19

19. All they that know thee among the people shall be astonished at thee: thou shalt be a terror, and never shalt thou be any more.

Think of God's garment, Lucifer , stained or being fired. Meditation. Why standest thou afar off, O Lord? Why hidest thou thyself in times of trouble?

SATAN   20 BILLION BC+/- -7000BC+/-

THE REBELLION

Lucifer instead of using his wise head to repent decided to rebel against God because he was shamed and was very proud and he thought he was too beautiful to undergo such shame.

Ezekiel 28:17

17. Thine heart was lifted up because of thy beauty, thou hast corrupted thy wisdom by reason of thy brightness: I will cast thee to the ground, I will lay thee before kings, that they may behold thee.

I Timothy 3:6

6. Not a novice, lest being lifted up with pride he fall into the condemnation of the devil.

That has to do with priests and how they should not be. Satan was a "novice" , that's why he fell. He fell because of pride.

Think of Lucifer's pride. Meditation. The wicked in his pride doth persecute the poor: let them be taken in the devices that they have imagined.

SATAN   20 BILLION BC+/- - 7000BC+/-

CHAOS, LIES, AND DARKNESS

Between Genesis 1:1 and 1:2 is millions +/- of years of Satan's rule, or Lucifer's rule in heaven. Then Lucifer brought chaos to God's perfect heaven when he decided to rebel. He lied to the Angels and told them to fight God and God should share His praise with them also. He lied to the Angels and tried to get them to turn against God. So God's perfect creation had lies and chaos in it. The "deep" in the next verse is the "political sea" and the "waters" means "political circles" of Angels.

Genesis 1:2

2. And the earth was without form, and void; and darkness was upon the face of the deep.
     And the Spirit of God moved upon the face of the waters.

God never abandoned His good Angels but His Holy Spirit went about saving His good Angels, His spirit moved among the "waters"as it does on earth to day to Christians saved the good Angels of heaven when Lucifer rebelled. Not all the Angels went with Lucifer because God's Spirit was there. Only the angels who were created after the big bang went with Lucifer.

Think of how Lucifer brought darkness and chaos and lies to God's perfect heaven. Meditation. For the wicked boasteth of his heart's desire, and blesseth the covetous, whom the Lord abhorreth.

SATAN   20 BILLION BC-7000BC+/-

THE LIGHT APPEARS.

Then God said " Let there be Light". He did not say "Let there be photons" but He meant "Let there be Jesus"- who is the Light of John 1:1-9. And Jesus appeared in heaven.

Genesis 1:3

3. And God said, Let there be light: and there was light.
Think of the Light Jesus Christ appearing in heaven to rally the good Angels. Meditation. Have mercy upon me, O Lord; consider my trouble which I suffer of them that hate me, thou that liftest me up from the gates of death:

SATAN   20 BILLION BC+/- - 7000 BC+/-

THE DIVISION OF THE GOOD ANGELS FROM THE BAD ANGELS.

Then God divided the good Angels from the bad angels. The good stayed with Jesus the Light and the bad stayed with Satan the Night.

Genesis 1:4

4. And God saw the light, that it was good: and God divided the light from the darkness.

Think of the division of Light and Darkness.

SATAN   20 BILLION BC+/- - 7000BC+/-

MORNING FIGHTS EVENING.

There was a battle between Jesus the Morning and Satan the evening the very first day they met.

Genesis 1:5

5. And God called the light Day, and the darkness he called Night. And the evening and the morning were the first day.

Think of the Morning fighting evening the first day, Jesus fought Satan the very first day. Meditation. The wicked, through the pride of his countenance, will not seek after God: God is not in all his thoughts.

SATAN   20 BILLION BC+/- - 7000 BC+/-

THE CREATION OF THE BARRIER, BETWEEN HEAVEN AND EARTH.

Genesis 1:6

6. And God said, Let there be a firmament in the midst of the waters, and let it divide the waters from the waters.

" waters" means "politics" or "political circles"
Think of the firmament created between heaven and earth. Meditation. Sing praises to the Lord, which dwelleth in Zion: declare among the people His doings.

SATAN   20 BILLION BC+/- - 7000 BC+/-

Genesis 1:7

7. And God made the firmament, and divided the waters which were under the firmament from the waters which were above the firmament: and it was so.

God divided the politics of heaven from the politics of the earth so they never mesh. That's why we can only get to heaven through death and no one can come back to earth.

Genesis 1:7-8

7. And God made the firmament, and divided the waters which were under the firmament from the waters which were above the firmament: and it was so.

8. And God called the firmament Heaven. And the evening and the morning were the second day.

There was a battle between Jesus the " Morning" and Satan the "evening" on the second day. Think of the heavens and the earth. Meditation. The Lord is in His holy temple, the Lord's throne is in heaven: His eyes behold, His eyelids try, the children of men.

SATAN   600 MILLION BC+/- -7000BC+/-

HUMANS CREATED ON THE EARTH

Then the true non symbolic creation of the earth began and it took God 600 million years to do it, but time was accelerated between heaven and earth because I don't believe the Angels had to wait 600 million years for the next phase of the Invisible war to go on. We call this stage of Genesis 1:9-31 "evolution", but it is God guided evolution so that the Adam creation was favored for the earth was created for Adam. Remember the Great volunteering. Lucifer never knew of us or what happened before his creation, a fatal mistake as they are finding out today.

Think of Adam being created taking God 600 million years +/-. Meditation. If the foundations be destroyed, what can the righteous do?

SATAN   7000-6000BC+/-

THE GARDEN

God put Adam the finished creation into the garden of Eden. All the other cavemen were insignificant , only Adam was chosen to live in the artificial garden of Eden. He probably wandered into it or was led into it. The garden of Eden is in Israel today and God gave Adam one rule. The Spirit of Adam came from a Christian from above the heavens from where all Christians come from. The body was already created from monkeys, but the spirits that inhabits our bodies come from heaven. The spirits of evil people come from below.

Think of the garden of Eden which is Israel today. Meditation. The Lord also will be a refuge for the oppressed, a refuge in times of trouble.

SATAN   6000BC+/-

ADAM AND EVE.

God created Adam and Eve. They both had fathers and mothers, but that's insignificant because their spirits came from above the heavens and they both ended up in the garden.

Think of Adam meeting Eve in the garden. Meditation. O Lord our Lord, how excellent is thy name in all the earth! Who hast set thy glory above the heavens.

SATAN   6000 BC+/-

DUST FOR SATAN THE SERPENT

Satan attacked Adam through Eve and tried to get Adam to be on his side but that failed when God made the rules of the invisible war, the rule that Eve's seed should hate Satan's seed forever and that a Child of Eve would kill Satan one day. That was Jesus.

Genesis 3:15

15. And I will put enmity between thee and the woman, and between thy seed and her seed; it shall bruise thy head, and thou shalt bruise his heel.

"Dust" means "frustration".

Think of the frustration that Satan will eat all his life until his head is bruised and becomes a dragon.

Meditation. His mouth is full of cursing and deceit and fraud; under his tongue is mischief and vanity.

SATAN   6000 BC+/-

THE CURSE OF LUCIFER

God cursed Lucifer and said he would be the lowest of all creatures and that he would eat dust (frustration) all the days of his life.

Genesis 3:14

14. And the Lord God said unto the serpent, Because thou hast done this, thou art cursed above all cattle, and above every beast of the field; upon thy belly shalt thou go, and dust shalt thou eat all the days of thy life:

Think of the curse of dust. Meditation. Sing praises to the Lord, which dwelleth in Zion: declare among the people His doings.

SATAN   6000BC+/-

CAIN

Satan tried to snuff out Adams seed by tempting Cain to kill Abel his brother thus eliminating the two.

"Sin" is Satan in this next verse when God warned Cain of Satan's desire for him. 1/3 of all the angels wanted to destroy Cain.

Genesis 4:6-7

6. And the Lord said unto Cain, Why art thou wroth? and why is thy countenance fallen?
7. If thou doest well, shalt thou not be accepted? and if thou doest not well, sin lieth at the door. And unto thee shall be his desire, and thou shalt rule over him.

Cain actually killed Abel later on. Adam had more children. Cain did not marry his sisters but he went out into the communities outside the garden and got married for there were people outside of the garden from Chapter 1 Genesis.

Think of Cain killing his brother Abel. Meditation. He hath said in his heart, God hath forgotten: he hideth His face; He will never see it.

SATAN   6000 BC+/-

SEX WITH SHEEP OR MANKIND BY SATAN AND HIS DEMONS.

Then Lucifer and his angels who came from heaven to earth (were visible as men) had sex with humanbeings. But God destroyed that race of creatures that were born with the flood.

Genesis 6:1-8

1. And it came to pass, when men began to multiply on the face of the earth, and daughters were born unto them,
2. That the sons of God saw the daughters of men that they were fair; and they took them wives of all which they chose.
3. And the Lord said, My spirit shall not always strive with man, for that he also is flesh: yet his days shall be an hundred and twenty years.
4. There were giants in the earth in those days; and also after that, when the sons of God came in unto the daughters of men, and they bare children to them, the same became mighty men which were of old, men of renown.
5. And God saw that the wickedness of man was great in the earth, and that every imagination of the thoughts of his heart was only evil continually.
6. And it repented the Lord that he had made man on the earth, and it grieved him at his heart.
7. And the Lord said, I will destroy man whom I have created from the face of the earth; both man, and beast, and the creeping thing, and the fowls of the air; for it repenteth me that I have made them.
8. But Noah found grace in the eyes of the Lord.

Think of the flood. Meditation. Break thou the arm of the wicked and the evil man: seek out his wickedness till thou find none.

SATAN   6000 BC+/- - 5000BC+/-

SATAN AND DEMONS MADE INVISIBLE.

After the flood God made Satan and his angels invisible to us humans so they wouldn't have sex with us and it has been that way ever since.
Think of Satan and his demons made invisible by the Lord. Meditation. The Lord is King forever and ever: the heathen are perished out of His land.

SATAN   2166 BC+/-

ABRAHAM

Satan hated Abraham and his attempted sacrifice of Isaac. So Satan said people can sacrifice their sons to him also. So the tradition was started in Canaan of people passing their children through the fire to Satan,

Psalm 106:37

37. Yea, they sacrificed their sons and their daughters unto devils,

Think of Satan watching Abraham attempted sacrifice of Isaac and copying it for real. Meditation. He sitteth in the lurking places of the villages: in the secret places doth he murder the innocent: his eyes are privily set against the poor.

SATAN   2166 BC +/-

SODOM

Jesus destroyed Sodom a stronghold of Satan. Satan and his demons had fallen so far down from the days of heaven to become homosexuals in Sodom. They found another way of having sex with humans. So Jesus after talking to Abraham destroyed Sodom.

Think of the fire coming down on the city of Sodom. Meditation. The Lord is known by the judgment which He executeth: the wicked is snared in the work of his own hands.

SATAN   1800 BC+/-

EGYPT AND ISRAEL

The Lord sent His nation to Egypt to grow up but Satan turned the Egyptians against the Israelites without a cause.

Isaiah 52:4

4. For thus saith the Lord God, My people went down aforetime into Egypt to sojourn there; and the Assyrian oppressed them without cause.

The Assyrian in Isaiah is Satan. Satan had the Egyptians worshipping the host of heaven or his demons.

Think of Israel being tortured in Egypt. Meditation. Lord, thou hast heard the desire of the humble: thou wilt cause thine ear to hear.

SATAN   1406 BC +/-

MOSES AND THE PLAGUES.

The plagues were designed to discredit the gods of Egypt. For example the darkness was designed to discredit the god Ra the sun god of Egypt.

Think of the plague of darkness. Meditation. But the Lord shall endure forever: He hath prepared His throne for judgment.

SATAN   1406 BC+/-

GOD JUDGES THE gods OF EGYPT.

After the plagues of Moses, God judged the gods of Egypt, Satan and his demons. God turned the angels of Satan to look like the frogs, scarab beetles, caterpillars, lice, grasshoppers and flies that the Egyptians worshipped. That's why in Revelation 16:13 Satan's angels looked like frogs. Also lice demons inhabited the man with a legion in the days of Christ. How do you think 6000 angels could fit into one person? They must have been very small. Today people worship lice in some societies, or talk about the lord of the flies as being a pestilence god or have movies with scarab beetles in them. (Indiana Jones). There is also scarab beetles on the cover of a Journey album. Just look around, do you think the fantasy pictures of beautiful women with butterfly wings or fairies is just coincidence ? God made the angels of Satan to look like caterpillars and flies and frogs. They are just expressing themselves through our Art. That's where Kermit the frog and the frog culture of kids playing with frogs come from. He represents the demons of Chpt 16:13 Revelation.

13. And I saw three unclean spirits like frogs come out of the mouth of the dragon, and out of the mouth of the beast, and out of the mouth of the false prophet.

14. For they are the spirits of devils, working miracles, which go forth unto the kings of the earth and of the whole world, to gather them to the battle of that great day of God Almighty.

Think of Kermit the frog and the frog culture as being highly suspicious. Meditation. Blessed is the man that walketh not in the counsel of the ungodly, nor standeth in the way of sinners, nor sitteth in the seat of the scornful.

SATAN   1400 BC+/-

THE CALF

It was Satan who made the children of Israel make the calf idol in the desert. Satan pursued the children of Israel into the wilderness to try to destroy them.

Think of how evil it was the calf idol was and the children of Israel dancing naked around it. Meditation. For the Lord knoweth the way of the righteous: but the way of the ungodly shall perish.

SATAN   1406BC+/-

JOSHUA

It was Satan who gathered the Canaanites against the Israelites but God destroyed them.

Think of the sun and moon standing still for Israel. Meditation. Lord, how are they increased that trouble me! Many are they that rise up against me.

SATAN   1400 BC+/-

JUDGES

In Judges 5:19-21 there is a prophecy of Africa or the Canaanites coming to the aid of the Angels before the Second Coming. So God did not abandon the Canaanites to Satan.

Think of the Angels fighting against Satan before the Second Coming. Meditation. Many there be which say of my soul, There is no help for him in God.

SATAN   1050 BC+/-

DAVID

David had a run in with Satan many times and it was Satan who was trying to destroy David. David knew this and he wrote many psalms saying the "mighty" were against him. It was Satan who made David number the people. David also called Satan and the demons " the workers of iniquity". That was his name for them.

Think of David being tempted to number the people. Meditation. But thou, O Lord, art a shield for me; my glory, and the lifter up of mine head.

SATAN   2166 BC+/-

JOB

In Job we see the sinister nature of Satan. So Satan is not a thought or our desires. He is a living creation a spirit being.

Job Chpt 1,2

1. There was a man in the land of Uz, whose name was Job; and that man was perfect and upright, and one that feared God, and eschewed evil.
2. And there were born unto him seven sons and three daughters.
3. His substance also was seven thousand sheep, and three thousand camels, and five hundred yoke of oxen, and five hundred she asses, and a very great household; so that this man was the greatest of all the men of the east.
4. And his sons went and feasted in their houses, every one his day; and sent and called for their three sisters to eat and to drink with them.
5. And it was so, when the days of their feasting were gone about, that Job sent and sanctified them, and rose up early in the morning, and offered burnt offerings according to the number of them all: for Job said, It may be that my sons have sinned, and cursed God in their hearts. Thus did Job continually.
6. Now there was a day when the sons of God came to present themselves before the Lord, and Satan came also among them.
7. And the Lord said unto Satan, Whence comest thou? Then Satan answered the Lord, and said, From going to and fro in the earth, and from walking up and down in it.
8. And the Lord said unto Satan, Hast thou considered my servant Job, that there is none like him in the earth, a perfect and an upright man, one that feareth God, and escheweth evil?
9. Then Satan answered the Lord, and said, Doth Job fear God for nought?
10. Hast not thou made an hedge about him, and about his house, and about all that he hath on every side? thou hast blessed the work of his hands, and his substance is increased in the land.
11. But put forth thine hand now, and touch all that he hath, and he will curse thee to thy face.
12. And the Lord said unto Satan, Behold, all that he hath is in thy power; only upon himself put not forth thine hand. So Satan went forth from the presence of the Lord.
13. And there was a day when his sons and his daughters were eating and drinking wine in their eldest brother's house:

14. And there came a messenger unto Job, and said, The oxen were plowing, and the asses feeding beside them:

15. And the Sabeans fell upon them, and took them away; yea, they have slain the servants with the edge of the sword; and I only am escaped alone to tell thee.

16. While he was yet speaking, there came also another, and said, The fire of God is fallen from heaven, and hath burned up the sheep, and the servants, and consumed them; and I only am escaped alone to tell thee.

17. While he was yet speaking, there came also another, and said, The Chaldeans made out three bands, and fell upon the camels, and have carried them away, yea, and slain the servants with the edge of the sword; and I only am escaped alone to tell thee.

18. While he was yet speaking, there came also another, and said, Thy sons and thy daughters were eating and drinking wine in their eldest brother's house:

19. And, behold, there came a great wind from the wilderness, and smote the four corners of the house, and it fell upon the young men, and they are dead; and I only am escaped alone to tell thee.

20. Then Job arose, and rent his mantle, and shaved his head, and fell down upon the ground, and worshipped,

21. And said, Naked came I out of my mother's womb, and naked shall I return thither: the Lord gave, and the Lord hath taken away; blessed be the name of the Lord.

22. In all this Job sinned not, nor charged God foolishly.

Job 2

1. Again there was a day when the sons of God came to present themselves before the Lord, and Satan came also among them to present himself before the Lord.

2. And the Lord said unto Satan, From whence comest thou? And Satan answered the Lord, and said, From going to and fro in the earth, and from walking up and down in it.

3. And the Lord said unto Satan, Hast thou considered my servant Job, that there is none like him in the earth, a perfect and an upright man, one that feareth God, and escheweth evil? and still he holdeth fast his integrity, although thou movedst me against him, to destroy him without cause.

4. And Satan answered the Lord, and said, Skin for skin, yea, all that a man hath will he give for his life.

5. But put forth thine hand now, and touch his bone and his flesh, and he will curse thee to thy face.

6. And the Lord said unto Satan, Behold, he is in thine hand; but save his life.

7. So went Satan forth from the presence of the Lord, and smote Job with sore boils from the sole of his foot unto his crown.

8. And he took him a potsherd to scrape himself withal; and he sat down among the ashes.

9. Then said his wife unto him, Dost thou still retain thine integrity? curse God, and die.

10. But he said unto her, Thou speakest as one of the foolish women speaketh. What? shall we receive good at the hand of God, and shall we not receive evil? In all this did not Job sin with his lips.

11. Now when Job's three friends heard of all this evil that was come upon him, they came every one from his own place; Eliphaz the Temanite, and Bildad the Shuhite, and Zophar

the Naamathite: for they had made an appointment together to come to mourn with him and to comfort him.

12. And when they lifted up their eyes afar off, and knew him not, they lifted up their voice, and wept; and they rent every one his mantle, and sprinkled dust upon their heads toward heaven.

13. So they sat down with him upon the ground seven days and seven nights, and none spake a word unto him: for they saw that his grief was very great.

Think of Satan attacking St. Job. Meditation. Why standest thou afar off, O Lord? Why hidest thou thyself in times of trouble ?

SATAN   2166 BC +/-

SATAN THE BEHEMOTH.

In Job 40:19 God calls Satan the behemoth of the earth for he is the "chief of the ways of God". This knowledge is from the days when he was a highpriest. See verse 19 the giveaway.

Job 40:15-24

15. Behold now behemoth, which I made with thee; he eateth grass as an ox.
16. Lo now, his strength is in his loins, and his force is in the navel of his belly.
17. He moveth his tail like a cedar: the sinews of his stones are wrapped together.
18. His bones are as strong pieces of brass; his bones are like bars of iron.
19. He is the chief of the ways of God: he that made him can make his sword to approach unto him.
20. Surely the mountains bring him forth food, where all the beasts of the field play.
21. He lieth under the shady trees, in the covert of the reed, and fens.
22. The shady trees cover him with their shadow; the willows of the brook compass him about.
23. Behold, he drinketh up a river, and hasteth not: he trusteth that he can draw up Jordan into his mouth.
24. He taketh it with his eyes: his nose pierceth through snares.

Many theologians have missed the Behemoth as being Satan. Jordan is Christianity in verse 22.

Think of the Behemoth Satan among the trees or the nations. Meditation. Consider and hear me, O Lord my God: lighten mine eyes, lest I sleep the sleep of death.

SATAN   2166 BC+/-

JOB

God also calls Satan Leviathan, the give away is verse 34 chapter 41 Job.

Job 41:1

1. Canst thou draw out leviathan with an hook? or his tongue with a cord which thou lettest down?

Job 41:34

34. He beholdeth all high things: he is a king over all the children of pride.

Isaiah 27:1

1. In that day the Lord with his sore and great and strong sword shall punish leviathan the piercing serpent, even leviathan that crooked serpent; and he shall slay the dragon that is in the sea.

That meant "political sea"

Job 41:1-18

1. Canst thou draw out leviathan with an hook? or his tongue with a cord which thou lettest down?
2. Canst thou put an hook into his nose? or bore his jaw through with a thorn?
3. Will he make many supplications unto thee? will he speak soft words unto thee?
4. Will he make a covenant with thee? wilt thou take him for a servant for ever?
5. Wilt thou play with him as with a bird? or wilt thou bind him for thy maidens?
6. Shall the companions make a banquet of him? shall they part him among the merchants?
7. Canst thou fill his skin with barbed irons? or his head with fish spears?
8. Lay thine hand upon him, remember the battle, do no more.
9. Behold, the hope of him is in vain: shall not one be cast down even at the sight of him?
10. None is so fierce that dare stir him up: who then is able to stand before me?
11. Who hath prevented me, that I should repay him? whatsoever is under the whole heaven is mine.
12. I will not conceal his parts, nor his power, nor his comely proportion.
13. Who can discover the face of his garment? or who can come to him with his double bridle?
14. Who can open the doors of his face? his teeth are terrible round about.
15. His scales are his pride, shut up together as with a close seal.
16. One is so near to another, that no air can come between them.
17. They are joined one to another, they stick together, that they cannot be sundered.
18. By his neesings a light doth shine, and his eyes are like the eyelids of the morning.

Think of Leviathan as being Satan or the Dragon. Meditation. Let all mine enemies be ashamed and sore vexed: let them return and be ashamed suddenly.

SATAN   2166 BC+/-

JOB 41:19

This is where Satan and men got the image that dragons spue out fire. It is because God said Satan or Leviathan spues our fire and Satan has made the vision public worldwide in all societies.

Job 41:19-20

19. Out of his mouth go burning lamps, and sparks of fire leap out.
20. Out of his nostrils goeth smoke, as out of a seething pot or caldron.

Think of Satan the Dragon the lives in the political sea spewing out political fire. Meditation. For there is no faithfulness in their mouth; their inward part is very wickedness; their throat is an open sepulchre; they flatter with their tongue.

SATAN   2166 BC+/-

SATANS HEART IS LIKE A MILLSTONE

Satan is completely ruthless. He has a heart of stone. Look what he did to the Jews in WWII.

Job 41:21-24

21. His breath kindleth coals, and a flame goeth out of his mouth.
22. In his neck remaineth strength, and sorrow is turned into joy before him.
23. The flakes of his flesh are joined together: they are firm in themselves; they cannot be moved.
24. His heart is as firm as a stone; yea, as hard as a piece of the nether millstone.

Think of Satan's heart. It is like a stone, completely ruthless. Meditation. Destroy thou them, O God; let them fall by their own counsels; cast them out in the multitude of their transgressions; for they have rebelled against thee.

SATAN   2166 BC +/-

SATAN IS THE MASTER OF THE POLITICAL SEA AMONG MEN.

In verse 31 God says Satan makes the political sea to boil with wars and contentions. I sometimes fear what he will do to this book and to me.

Job 41:25-31

25. When he raiseth up himself, the mighty are afraid: by reason of breakings they purify themselves.
26. The sword of him that layeth at him cannot hold: the spear, the dart, nor the habergeon.
27. He esteemeth iron as straw, and brass as rotten wood.
28. The arrow cannot make him flee: slingstones are turned with him into stubble.
29. Darts are counted as stubble: he laugheth at the shaking of a spear.
30. Sharp stones are under him: he spreadeth sharp pointed things upon the mire.
31. He maketh the deep to boil like a pot: he maketh the sea like a pot of ointment.

But God is the King of the political sea.

Think of Leviathan and his sharks the demons in the political sea. Meditation. Depart from me, all ye workers of iniquity; for the Lord hath heard the voice of my weeping.

SATAN   2166 BC +/-

JOB

Satan beholds all high things and wants to be God. He is the king of the children of pride his demons.

Job 41:32-34

32. He maketh a path to shine after him; one would think the deep to be hoary.
33. Upon earth there is not his like, who is made without fear.
34. He beholdeth all high things: he is a king over all the children of pride.

Theologians look through all the recent bibles that were written and see how Satan has tampered with the Bible and exalting himself. Some Bibles he said ,"He is the Monarch over all that he sees" But the KJV is still the most accurate Bible that there is.

Think of Leviathan as king over the children of pride. Meditation. But let all those that put their trust in thee rejoice: let them ever shout for joy, because thou defendest them: let them also that love thy name be joyful in thee.

SATAN   1050 BC+/-

LEVIATHAN

Leviathan is mentioned in psalm 104:26 and Psalm 74:14

When God destroyed Satan at the Second Coming and divulged all the information about him to the people of the earth, Psalm 74:14 recorded it.

Psalm 74:14

14. Thou brakest the heads of leviathan in pieces, and gavest him to be meat to the people inhabiting the wilderness.

Psalm 104:26

26. There go the ships: there is that leviathan, whom thou hast made to play therein.

Think of Leviathan playing in the political sea. Meditation. My flesh and my heart faileth: but God is the strength of my heart, and my portion for ever.

SATAN   1056 BC+/-

THE MIGHTY

The Mighty are the Angels and David talks about the demons bothering him.

Psalm 82

1. God standeth in the congregation of the mighty; he judgeth among the gods.
2. How long will ye judge unjustly, and accept the persons of the wicked? Selah.
3. Defend the poor and fatherless: do justice to the afflicted and needy.
4. Deliver the poor and needy: rid them out of the hand of the wicked.
5. They know not, neither will they understand; they walk on in darkness: all the foundations of the earth are out of course.
6. I have said, Ye are gods; and all of you are children of the most High.
7. But ye shall die like men, and fall like one of the princes.
8. Arise, O God, judge the earth: for thou shalt inherit all nations.

Think of the Mighty stand before God who is Jesus. Meditation. But it is good for me to draw near to God: I have put my trust in the Lord God, that I may declare all thy works.

SATAN   605 BC +/-

ISRAEL FALLS.

Israel fell to Satan and God put them away, out of His sight for thousands of years until today the 1940's.

Think of the Captivity to Satan's lands the habitations of cruelty. Meditation. Remember thy congregation, which thou hast purchased of old; the rod of thine inheritance, which thou hast redeemed; this mount Zion, wherein thou dwelt.

SATAN   2010 AD+/- -40 BILLION AD+/-

PROVERBS

After Satan comes out of the bottomless pit he will have learned nothing from his experience, for the proverb says.

Proverb 27:22

22. Though thou shouldest bray a fool in a mortar among wheat with a pestle, yet will not his foolishness depart from him.

Think of Satan in the bottomless pit and never learning anything. Meditation. For, lo, they that are far from thee shall perish: thou hast destroyed all them that go a-whoring from thee.

SATAN   1000 BC+/-

PROVERB

Also this next proverb says that even when the anti Christ beast joins hands with Satan they will both fall.

Proverbs 11:21

21. Though hand join in hand, the wicked shall not be unpunished: but the seed of the righteous shall be delivered.

Think of the Beast and Satan fighting against God together. Meditation. Thou brakest the heads Leviathan in pieces, and gavest him to be meat to the people inhabiting the wilderness.

SATAN   790 BC+/-

ISAIAH

In Isaiah 10:24 the Lord says that Satan before the Second Coming would lift up his hand against the children of Israel- the Jews – as he did in Egypt. Isaiah 10:24 is Satan's second attempt to wipe out the Jews in WWII.

Isaiah 10:24

24. Therefore thus saith the Lord God of hosts, O my people that dwellest in Zion, be not afraid of the Assyrian: he shall smite thee with a rod, and shall lift up his staff against thee, after the manner of Egypt.

Think of Isaiah's prophecy about WWII. Meditation. O God, why hast thou cast us off forever? Why doth thine anger smoke against the sheep of thy pasture.

SATAN   2010 AD+/-

THE SECOND COMING.

Chapter 14 Isaiah is really about Satan, post WWII days and the Second Coming of Christ. The king of Babylon is Satan and the fir trees are the nations. Satan is being burnt in the bottomless pit and none hindereth.

Isaiah 14:1-8

1. For the Lord will have mercy on Jacob, and will yet choose Israel, and set them in their own land: and the strangers shall be joined with them, and they shall cleave to the house of Jacob.
2. And the people shall take them, and bring them to their place: and the house of Israel shall possess them in the land of the Lord for servants and handmaids: and they shall take them captives, whose captives they were; and they shall rule over their oppressors.
3. And it shall come to pass in the day that the Lord shall give thee rest from thy sorrow, and from thy fear, and from the hard bondage wherein thou wast made to serve,
4. That thou shalt take up this proverb against the king of Babylon, and say, How hath the oppressor ceased! the golden city ceased!
5. The Lord hath broken the staff of the wicked, and the sceptre of the rulers.
6. He who smote the people in wrath with a continual stroke, he that ruled the nations in anger, is persecuted, and none hindereth.
7. The whole earth is at rest, and is quiet: they break forth into singing.
8. Yea, the fir trees rejoice at thee, and the cedars of Lebanon, saying, Since thou art laid down, no feller is come up against us.

9. Hell from beneath is moved for thee to meet thee at thy coming: it stirreth up the dead for thee, even all the chief ones of the earth; it hath raised up from their thrones all the kings of the nations.
10. All they shall speak and say unto thee, Art thou also become weak as we? art thou become like unto us?
11. Thy pomp is brought down to the grave, and the noise of thy viols: the worm is spread under thee, and the worms cover thee.
12. How art thou fallen from heaven, O Lucifer, son of the morning! how art thou cut down to the ground, which didst weaken the nations!
13. For thou hast said in thine heart, I will ascend into heaven, I will exalt my throne above the stars of God: I will sit also upon the mount of the congregation, in the sides of the north:
14. I will ascend above the heights of the clouds; I will be like the most High.
15. Yet thou shalt be brought down to hell, to the sides of the pit.
16. They that see thee shall narrowly look upon thee, and consider thee, saying, Is this the man that made the earth to tremble, that did shake kingdoms;
17. That made the world as a wilderness, and destroyed the cities thereof; that opened not the house of his prisoners?
18. All the kings of the nations, even all of them, lie in glory, every one in his own house.

Think of Satan in the bottomless pit. Meditation. Remember this that the enemy hath reproached, O Lord, and that the foolish people have blasphemed thy name.

SATAN   2010 AD+/-

THE SECOND COMING

The people in hell are excited to meet Satan.

Isaiah 14:9-10

9. Hell from beneath is moved for thee to meet thee at thy coming: it stirreth up the dead for thee, even all the chief ones of the earth; it hath raised up from their thrones all the kings of the nations.
10. All they shall speak and say unto thee, Art thou also become weak as we? art thou become like unto us?

Think of the people in hell excited to meet Satan. Meditation. Whither shall I go from thy Spirit? Or whither shall I flee from thy presence O Lord. If I ascend up into heaven, thou art there: if I make my bed in hell, behold, thou art there.

SATAN   2010AD+/-

SECOND COMING.

Satan's rockin roll (viols) and movies (pomp) are brought down to the grave with him.

Isaiah 14:11-15

11. Thy pomp is brought down to the grave, and the noise of thy viols: the worm is spread under thee, and the worms cover thee.
12. How art thou fallen from heaven, O Lucifer, son of the morning! how art thou cut down to the ground, which didst weaken the nations!
13. For thou hast said in thine heart, I will ascend into heaven, I will exalt my throne above the stars of God: I will sit also upon the mount of the congregation, in the sides of the north:
14. I will ascend above the heights of the clouds; I will be like the most High.
15. Yet thou shalt be brought down to hell, to the sides of the pit.

To split hairs groups like Madonna will go to hell for dragging Mary's name through the dirt, Metallica for exalting the Beast, Ozzy whom Satan loves so much and even rewarded him with a TV show and all the other groups (2112 Rush) etc will be in hell. They can repent if they want to today before Christ comes back. Movies are almost endless, but it lately I noticed Satan has been exalting the Secret Service culture. I know why, but its better not said because it might spook the sheep. But other movies like Diablo, and reign of fire , the hobbit series with sorcery and Science fiction space movies where Jesus and God has been eliminated etc. Just look around. All that is Satan and its going down with him to his grave.

Think of Satan and his viols broken in hell. Meditation. O Give thanks unto the Lord; for He is good: for His mercy endureth forever.

SATAN   2010 AD+/-

SATAN IS KICKED OUT OF HELL

The people in hell looked at Satan narrowly when they saw him and they kicked him out of hell his grave and threw him into the bottomless pit.

Isaiah 14 :16-20

16. They that see thee shall narrowly look upon thee, and consider thee, saying, Is this the man that made the earth to tremble, that did shake kingdoms;
17. That made the world as a wilderness, and destroyed the cities thereof; that opened not the house of his prisoners?
18. All the kings of the nations, even all of them, lie in glory, every one in his own house.
19. But thou art cast out of thy grave like an abominable branch, and as the raiment of those that are slain, thrust through with a sword, that go down to the stones of the pit; as a carcase trodden under feet.
20. Thou shalt not be joined with them in burial, because thou hast destroyed thy land, and slain thy people: the seed of evildoers shall never be renowned.

Think of Satan and his demons kicked out of hell by the people there. Meditation. O give thanks unto the God of gods: for His mercy endureth for ever.

SATAN   2010 AD+/-

SATAN WANTED A LEGEND.

Isaiah 14:20 **"....: The** seed of evildoers shall never be renowned."

Satan wanted a legend to be remembered by when he and his angels went into the bottomless pit. Like when Metallica sings that song. " ... they were watching us, as we were all flying away".. The Bible says this will all happen near the Second Coming. The whole chapter 14 is a future prophecy of our days around the year 2000 +/-. Today the Lord says that He will kill off everyone associated with Satan, from the Hell's angels motorcycle gangs to the witches of Salem, for Satan intended that culture of people take over the world (gangsters) and replace Christians in the cities of the world.

Isaiah 14:21-28

21. Prepare slaughter for his children for the iniquity of their fathers; that they do not rise, nor possess the land, nor fill the face of the world with cities.
22. For I will rise up against them, saith the Lord of hosts, and cut off from Babylon the name, and remnant, and son, and nephew, saith the Lord.
23. I will also make it a possession for the bittern, and pools of water: and I will sweep it with the Besom of destruction, saith the Lord of hosts.
24. The Lord of hosts hath sworn, saying, Surely as I have thought, so shall it come to pass; and as I have purposed, so shall it stand:
25. That I will break the Assyrian in my land, and upon my mountains tread him under foot: then shall his yoke depart from off them, and his burden depart from off their shoulders.
26. This is the purpose that is purposed upon the whole earth: and this is the hand that is stretched out upon all the nations.
27. For the Lord of hosts hath purposed, and who shall disannul it? and his hand is stretched out, and who shall turn it back?
28. In the year that king Ahaz died was this burden.

Think of the gangsters exalted on TV and music groups like Bad company that exalt evil (song Bad Company, Bad Company) Meditation. O give thanks unto the God of heaven: for His mercy endureth forever.

<u>SATAN</u>   2010 AD+/-

SATAN WANTS TO NUKE THE WORLD AS A DRAGON

After Satan's rod or Nazi's was broken or destroyed in WWII, Satan became a dragon- a fiery flying serpent. He tried to nuke the world with the communist threat by escalating the cold war. A dragon is a creature that wants to destroy all mankind thus the metamorphisis of Satan.

Isaiah 14:29

29. Rejoice not thou, whole Palestina, because the rod of him that smote thee is broken: for out of the serpent's root shall come forth a cockatrice, and his fruit shall be a fiery flying serpent.

Think of Satan turning into a dragon and wanting to nuke the earth. Meditation. By the rivers of Babylon , there we sat down, yea, we wept when we remembered Zion.

SATAN   2010 AD+/-

THE SECOND COMING

But at the Second Coming God will destroy the root of evil- Satan and his demons and Jesus will destroy the remnant the human goats.

Isaiah 14:30

30. And the firstborn of the poor shall feed, and the needy shall lie down in safety: and I will kill thy root with famine, and he shall slay thy remnant.

Think of God the Father throwing Satan into the bottomless pit. Meditation. To Him that by wisdom made the heavens: for His mercy endureth forever.

SATAN   1984-2000 AD+/-

THE CARCASE.

The gate of Zion, the Church was in trouble when the Carcase of Mt 24:28 came around and was deceived by Satan, but he rebelled against Satan who had deceived him and he lost his marriage date- his appointed time. He later found the God of Israel. He is the messenger of Isaiah 14:32

Isaiah 14:31-32

31. Howl, O gate; cry, O city; thou, whole Palestina, art dissolved: for there shall come from the north a smoke, and none shall be alone in his appointed times.
32. What shall one then answer the messengers of the nation? That the Lord hath founded Zion, and the poor of his people shall trust in it.

Think of the Messenger of Isaiah 14:32 serving Jesus. Meditation. If I forget thee, O Jerusalem, let my right hand forget her cunning.

SATAN   2010 AD+/-

SATAN AND HIS DEMONS ARE PUNISHED.

At the Second Coming God will punish Satan and his demons who are the kings of the earth and after many days- 40 billion years they shall be visited for WWIII.

Isaiah 24:21-23

21. And it shall come to pass in that day, that the Lord shall punish the host of the high ones that are on high, and the kings of the earth upon the earth.
22. And they shall be gathered together, as prisoners are gathered in the pit, and shall be shut up in the prison, and after many days shall they be visited.
23. Then the moon shall be confounded, and the sun ashamed, when the Lord of hosts shall reign in mount Zion, and in Jerusalem, and before his ancients gloriously.

Think of Satan and his demons in the bottomless pit for many days. Meditation. O daughter of Babylon, who are to be destroyed; happy shall he be, that rewardeth thee as thou hast served us. Happy shall he be, that taketh and dasheth thy little ones against the stones.

SATAN   2010 AD+/-

THE LORDS SWORD.

"In that day" is the Second Coming and God will destroy Satan the dragon who lives in the political sea.

Isaiah 27:1

1. In that day the Lord with his sore and great and strong sword shall punish leviathan the piercing serpent, even leviathan that crooked serpent; and he shall slay the dragon that is in the sea.

Think of Leviathan being punished by the Lord's sword. Meditation. Come and see the works of God: He is terrible in His doing toward the children of men.

SATAN   00AD-2010 AD+/-

THE CHURCH'S LOVE IS THE LORD'S RED WINE.

The vineyard of the Lord is the Church and the "red wine" is Christianity and God said He will protect her from Satan who is trying to destroy her and setting up barriers against Him at the Second Coming.

Isaiah 27:2-5

2. In that day sing ye unto her, A vineyard of red wine.
3. I the Lord do keep it; I will water it every moment: lest any hurt it, I will keep it night and day.
4. Fury is not in me: who would set the briers and thorns against me in battle? I would go through them, I would burn them together.
5. Or let him take hold of my strength, that he may make peace with me; and he shall make peace with me.

Think of the Lord's vineyard the Church and how the Lord protects her. Meditation. For the Lord God is a sun and shield: the Lord will give grace and glory: no good thing will He withhold from them that walk uprightly.

SATAN   586 BC+/-

THE MOST PROUD.

In Jeremiah the Lord calls Satan the Most Proud.

Jeremiah 50:31-32

31. Behold, I am against thee, O thou most proud, saith the Lord God of hosts: for thy day is come, the time that I will visit thee.

32. And the most proud shall stumble and fall, and none shall raise him up: and I will kindle a fire in his cities, and it shall devour all round about him.

Think of Satan the most proud about to be destroyed. Meditation. All the horns of the wicked also will I cut off; but the horns of the righteous shall be exalted.

SATAN   20 BILLION BC-7000BC+/-

EZEKIEL 28

We go back to Ezekiel 28 where God records His original speech to Lucifer which started the whole war in Genesis. All the people who knew Satan originally – St. Michael and St. Gabriel were astonished at Lucifer's fall.

Ezekiel 28

1. The word of the Lord came again unto me, saying,

2. Son of man, say unto the prince of Tyrus, Thus saith the Lord God; Because thine heart is lifted up, and thou hast said, I am a God, I sit in the seat of God, in the midst of the seas; yet thou art a man, and not God, though thou set thine heart as the heart of God:

3. Behold, thou art wiser than Daniel; there is no secret that they can hide from thee:

4. With thy wisdom and with thine understanding thou hast gotten thee riches, and hast gotten gold and silver into thy treasures:

5. By thy great wisdom and by thy traffick hast thou increased thy riches, and thine heart is lifted up because of thy riches:

6. Therefore thus saith the Lord God; Because thou hast set thine heart as the heart of God;

7. Behold, therefore I will bring strangers upon thee, the terrible of the nations: and they shall draw their swords against the beauty of thy wisdom, and they shall defile thy brightness.

8. They shall bring thee down to the pit, and thou shalt die the deaths of them that are slain in the midst of the seas.

9. Wilt thou yet say before him that slayeth thee, I am God? but thou shalt be a man, and no God, in the hand of him that slayeth thee.

10. Thou shalt die the deaths of the uncircumcised by the hand of strangers: for I have spoken it, saith the Lord God.

11. Moreover the word of the Lord came unto me, saying,

12. Son of man, take up a lamentation upon the king of Tyrus, and say unto him, thus saith the Lord God; Thou sealest up the sum, full of wisdom, and perfect in beauty.

13. Thou hast been in Eden the garden of God; every precious stone was thy covering, the sardius, topaz, and the diamond, the Beryl, the onyx, and the jasper, the sapphire, the emerald, and the carbuncle, and gold: the workmanship of thy tabrets and of thy pipes was prepared in thee in the day that thou wast created.

14. Thou art the anointed cherub that covereth; and I have set thee so: thou wast upon the

holy mountain of God; thou hast walked up and down in the midst of the stones of fire.

15. Thou wast perfect in thy ways from the day that thou wast created, till iniquity was found in thee.

16. By the multitude of thy merchandise they have filled the midst of thee with violence, and thou hast sinned: therefore I will cast thee as profane out of the mountain of God: and I will destroy thee, O covering cherub, from the midst of the stones of fire.

17. Thine heart was lifted up because of thy beauty, thou hast corrupted thy wisdom by reason of thy brightness: I will cast thee to the ground, I will lay thee before kings, that they may behold thee.

18. Thou hast defiled thy sanctuaries by the multitude of thine iniquities, by the iniquity of thy traffick; therefore will I bring forth a fire from the midst of thee, it shall devour thee, and I will bring thee to ashes upon the earth in the sight of all them that behold thee.

Think of Lucifer becoming Satan. Meditation. Praise ye the Lord. Praise ye the Lord from the heavens: praise Him in the heights.

SATAN   600 BC+/-

DANIEL AND THE ANGEL

In Daniel we see that Angels were and are fighting over the earth.

Daniel 10:12-14

12. Then said he unto me, Fear not, Daniel: for from the first day that thou didst set thine heart to understand, and to chasten thyself before thy God, thy words were heard, and I am come for thy words.

13. But the prince of the kingdom of Persia withstood me one and twenty days: but, lo, Michael, one of the chief princes, came to help me; and I remained there with the kings of Persia.

14. Now I am come to make thee understand what shall befall thy people in the latter days: for yet the vision is for many days.

Think of the Angel that talked to Daniel. Meditation. Praise ye Him, all His Angels: praise ye Him, all His hosts.

SATAN   10 BC+/-

NEW TESTAMENT TIMES.

In Matthew we see Satan fighting John the Baptist . Jesus said in Matthew 11:12

Mt 11:12

12. And from the days of John the Baptist until now the kingdom of heaven suffereth violence, and the violent take it by force.

Think of John the Baptist fighting Satan. Meditation. Praise ye Him, sun and moon: praise Him, all ye stars of light.

SATAN   10BC+/-

SATAN KILLS THE LITTLE CHILDREN.

It was satan who killed all the children of Israel who lived on the coasts when Christ was born. He even knew that Jesus was in Egypt but he killed them anyway.

Matthew 2:16-18

16. Then Herod, when he saw that he was mocked of the wise men, was exceeding wroth, and sent forth, and slew all the children that were in Bethlehem, and in all the coasts thereof, from two years old and under, according to the time which he had diligently inquired of the wise men.
17. Then was fulfilled that which was spoken by Jeremy the prophet, saying,
18. In Rama was there a voice heard, lamentation, and weeping, and great mourning, Rachel weeping for her children, and would not be comforted, because they are not.

Think of Satan killing all the little children on the coasts of Israel. Meditation. Praise Him, ye heavens of heavens, and ye waters that be above the heavens.

SATAN   10 BC+/-

SATAN TEMPTS JESUS THE CREATOR.

Satan tempted Jesus his creator. Jesus did not use any supernatural weapon to destroy Satan but He used the written Word of God, the same weapon that all Christians have available to them- the Bible. A little word shall fell him.

Matthew 4:1-11

1. Then was Jesus led up of the Spirit into the wilderness to be tempted of the devil.
2. And when he had fasted forty days and forty nights, he was afterward an hungred.
3. And when the tempter came to him, he said, If thou be the Son of God, command that these stones be made bread.
4. But he answered and said, It is written, Man shall not live by bread alone, but by every word that proceedeth out of the mouth of God.
5. Then the devil taketh him up into the holy city, and setteth him on a pinnacle of the temple,
6. And saith unto him, If thou be the Son of God, cast thyself down: for it is written, He shall give his angels charge concerning thee: and in their hands they shall bear thee up, lest at any time thou dash thy foot against a stone.
7. Jesus said unto him, It is written again, Thou shalt not tempt the Lord thy God.

8. Again, the devil taketh him up into an exceeding high mountain, and sheweth him all the kingdoms of the world, and the glory of them;

9. And saith unto him, All these things will I give thee, if thou wilt fall down and worship me.

10. Then saith Jesus unto him, Get thee hence, Satan: for it is written, Thou shalt worship the Lord thy God, and him only shalt thou serve.

11. Then the devil leaveth him, and, behold, angels came and ministered unto him.

Think of Satan tempting Jesus. Meditation. Let them praise the name of the Lord: for He commanded, and they were created.

SATAN   10 BC+/-

THE PHARISEES

The Pharisees were possessed by demons and Satan, and tried to confuse Christ's words. That's where all those arguments and attempted murders came from.

Think of the Pharisees against Jesus. Meditation. Praise the Lord from the earth, ye dragons, and all deeps.

SATAN   10BC+/-

EVERLASTING PUNISHMENT.

Jesus said that Satan and his angels will be thrown into everlasting fire.

Matthew 25:41

41. Then shall he say also unto them on the left hand, Depart from me, ye cursed, into everlasting fire, prepared for the devil and his angels:

Think of the Lake of fire and how Satan will be burnt in it. Meditation. Praise ye the Lord. Sing unto the Lord a new song, and His praise in the congregation of saints.

SATAN   10 BC+/-

DEVICES

The devices of Satan against the Apostles were terrible. In Acts Satan tried to fight and kill the Apostles.

Think of Satan attacking the Apostles. Meditation. Let Israel rejoice in Him that made him: let the children of Zion be joyful in their King.

SATAN   600 AD+/-

ROME IS DESTROYED BY SATAN.

Jesus converted the whole Roman empire with His single act on the cross so Satan destroyed Rome because it had converted to Christianity.

Think of Rome destroyed by Satan. Meditation. For the Lord taketh pleasure in His people: He will beautify the meek with salvation.

SATAN   600-1000 AD+/-

ISLAM

Jesus converted the Goths who destroyed the Roman empire. So Satan invented Islam to try to destroy Christianity when the Goths and Barbarians who destroyed Rome were converted.

Think of Islam attacking the Crusaders. Meditation. Let the saints be joyful I glory: let them sing aloud upon their beds

SATAN   1930-1945 +/-

ISAIAH 10:24

In this time frame Satan tried to destroy the Jews so the prophecy of their return would not happen. This is when Isaiah Chpt 10:24 comes true.

24.   Therefore thus saith the Lord God of hosts, O my people that dwellest in Zion, be not afraid of the Assyrian: he shall smite thee with a rod, and shall lift up his staff against thee, after the manner of Egypt.

Think of WWII and Satan's attempt to wipe out the Jews so Israel would not be recreated. Meditation. Our feet shall stand within thy gates, O Jerusalem.

SATAN   1945-1984 AD+/-

THE RED DRAGON OF COMMUNISM.

After Satan failed with the Nazi's he tried communism and tried to destroy the Church with it. He became a dragon because dragon's want to destroy the whole human race with nukes.

Isaiah 14:29 came true.

29.   Rejoice not thou, whole Palestina, because the rod of him that smote thee is broken: for out of the serpent's root shall come forth a cockatrice, and his fruit shall be a fiery flying serpent.

Think of the Communist Dragon Meditation. Go from the presence of a foolish man, when thou perceivest not in him the lips of knowledge.

SATAN   1984-1985 +/- AD.

THE U.S.S.R FALLS

The carcase helped Jesus destroy the U.S.S.R.. That long awaited battle between Christians and communist Russia at the end of time was stopped by God with Isaiah 27:8

Isaiah 27:8

8. In measure, when it shooteth forth, thou wilt debate with it: he stayeth his rough wind in the day of the east wind.

Satan is debating with the expanding Church. " Roughwind" is Christian Jihad. " Wind" means "politics" . " East wind" is eastern politics- communism. So the day of Eastern wind is Eastern communism. God "Stayeth" His roughwind in the day of the east wind. He stopped the Jihad against Satan's communism , an operation the Carcase put together and was about to implement.

Isaiah 27:8.

8. In measure, when it shooteth forth, thou wilt debate with it: he stayeth his rough wind in the day of the east wind.

Think of Satan and communism stopped by Jesus and the Carcase. Meditation. Blessed be the Lord my strength, which teacheth my hands to war, and my fingers to fight.

SATAN   2010 AD+/–

SATAN USES ISLAM AND THE PEDOPHILE SCANDAL TO HURT THE CHURCH.

Jesus said the pedophile scandal would happen in Matthew and Mark. The pedophile scandal is what happened after Satan failed in converting the Carcase. The Carcase if the Earth of Revelation 12:16 and after he swallowed the political dictation of Satan (the flood) verse 2:17 says Satan went out and hurt the Church with the scandal and demon possessed suicide bombers against Israel and the Jews

Revelation 12:17

16. And the earth helped the woman, and the earth opened her mouth, and swallowed up the flood which the dragon cast out of his mouth.
17. And the dragon was wroth with the woman, and went to make war with the remnant of her seed, which keep the commandments of God, and have the testimony of Jesus Christ.

Matthew 18:6-7 6.

6. But whoso shall offend one of these little ones which believe in me, it were better for him that a millstone were hanged about his neck, and that he were drowned in the depth of the sea.
7. Woe unto the world because of offences! for it must needs be that offences come; but woe to that man by whom the offence cometh!

Mark 9:42

42. And whosoever shall offend one of these little ones that believe in me, it is better for him that a millstone were hanged about his neck, and he were cast into the sea.

Think on how Jesus knew Satan would attack and try to dirty the Church at the end of time. Meditation. Mine eyes shall be upon the faithful of the land, that they may dwell with Me: he shall serve Me

SATAN   2010 AD+/-

THE SECOND COMING.

The Second Coming took place right after chpt 12 Revelation with Chpt 13 Isaiah.
Chapter 13 Isaiah.

Isaiah 13

1. The burden of Babylon, which Isaiah the son of Amoz did see.
2. Lift ye up a banner upon the high mountain, exalt the voice unto them, shake the hand, that they may go into the gates of the nobles.
3. I have commanded my sanctified ones, I have also called my mighty ones for mine anger, even them that rejoice in my highness.
4. The noise of a multitude in the mountains, like as of a great people; a tumultuous noise of the kingdoms of nations gathered together: the Lord of hosts mustereth the host of the battle.
5. They come from a far country, from the end of heaven, even the Lord, and the weapons of his indignation, to destroy the whole land.
6. Howl ye; for the day of the Lord is at hand; it shall come as a destruction from the Almighty.
7. Therefore shall all hands be faint, and every man's heart shall melt:
8. And they shall be afraid: pangs and sorrows shall take hold of them; they shall be in pain as a woman that travaileth: they shall be amazed one at another; their faces shall be as flames.
9. Behold, the day of the Lord cometh, cruel both with wrath and fierce anger, to lay the land desolate: and he shall destroy the sinners thereof out of it.
10. For the stars of heaven and the constellations thereof shall not give their light: the sun shall be darkened in his going forth, and the moon shall not cause her light to shine.
11. And I will punish the world for their evil, and the wicked for their iniquity; and I will cause the arrogancy of the proud to cease, and will lay low the haughtiness of the terrible.
12. I will make a man more precious than fine gold; even a man than the golden wedge of Ophir.
13. Therefore I will shake the heavens, and the earth shall remove out of her place, in the wrath of the Lord of hosts, and in the day of his fierce anger.
14. And it shall be as the chased roe, and as a sheep that no man taketh up: they shall every man turn to his own people, and flee every one into his own land.
15. Every one that is found shall be thrust through; and every one that is joined unto them shall fall by the sword.

16. Their children also shall be dashed to pieces before their eyes; their houses shall be spoiled, and their wives ravished.

17. Behold, I will stir up the Medes against them, which shall not regard silver; and as for gold, they shall not delight in it.

18. Their bows also shall dash the young men to pieces; and they shall have no pity on the fruit of the womb; their eye shall not spare children.

19. And Babylon, the glory of kingdoms, the beauty of the Chaldees' excellency, shall be as when God overthrew Sodom and Gomorrah.

20. It shall never be inhabited, neither shall it be dwelt in from generation to generation: neither shall the Arabian pitch tent there; neither shall the shepherds make their fold there.

21. But wild beasts of the desert shall lie there; and their houses shall be full of doleful creatures; and owls shall dwell there, and Satyrs shall dance there.

22. And the wild beasts of the islands shall cry in their desolate houses, and dragons in their pleasant palaces: and her time is near to come, and her days shall not be prolonged.

Think of the Angels coming to earth to do sinners in. Meditation. The Lord is righteous in all His ways, and Holy in all His works.

SATAN   2010 AD+/-

THE BOTTOMLESS PIT

Satan is thrown into the bottomless pit.

Think of the bottomless pit and how Satan is thrown into it. Meditation. Cast forth lightning, and scatter them: shoot out thine arrows, and destroy them.

SATAN   2010-40 BILLION AD+/-

RELEASED OUT OF THE BOTTOMLESS PIT IN 40 BILLION AD+/-

After 40 billion years of torture Satan is released out of the bottomless pit.

Revelation 20:7

7. And when the thousand years are expired, Satan shall be loosed out of his prison,

Think of Satan and demons being released out of the pit. Meditation. Jerusalem is builded as a city that is compact together.

SATAN   40 BILLION AD+/-

SHY AT FIRST.

At first Satan and his demons were shy to come out into society, but they had a great curse on them from the Carcase.

Think of Satan and his demons stretch their legs and stop crying. Meditation. Blessed be the Lord, who hath not given us as a prey to their teeth.

SATAN   40 BILLION AD+/-

THE CREATION OF BABYLON

Then Satan went into the fringes of the universe and created a nation called Babylon the great to coexist with Christ's peaceful kingdom.

Think of the creation of evil Babylon. Meditation. Many a time have they afflicted me from my youth may Israel now say:

SATAN   40 BILLION AD+/-

CHRIST'S KINGDOM IS CONTAMINATED.

I John 4:1-3

1. Beloved, believe not every spirit, but try the spirits whether they are of God: because many false prophets are gone out into the world.
2. Hereby know ye the Spirit of God: Every spirit that confesseth that Jesus Christ is come in the flesh is of God:
3. And every spirit that confesseth not that Jesus Christ is come in the flesh is not of God: and this is that spirit of antichrist, whereof ye have heard that it should come; and even now already is it in the world.

I John 2:18-19

18. Little children, it is the last time: and as ye have heard that antichrist shall come, even now are there many antichrists; whereby we know that it is the last time.
19. They went out from us, but they were not of us; for if they had been of us, they would no doubt have continued with us: but they went out, that they might be made manifest that they were not all of us.

Think of the goats turning to Satan. Meditation. Many a time have they afflicted me from my youth: yet they have not prevailed against me.

SATAN   40 BILLION AD+/-

SATAN ATTACKS CHRIST'S KINGDOM.

Then Satan attacked Christs kingdom.

Ezekiel 38

1. And the word of the Lord came unto me, saying,
2. Son of man, set thy face against Gog, the land of Magog, the chief prince of Meshech and Tubal, and prophesy against him,
3. And say, Thus saith the Lord God; Behold, I am against thee, O Gog, the chief prince of Meshech and Tubal:

4. And I will turn thee back, and put hooks into thy jaws, and I will bring thee forth, and all thine army, horses and horsemen, all of them clothed with all sorts of armour, even a great company with bucklers and shields, all of them handling swords:

5. Persia, Ethiopia, and Libya with them; all of them with shield and helmet:

6. Gomer, and all his bands; the house of Togarmah of the north quarters, and all his bands: and many people with thee.

7. Be thou prepared, and prepare for thyself, thou, and all thy company that are assembled unto thee, and be thou a guard unto them.

8. After many days thou shalt be visited: in the latter years thou shalt come into the land that is brought back from the sword, and is gathered out of many people, against the mountains of Israel, which have been always waste: but it is brought forth out of the nations, and they shall dwell safely all of them.

9. Thou shalt ascend and come like a storm, thou shalt be like a cloud to cover the land, thou, and all thy bands, and many people with thee.

10. Thus saith the Lord God; It shall also come to pass, that at the same time shall things come into thy mind, and thou shalt think an evil thought:

11. And thou shalt say, I will go up to the land of unwalled villages; I will go to them that are at rest, that dwell safely, all of them dwelling without walls, and having neither bars nor gates,

12. To take a spoil, and to take a prey; to turn thine hand upon the desolate places that are now inhabited, and upon the people that are gathered out of the nations, which have gotten cattle and goods, that dwell in the midst of the land.

13. Sheba, and Dedan, and the merchants of Tarshish, with all the young lions thereof, shall say unto thee, Art thou come to take a spoil? hast thou gathered thy company to take a prey? to carry away silver and gold, to take away cattle and goods, to take a great spoil?

14. Therefore, son of man, prophesy and say unto Gog, Thus saith the Lord God; In that day when My people of Israel dwelleth safely, shalt thou not know it?

15. And thou shalt come from thy place out of the north parts, thou, and many people with thee, all of them riding upon horses, a great company, and a mighty army:

16. And thou shalt come up against My people of Israel, as a cloud to cover the land; it shall be in the latter days, and I will bring thee against my land, that the heathen may know me, when I shall be sanctified in thee, O Gog, before their eyes.

17. Thus saith the Lord God; Art thou he of whom I have spoken in old time by my servants the prophets of Israel, which prophesied in those days many years that I would bring thee against them?

18. And it shall come to pass at the same time when Gog shall come against the land of Israel, saith the Lord God, that my fury shall come up in my face.

19. For in my jealousy and in the fire of my wrath have I spoken, surely in that day there shall be a great shaking in the land of Israel;

20. So that the fishes of the sea, and the fowls of the heaven, and the beasts of the field, and all creeping things that creep upon the earth, and all the men that are upon the face of the earth, shall shake at my presence, and the mountains shall be thrown down, and the steep places shall fall, and every wall shall fall to the ground.

21. And I will call for a sword against him throughout all my mountains, saith the Lord God: every man's sword shall be against his brother.

22. And I will plead against him with pestilence and with blood; and I will rain upon him,

and upon his bands, and upon the many people that are with him, an overflowing rain, and great hailstones, fire, and brimstone.

23. Thus will I magnify myself, and sanctify myself; and I will be known in the eyes of many nations, and they shall know that I am the Lord.

Think of Satan's hordes attacking Christ's kingdom and a great civil war ensues. Meditation Why do the heathen rage, and the people imagine a vain thing?

<u>SATAN</u>   <u>40 BILLION AD</u>

CHAPTER 13 REVELATION COMES TRUE IN THIS TIME FRAME.

Revelation 13

1. And I stood upon the sand of the sea, and saw a beast rise up out of the sea, having seven heads and ten horns, and upon his horns ten crowns, and upon his heads the name of blasphemy.

2. And the beast which I saw was like unto a leopard, and his feet were as the feet of a bear, and his mouth as the mouth of a lion: and the dragon gave him his power, and his seat, and great authority.

3. And I saw one of his heads as it were wounded to death; and his deadly wound was healed: and all the world wondered after the beast.

4. And they worshipped the dragon which gave power unto the beast: and they worshipped the beast, saying, Who is like unto the beast? who is able to make war with him?

5. And there was given unto him a mouth speaking great things and blasphemies; and power was given unto him to continue forty and two months.

6. And he opened his mouth in blasphemy against God, to blaspheme his name, and his tabernacle, and them that dwell in heaven.

7. And it was given unto him to make war with the saints, and to overcome them: and power was given him over all kindreds, and tongues, and nations.

8. And all that dwell upon the earth shall worship him, whose names are not written in the book of life of the Lamb slain from the foundation of the world.

9. If any man have an ear, let him hear.

10. He that leadeth into captivity shall go into captivity: he that killeth with the sword must be killed with the sword. Here is the patience and the faith of the saints.

11. And I beheld another beast coming up out of the earth; and he had two horns like a lamb, and he spake as a dragon.

12. And he exerciseth all the power of the first beast before him, and causeth the earth and them which dwell therein to worship the first beast, whose deadly wound was healed.

13. And he doeth great wonders, so that he maketh fire come down from heaven on the earth in the sight of men,

14. And deceiveth them that dwell on the earth by the means of those miracles which he had power to do in the sight of the beast; saying to them that dwell on the earth, that they should make an image to the beast, which had the wound by a sword, and did live.

15. And he had power to give life unto the image of the beast, that the image of the beast

should both speak, and cause that as many as would not worship the image of the beast should be killed.

16. And he causeth all, both small and great, rich and poor, free and bond, to receive a mark in their right hand, or in their foreheads:

17. And that no man might buy or sell, save he that had the mark, or the name of the beast, or the number of his name.

18. Here is wisdom. Let him that hath understanding count the number of the beast: for it is the number of a man; and his number is Six hundred threescore and six.

Think of the Wicked one. Meditation. But thou, O Lord, art a shield for me; my glory, and the lifter up of mine head.

SATAN   40 BILLION AD+/-

CIVIL WAR IN THE UNIVERSE.

The universe wide civil war is explained in Ezekiel.

Ezekiel 39

1. Therefore, thou son of man, prophesy against Gog, and say, Thus saith the Lord God; Behold, I am against thee, O Gog, the chief prince of Meshech and Tubal:

2. And I will turn thee back, and leave but the sixth part of thee, and will cause thee to come up from the north parts, and will bring thee upon the mountains of Israel:

3. And I will smite thy bow out of thy left hand, and will cause thine arrows to fall out of thy right hand.

4. Thou shalt fall upon the mountains of Israel, thou, and all thy bands, and the people that is with thee: I will give thee unto the ravenous birds of every sort, and to the beasts of the field to be devoured.

5. Thou shalt fall upon the open field: for I have spoken it, saith the Lord God.

6. And I will send a fire on Magog, and among them that dwell carelessly in the isles: and they shall know that I am the Lord.

7. So will I make my holy name known in the midst of my people Israel; and I will not let them pollute my holy name any more: and the heathen shall know that I am the Lord, the Holy One in Israel.

8. Behold, it is come, and it is done, saith the Lord God; this is the day whereof I have spoken.

9. And they that dwell in the cities of Israel shall go forth, and shall set on fire and burn the weapons, both the shields and the bucklers, the bows and the arrows, and the handstaves, and the spears, and they shall burn them with fire seven years:

10. So that they shall take no wood out of the field, neither cut down any out of the forests; for they shall burn the weapons with fire: and they shall spoil those that spoiled them, and rob those that robbed them, saith the Lord God.

11. And it shall come to pass in that day, that I will give unto Gog a place there of graves in Israel, the valley of the passengers on the east of the sea: and it shall stop the noses of the passengers: and there shall they bury Gog and all his multitude: and they shall call it the valley of Hamongog.

12. And seven months shall the house of Israel be burying of them, that they may cleanse the land.

13. Yea, all the people of the land shall bury them; and it shall be to them a renown the day that I shall be glorified, saith the Lord God.

14. And they shall sever out men of continual employment, passing through the land to bury with the passengers those that remain upon the face of the earth, to cleanse it: after the end of seven months shall they search.

15. And the passengers that pass through the land, when any seeth a man's bone, then shall he set up a sign by it, till the buriers have buried it in the valley of Hamongog.

16. And also the name of the city shall be Hamonah. Thus shall they cleanse the land.

17. And, thou son of man, thus saith the Lord God; Speak unto every feathered fowl, and to every beast of the field, assemble yourselves, and come; gather yourselves on every side to my sacrifice that I do sacrifice for you, even a great sacrifice upon the mountains of Israel, that ye may eat flesh, and drink blood.

18. Ye shall eat the flesh of the mighty, and drink the blood of the princes of the earth, of rams, of lambs, and of goats, of bullocks, all of them fatlings of Bashan.

19. And ye shall eat fat till ye be full, and drink blood till ye be drunken, of my sacrifice which I have sacrificed for you.

20. Thus ye shall be filled at my table with horses and chariots, with mighty men, and with all men of war, saith the Lord God.

21. And I will set my glory among the heathen, and all the heathen shall see my judgment that I have executed, and my hand that I have laid upon them.

22. So the house of Israel shall know that I am the Lord their God from that day and forward.

23. And the heathen shall know that the house of Israel went into captivity for their iniquity: because they trespassed against me, therefore hid I my face from them, and gave them into the hand of their enemies: so fell they all by the sword.

24. According to their uncleanness and according to their transgressions have I done unto them, and hid my face from them.

25. Therefore thus saith the Lord God; Now will I bring again the captivity of Jacob, and have mercy upon the whole house of Israel, and will be jealous for my holy name;

26. After that they have borne their shame, and all their trespasses whereby they have trespassed against me, when they dwelt safely in their land, and none made them afraid.

27. When I have brought them again from the people, and gathered them out of their enemies' lands, and am sanctified in them in the sight of many nations;

28. Then shall they know that I am the Lord their God, which caused them to be led into captivity among the heathen: but I have gathered them unto their own land, and have left none of them any more there.

29. Neither will I hide my face any more from them: for I have poured out my spirit upon the house of Israel, saith the Lord God.

Think of Satan's forces defeated by Christians and by fire and brimstone. Meditation. Kiss the Son, lest He be angry, and ye perish from the way, when His wrath is kindled but a little. Blessed are all they that put their trust in Him.

SATAN   40 BILLION AD+/-

SATAN IS THROWN INTO THE LAKE OF FIRE FOREVER.

Revelation 20:9-10

9. And they went up on the breadth of the earth, and compassed the camp of the saints about, and the beloved city: and fire came down from God out of heaven, and devoured them.
10. And the devil that deceived them was cast into the lake of fire and brimstone, where the beast and the false prophet are, and shall be tormented day and night for ever and ever.

Think of how good it is that Satan who started out as Lucifer ruling the Angels is thrown into the core of the collapsing universe. The Lord defeated him Righteously. Meditation. Blessed is the man that walketh not in the counsel of the ungodly, nor standeth in the way of sinners, nor sitteth in the seat of the scornful. But his delight is in the law of the Lord; and in His law doth he meditate day and night.

The End of book Satan

CHAPTER THREE
THE BEAST. SATAN HOMOSEXUAL HUSBAND

Isaiah 28:12 " To whom He said, This is the rest wherewith ye may cause the weary to rest: and this is the refreshing: yet they would not hear"

This book is new material for Christians and the Church about the beast, the anti Christ.

THE ANTICHRIST IS REALLY AN ANGEL WHO WAS CREATED BY GOD TO DESTROY NATIONS, BECAUSE HE DOES NOT DO THAT KIND OF WORK HIMSELF. BUT THIS ANGEL REBELLED AND SERVED SATAN. HE IS THE MILITARY PLANNER OF ISLAM, NAZI GERMANY, THE U.S.S.R. THIS ANGEL EXISTED THROUGHOUT HISTORY HELPING SATAN. (God introduces him in Isaiah 54:16, The Waster, the smith, the Beast 666). ONE DAY - 40 BILLION YEARS FROM NOW HE WILL POSSESS A DEAD BODY OF A KILLED KING AND THAT BODY WILL COME BACK TO LIFE LIKE JESUS DID IN THREE DAYS. AND THEY WORSHIPPED THE BEAST AND SATAN THE DRAGON. VERY SPOOKY.

BUT MANY PEOPLE MISSED ISAIAH 54:16 WHERE GOD FIRST MENTIONS HIM AS AN ANGEL. THEOLOGIANS MISSED THAT AND NOW THEY CONJURE UP A HUMAN BEING AS THE ANTICHRIST WHO WILL TAKE OVER THE WHOLE WORLD. THIS BOOK SETS EVERYTHING RIGHT AND HELPS THE CHURCH UNDERSTAND ABOUT THE REBEL ANGELS OF SATAN. SATAN'S HUSBAND.

CONCERNING THE CHURCH THE LORD SAYS.

14. In righteousness shalt thou be established: thou shalt be far from oppression; for thou shalt not fear: and from terror; for it shall not come near thee.
15. Behold, they shall surely gather together, but not by me: whosoever shall gather together against thee shall fall for thy sake.
16. Behold, I have created the smith that bloweth the coals in the fire, and that bringeth forth an instrument for his work; and I have created the waster to destroy.
17. No weapon that is formed against thee shall prosper; and every tongue that shall rise against thee in judgment thou shalt condemn. This is the heritage of the servants of the Lord, and their righteousness is of me, saith the Lord.

THE BEAST. The antichrist, the abomination of desolation, the waster, the smith.

I have met many young Americans who have asked me if they were the beast. Some desperately want to be the anti Christ. I have met some people who have tattooed 666 on their hands, others just simply worship Satan outright. They want to so desperately want to be the person that the rockin roll groups are glorifying and exalting. They just want to be someone.

Satan really doesn't have problems finding recruits to serve him, but Iam here to tell these new children of Satan and the Beast that they can never be the Beast because the Beast is not a man but an angel. 40 billion years from now this angel will physically take over the body of a dead man and bring him back to life, but the soul of that man probably went to heaven and all the people worshipped that dead mans body as they did Jesus for he was resurrected from the dead. That's 40 billion years from now, so I really feel sorry to tell these young new Satanists that they cant be the Beast. If you are really sad that your not the anti Christ and not the person all the rockinroll groups are glorifying – Iam sorry. But if your just a serious student of the Bible and want to hear who the anti Christ really is, read on.

Who is the beast? And where did he come from?

ISAIAH

The very first time that the Beast is mentioned in the Bible is by God in the book of Isaiah. If you don't understand these passages you'll never know who the Beast is. In Chapter 54 God is talking to His Church at the Second Coming of Jesus, (somewhere after and near the year 2000.)

He tells her to increase and not decrease for Jesus Christ is back. He says that the world, even the West rejected the Church and no one took her to be her protector. He says that He, God , is her Husband and the Creator of the Church His wife. He also says that there will be a group of individuals who will try to attack the Church (gather together powers against the Church) but they will not prevail. He also says that He created an angel whose job is to destroy nations. He creates weapons using God's knowledge and destroys any nation that God wants him to . Arrow smith the rock group is named after him, and so is Megadeath and some minor other groups. But God calls him in Isaiah the "Smith" and the "Waster". God gives a hint here in Isaiah that one day this creature will rebel against God and serve Satan and try to destroy the Church of Jesus. But God says no weapon created can destroy Christ's Church, for the attempt has been made so many times in history by the forces of Satan.

Isaiah 54:15-17

15. Behold, they shall surely gather together, but not by me: whosoever shall gather together against thee shall fall for thy sake.
16. Behold, I have created the smith that bloweth the coals in the fire, and that bringeth forth an instrument for his work; and I have created the waster to destroy.
17. No weapon that is formed against thee shall prosper; and every tongue that shall rise against thee in judgment thou shalt condemn. This is the heritage of the servants of the Lord, and their righteousness is of me, saith the Lord.

So God created an angel called the waster to destroy nations and that's who the beast is. He is not a man, so too bad you cant be the anti Christ.

DANIEL

The next time that the Beast is mentioned, where God makes no secret about his defection is in Daniel. God who creates perfect angels now calls the "Waster"- the abomination that maketh desolate or the abomination that wastes.

Daniel 11:31

31. And arms shall stand on his part, and they shall pollute the sanctuary of strength, and shall take away the daily sacrifice, and they shall place the abomination that maketh desolate.

This section of Daniel is not talking about the battle before the Second Coming but is really talking about Magog and Gog 1000 Christ years after the Second Coming. I will return to this Chapter later in the history of the beast for this prophecy is 40 billion years away. Now the Beast must have turned to Satan when Jesus Christ preached the gospel of peace. For some reason the angel who was in heaven with all the heavenly host did not like Jesus, a fatal mistake. So actually if it was written in the days of Daniel in heaven, Christ's plan for the redemption of the earth was revealed then and all the Angels took sides.

God described the last days or the walk of Jesus. He let Satan devise a death for Jesus so he could break Him, for the crucifixion was created solely for Jesus. Also Satan was giving some limited powers to make visions to use after Jesus died and went to heaven. These miracles are the Fatima miracles, the miracles of Mohammed hearing voices and many other such things. Those are the miracles that God gave Satan to defend himself, but he had to use them sparingly because he had to use them on the Carcase of Mathew 2428 in that great battle of Angels in Revelation 12. Don't worry everything will be in chronological order, but a great event happened 700 B.C in the days of Daniel. The heavens were shaken and those who fell, fell.

Then the Beast and Satan fought John the Baptist and Jesus says in Mt 11:12.

Matthew 11:12

12. And from the days of John the Baptist until now the kingdom of heaven suffereth violence, and the violent take it by force.

So the Beast fought John the Baptist and failed. He and Satan engineered the insurrections against the Romans at Christ's birth- in the days of the taxation. Jesus warns the Carcase a special sheep of the year 2000 and the people of 40 billion A.D about the violence of the Beast or the angel of desolation.

Matthew 24:14-15

14. And this gospel of the kingdom shall be preached in all the world for a witness unto all nations; and then shall the end come.
15. When ye therefore shall see the abomination of desolation, spoken of by Daniel the prophet, stand in the holy place, (whoso readeth, let him understand:)

Matthew 24 coming true is dependent on Verse 24:28. You have to understand that the whole war at the end of time or the Second Coming could not happen if the Carcase of Matthew 24:28 did not want it to happen.

Matthew 24:28

28. For wheresoever the carcase is, there will the eagles be gathered together.

That meant that there was a condition in which that terrible war of the anti Christ was supposed to happen. It depended on the Carcase. The Eagles are Jesus and the other eagle is Satan. A carcase is a dead person or a person who is dead to the world, dead to the world of Satan. So all Christians are Carcases according to the gospel of Paul- Crucified in Him. But lets go on to II Thessa 2:3-12. In II Thessa we see the Beast called the Wicked one who exalts himself above God. We will see how this fits in chronologically. The last time we hear about the Beast is in Revelation. After being thrown into the bottomless pit for 40 billion years at the Second Coming he is taking out and performs the prophecy of Chpt 13 Revelation. Chpt 13 is a blow up of Chpt 20:7-10 Revelation. The final destruction of the Beast is the Lake of fire. I will put everything in historical order and it will all make sense to you, but at least you will know that the Beast is not a man but an angel. That he will possess the shell of a man and make that body be worshipped by billions of people in WWIII billions of years from now. So lets start our story about this creation that God created and whom Christians are profoundly in and Satanists worship and glorify in songs.

MAP OF TIME   20 BILLION B.C.

THE BIG BANG HAPPENED AROUND THIS TIME

Twenty billion years ago our universe expanded from being a singularity. What happened before is written in another book- What the Bible says about the collapse of the universe, Life before the big bang, the 200 billion year history of Christianity- *the invisible war.*, but it is this side of the big bang that the Beast was created by Jesus.

Think of the big bang of this universe. Meditation I was glad when they said unto me, Let us go into the house of the Lord.

MAP OF TIME   20 BILLION B.C-7000B.C +/-

CREATION OF THE BEAST.

Jesus created Lucifer and his angels and the beast after the big bang. Lucifer rebelled against God in Ezekiel chpt 28. When Satan and his demons rebelled against God the Beast angel did not rebel with them, but was a servant of God- The God of Israel. There were no nations created then, so he was unemployed. But the Bible says he rebelled when the heavens were shaken a second time and this happened in the days of Daniel.

Hebrews 12:26-27

26. Whose voice then shook the earth: but now he hath promised, saying, Yet once more I shake not the earth only, but also heaven.
27. And this word, Yet once more, signifieth the removing of those things that are shaken, as of things that are made, that those things which cannot be shaken may remain.

Think of the Creation of the Beast. Meditation. Our feet shall stand within thy gates, O Jerusalem.

MAP OF TIME   605 B.C+/-

THE BEAST DESTROYS EGYPT

When the nations were created after the flood the Beast was given the task of destroying nations. One of the greatest nations he destroyed in history was Egypt.

Think of the destruction of Egypt. Meditation. Jerusalem is builded as a city that is compact together.

Whither the tribes go up, the tribes of the Lord, unto the testimony of Israel, to give thanks unto the name of the Lord.

MAP OF TIME   627 BC +/-

THE BEAST DESTROYS ASSYRIA

The Beast destroyed many nations small and great throughout the planet as God dictated, for God doesn't do that kind of work Himself, but lets His creatures do it for Him. Assyria fell by the hand of the Waster or Smith.

Think of Assyria destroyed. Meditation. For there are set thrones of judgment, the thrones of the house of David. Pray for the peace of Jerusalem: they shall prosper that love thee.

MAP OF TIME   700 B.C +/-

DANIEL

The heavens were shook in the days of Daniel and all the Angels took sides when Christ revealed His plan for mankind. The Beast rebelled and served Satan

Think of the Beast turning to Satan. Meditation If it had not been the Lord who was on our side, when their wrath was kindled against us: Then the waters had overwhelmed us, the stream had gone over our soul.

MAP OF TIME   0.0.B.C-00 AD +/-

NEW TESTAMENT ERA.

Jesus mentions the Beast and said he was against Him. It was Satan and the Beast who killed all the children on the coasts of Israel. It was Satan and the Beast who caused the insurrection in the days of Christ's birth (the taxation). Jesus converted the whole Roman empire with His act on the cross- so Satan and the Beast destroyed Rome with the Goth's and the Barbarians.

Think of the Beast destroying Rome because they believed in Jesus. Meditation. Blessed be the Lord, who hath not given us as a prey to their teeth.

MAP OF TIME   400-600 AD+/-

ISLAM

Jesus then converted the Goths and Barbarians after the fall of Rome. So Satan and the Beast decided to destroy to destroy the Goths, Visgoths and the Germanic tribes for converting. Thus the crusades. Satan was the religious founder of Islam and the Beast was the military leader. Together they tried to destroy the Christian West. The Beast made an attack through turkey and swept down through North Africa into Spain to pincer the Christians. But they failed when God turned the battle and Jerusalem was recaptured by the Christians. Satan tried to negate Christ's teaching of living by the Spirit with living by the Law or Sheria which means the Law.

Think of the beast trying to surround the Christians. Meditation. Our soul is escaped as a bird out of the snare of the fowler: the snare is broken, and we are escaped.

<u>MAP OF TIME</u>   <u>1930-1945 A.D +/-</u>

NAZISM

Many small battles took place as history went on but nothing big came after Islam unless you count the destruction of kings and kingships. Then the prophecy of Israel's return came to be true. The time came. Israel was to become a nation just before the return of Jesus Christ. So the Beast and Satan tried to wipe out all the Jews so the prophecy wouldn't happen. No Jews, no Israel. It was the Beast who executed all of Germany's early successes in the war. It was Satan who engineered all of Germany's glory prior to the war. It was demons who exposed hiding Jews to the police. But the God of Israel fought and in 4 years Germany was dead and Israel was born. 8 million Jews died in that war but 43 million Gentiles died for the Jews. God won.

Think of the Beasts attempt to wipe out the Jews. Meditation. Our help is in the name of the Lord, who made heaven and earth.

<u>MAP OF TIME</u>   <u>1945-2000A.D+/-</u>

COMMUNISM

After Nazism the Beast and Satan decided to attack the Church as the big red dragon of communism. Satan created communist doctrine and together they attempted to spread it around the world. But this plan was cut short at the emergence of the Carcase of Matthew 24:28 and the U.S.S.R. was destroyed in the Invisible war.

Think of the communist attempt by the beast to destroy the Church. Meditation. They that trust in the Lord shall be as mount Zion, which cannot be removed, but abideth forever.

<u>MAP OF TIME</u>   <u>1984-2010 A.D</u>

THE CARCASE

The carcase is a very important cog in the Invisible war. Nobody has evr mentioned him, except by this author. Ive met the Carcase.

Matthew 24:28 says.

28. For wheresoever the carcase is, there will the eagles be gathered together.

The Eagles are Jesus and Satan and the work of the Carcase is to welcome Jesus Christ. The Carcase could prepare Christ's welcome by Christianizing the planet through a great war or he could just ask Jesus to take over his burdens and come in peace. Apparently he chose the peaceful route and that negates almost the whole chpt- all the wars of Chpt 24:15-22 will not come true. Jesus will come in peace. That's why verse 28 was inserted into the Chpt. It is conditional that that war happen. It takes careful reading to put it into context to determine that everything hinged on verse 28.

Think of the Carcase being tempted by Satan and the Beast. Meditation. There were they in great fear: for God is in the generation of the righteous.

THE BEAST USES ISLAM AND THE PEDOPHILE SCANDEL TO DESTROY THE CHURCH.

After trying to use the Carcase to destroy the Church with a war where Africa was supposed to be united and become like another Germany, the Beast and Satan were bankrupt, so they decided to use Islam and demon possessed suicide bombers to destroy Israel and the pedophile scandal to destroy the Church and Revelation 12:17 came true. Next on the agenda is Chpt 13 Isaiah. Not chpt 13 Revelation which is 40 billion years away.

Jesus knew about the pedophile scandal and He talked about it in Mathew 18:6-7. Look it up. He said offences would come.

Think of the Beast and Satan trying to destroy the Church just before Jesus returned. Meditation. Make a joyful noise unto the Lord, all ye lands.

THE SECOND COMING OF JESUS CHRIST.

The Second Coming is a very great event. Its in the life of the Carcase and it is the end of the Beast for 40 billion years. At the Second Coming he will be thrown into the bottomless pit by God the Father. In the last days they tried to create a society of Satanists, Satan's children to replace Christians. From the witches of Salem, Halloween to the Hell's angels using the propaganda machine called Hollywood, they tried to build a nation of Satanist's worldwide. We call these children of evil "gangsters" and they are supposed to replace Christians. But God said He will kill them off in Isaiah 14:20-23. Also knowing their end was near, Satan tried to make themselves into a legend like in the song Bad company- Bd Company, which is the national anthem of Satan hood. Another song is the one that says "my soul is on fire" as they mock the fires of the bottomless pit. Isaiah 59:5-6

5. They hatch cockatrice' eggs, and weave the spider's web: he that eateth of their eggs dieth, and that which is crushed breaketh out into a viper.
6. Their webs shall not become garments, neither shall they cover themselves with their works: their works are works of iniquity, and the act of violence is in their hands.

But God the Father destroyed the root of evil, Satan and demons, and threw them into the bottomless pit and Jesus will throw the remnant, the humans into hell at the Second Coming.

Isaiah 14:30

30. And the firstborn of the poor shall feed, and the needy shall lie down in safety: and I will kill thy root with famine, and he shall slay thy remnant.

Psalm 110 is a blueprint of the Second coming

Psalm 110

1. The Lord said unto my Lord, Sit thou at my right hand, until I make thine enemies thy footstool.

2. The Lord shall send the rod of thy strength out of Zion: rule thou in the midst of thine enemies.
3. Thy people shall be willing in the day of thy power, in the beauties of holiness from the womb of the morning: thou hast the dew of thy youth.
4. The Lord hath sworn, and will not repent, Thou art a priest for ever after the order of Melchizedek.
5. The Lord at thy right hand shall strike through kings in the day of his wrath.
6. He shall judge among the heathen, he shall fill the places with the dead bodies; he shall wound the heads over many countries.
7. He shall drink of the brook in the way: therefore shall he lift up the head.

Isaiah 13 is also a blueprint of the Second Coming as Isaiah 24 is . In chpt 13 the Angels are the Sanctified ones and they are coming to earth to do the sinners in.

Isaiah 13

1. The burden of Babylon, which Isaiah the son of Amoz did see.
2. Lift ye up a banner upon the high mountain, exalt the voice unto them, shake the hand, that they may go into the gates of the nobles.
3. I have commanded my sanctified ones, I have also called my mighty ones for mine anger, even them that rejoice in my highness.
4. The noise of a multitude in the mountains, like as of a great people; a tumultuous noise of the kingdoms of nations gathered together: the Lord of hosts mustereth the host of the battle.
5. They come from a far country, from the end of heaven, even the Lord, and the weapons of his indignation, to destroy the whole land.
6. Howl ye; for the day of the Lord is at hand; it shall come as a destruction from the Almighty.
7. Therefore shall all hands be faint, and every man's heart shall melt:
8. And they shall be afraid: pangs and sorrows shall take hold of them; they shall be in pain as a woman that travaileth: they shall be amazed one at another; their faces shall be as flames.
9. Behold, the day of the Lord cometh, cruel both with wrath and fierce anger, to lay the land desolate: and he shall destroy the sinners thereof out of it.
10. For the stars of heaven and the constellations thereof shall not give their light: the sun shall be darkened in his going forth, and the moon shall not cause her light to shine.
11. And I will punish the world for their evil, and the wicked for their iniquity; and I will cause the arrogancy of the proud to cease, and will lay low the haughtiness of the terrible.
12. I will make a man more precious than fine gold; even a man than the golden wedge of Ophir.
13. Therefore I will shake the heavens, and the earth shall remove out of her place, in the wrath of the Lord of hosts, and in the day of his fierce anger.
14. And it shall be as the chased roe, and as a sheep that no man taketh up: they shall every man turn to his own people, and flee every one into his own land.
15. Every one that is found shall be thrust through; and every one that is joined unto them shall fall by the sword.

16. Their children also shall be dashed to pieces before their eyes; their houses shall be spoiled, and their wives ravished.

17. Behold, I will stir up the Medes against them, which shall not regard silver; and as for gold, they shall not delight in it.

18. Their bows also shall dash the young men to pieces; and they shall have no pity on the fruit of the womb; their eye shall not spare children.

19. And Babylon, the glory of kingdoms, the beauty of the Chaldees' excellency, shall be as when God overthrew Sodom and Gomorrah.

20. It shall never be inhabited, neither shall it be dwelt in from generation to generation: neither shall the Arabian pitch tent there; neither shall the shepherds make their fold there.

21. But wild beasts of the desert shall lie there; and their houses shall be full of doleful creatures; and owls shall dwell there, and Satyrs shall dance there.

22. And the wild beasts of the islands shall cry in their desolate houses, and dragons in their pleasant palaces: and her time is near to come, and her days shall not be prolonged.

When the Bible says the Moon will turn red it means that Jesus the Moon will tread the grapes of wrath and will stain His robe red, thus the Moon turning red. When the Bible says the Sun will be darkened before the Second Coming it means that God the Father who is the Sun will be angry. "Darkened" means angry in the old days. Also when the Bible says that the heavens will be pulled back like a scroll, that's literal, space which is billions of times more rigid then steel will be ripped open and another dimension, Heaven, will come down to meet the earth and the Angels will come down. The Second Coming starts at the end of Chpt 12 Revelation. Chpt 13 Isaiah is next after Chpt 12 Revelation. Chpt 13 Revelation is 40 billion years from now.

Think of the heavens being ripped open at the Second Coming. Meditation. He hath remembered His mercy and His truth toward the house of Israel: all the ends of the earth have seen the salvation of our God.

MAP OF TIME _____ 2010 AD+/-

THE BOTTOMLESS PIT.

The Beast rebelled against Jesus- so Jesus created a king of destroyers and millions of destroyers to serve Him instead of the Beast. Had the Beast stayed with Jesus, he could have been given the job of St. Abaddon. St Abaddon is a king of destroyers. Jesus created him to torture Satan and his demons. St. Abaddon is first mentioned in St. Job 18:14 as the king of terrors.

People will not be thrown into the bottomless pit but only the Beast, Satan and his demons. They are the Chief Criminals there. St Abaddon and his warriors are immune to the fire. The Bible says the Beast "is not" for 40 billion years or 1000 Christ years. The reason I call Abaddon a saint is because anyone who tortures Satan is a saint to me.

Think on how the Beast is thrown into the bottomless pit. Meditation. I will set no wicked thing before mine eyes: I hate the work of them that turn aside; it shall not cleave to Me.

MAP OF TIME _____ 2010AD+/- 40 BILLION AD+/-

BLUE SHIFT

The universe expands for billions of years and in 40 billion years it starts to contract. The core of the collapsing universe is called the Lake of fire by Christians. At this time the 1000 years of peace will be finished and the human race expanded to the far reaches of the universe. Satan and his demons are released out of the bottomless pit and the Bible says "he is".

Revelation 20:7

7. And when the thousand years are expired, Satan shall be loosed out of his prison,
When Jesus says Satan He means the whole nation of Satan.
Think of the Beast being released out of the bottomless pit. Meditation: Whoso privily slandereth his neighbour, him will I cut off: him that hath an high look and a proud heart will not I suffer.

<u>MAP OF TIME</u>   40 BILLION AD+/-

THE BEAST AND SATAN TEMPT THE NATIONS

Revelation 20:8-9 says the Beast and Satan went out and created a marvelous nation in the fringes of the universe with the pomp of Germany as they did in WWII. The human race had expanded far into the universe. Ezekiel chpt 38 tells the story of what happened.

Ezekiel 38

1. And the word of the Lord came unto me, saying,
2. Son of man, set thy face against Gog, the land of Magog, the chief prince of Meshech and Tubal, and prophesy against him,
3. And say, Thus saith the Lord God; Behold, I am against thee, O Gog, the chief prince of Meshech and Tubal:
4. And I will turn thee back, and put hooks into thy jaws, and I will bring thee forth, and all thine army, horses and horsemen, all of them clothed with all sorts of armour, even a great company with bucklers and shields, all of them handling swords:
5. Persia, Ethiopia, and Libya with them; all of them with shield and helmet:
6. Gomer, and all his bands; the house of Togarmah of the north quarters, and all his bands: and many people with thee.
7. Be thou prepared, and prepare for thyself, thou, and all thy company that are assembled unto thee, and be thou a guard unto them.
8. After many days thou shalt be visited: in the latter years thou shalt come into the land that is brought back from the sword, and is gathered out of many people, against the mountains of Israel, which have been always waste: but it is brought forth out of the nations, and they shall dwell safely all of them.
9. Thou shalt ascend and come like a storm, thou shalt be like a cloud to cover the land, thou, and all thy bands, and many people with thee.
10. Thus saith the Lord God; It shall also come to pass, that at the same time shall things come into thy mind, and thou shalt think an evil thought:
11. And thou shalt say, I will go up to the land of unwalled villages; I will go to them that are at rest, that dwell safely, all of them dwelling without walls, and having neither bars nor gates,
12. To take a spoil, and to take a prey; to turn thine hand upon the desolate places that are

now inhabited, and upon the people that are gathered out of the nations, which have gotten cattle and goods, that dwell in the midst of the land.

13. Sheba, and Dedan, and the merchants of Tarshish, with all the young lions thereof, shall say unto thee, Art thou come to take a spoil? hast thou gathered thy company to take a prey? to carry away silver and gold, to take away cattle and goods, to take a great spoil?

14. Therefore, son of man, prophesy and say unto Gog, Thus saith the Lord God; In that day when My people of Israel dwelleth safely, shalt thou not know it?

15. And thou shalt come from thy place out of the north parts, thou, and many people with thee, all of them riding upon horses, a great company, and a mighty army:

16. And thou shalt come up against My people of Israel, as a cloud to cover the land; it shall be in the latter days, and I will bring thee against my land, that the heathen may know me, when I shall be sanctified in thee, O Gog, before their eyes.

17. Thus saith the Lord God; Art thou he of whom I have spoken in old time by my servants the prophets of Israel, which prophesied in those days many years that I would bring thee against them?

18. And it shall come to pass at the same time when Gog shall come against the land of Israel, saith the Lord God, that my fury shall come up in my face.

19. For in my jealousy and in the fire of my wrath have I spoken, surely in that day there shall be a great shaking in the land of Israel;

20. So that the fishes of the sea, and the fowls of the heaven, and the beasts of the field, and all creeping things that creep upon the earth, and all the men that are upon the face of the earth, shall shake at my presence, and the mountains shall be thrown down, and the steep places shall fall, and every wall shall fall to the ground.

21. And I will call for a sword against him throughout all my mountains, saith the Lord God: every man's sword shall be against his brother.

22. And I will plead against him with pestilence and with blood; and I will rain upon him, and upon his bands, and upon the many people that are with him, an overflowing rain, and great hailstones, fire, and brimstone.

23. Thus will I magnify myself, and sanctify myself; and I will be known in the eyes of many nations, and they shall know that I am the Lord.

Think of the outer fringes of the universe being contaminated with Babylon. Meditation. Mine eyes shall be upon the faithful of the land, that they may dwell with Me: he that walketh in a perfect way, he shall serve Me.

MAP OF TIME   40 BILLION AD+/-

THE BEAST GATHERS THE NATIONS AGAINST CHRIST.

The nations commit fornication with the new nation. Jesus who is in the universe in Jerusalem planet is perturbed that people have turned to Satan's physical and spiritual nation again. After about 2000 years or a season, Christian children fret against Jesus and turn to Satan. Then there are wars in Christ's peaceful kingdom again after 40 billion years of peace.

Think of Satan causing wars again. Meditation. In thee, O Lord, do I put my trust; let me never be ashamed: deliver me in thy righteousness.

MAP OF TIME   40 BILLION AD+/-

KINGS ARE CHANGED.

Satan sets up his kings instead of Christ's appointed kings and the Bible says they have power for one hour with the Beast.

Revelation 17:9-12

9. And here is the mind which hath wisdom. The seven heads are seven mountains, on which the woman sitteth.
10. And there are seven kings: five are fallen, and one is, and the other is not yet come; and when he cometh, he must continue a short space.
11. And the beast that was, and is not, even he is the eighth, and is of the seven, and goeth into perdition.
12. And the ten horns which thou sawest are ten kings, which have received no kingdom as yet; but receive power as kings one hour with the beast.

Think of the kings serving the Beast. Meditation. Bow down thine ear to me; deliver me speedily: be thou my strong rock, for an house of defence to save me.

MAP OF TIME   40 BILLION AD+/-

DANIELS PROPHECY

This is where Daniel's prophecy Chpt 11:29 fits in. The appointed time is 40 billion years away. So between 11:28 and 11:29 is 40 billion years just like there is a long time between Genesis 1:1 and Genesis 1:2. One of the kings is killed by Satan and his body is resurrected by the Beast. Wounded by a sword unto death. Satan tried to set up Ronald Wilson Reagan that way when he got shot. It was all a set up to smear him. But anyway the body they put to death is possessed by the abomination of desolation and people worship him just like Jesus. Christians are killed and hunted down with the help of demons, just like the Jews were hunted down by the Nazi's with a little help.

Daniel 11:29-45

29. At the time appointed he shall return, and come toward the south; but it shall not be as the former, or as the latter.
30. For the ships of Chittim shall come against him: therefore he shall be grieved, and return, and have indignation against the holy covenant: so shall he do; he shall even return, and have intelligence with them that forsake the holy covenant.
31. And arms shall stand on his part, and they shall pollute the sanctuary of strength, and shall take away the daily sacrifice, and they shall place the abomination that maketh desolate.
32. And such as do wickedly against the covenant shall he corrupt by flatteries: but the people that do know their God shall be strong, and do exploits.
33. And they that understand among the people shall instruct many: yet they shall fall by the sword, and by flame, by captivity, and by spoil, many days.
34. Now when they shall fall, they shall be holpen with a little help: but many shall cleave to them with flatteries.

35. And some of them of understanding shall fall, to try them, and to purge, and to make them white, even to the time of the end: because it is yet for a time appointed.

36. And the king shall do according to his will; and he shall exalt himself, and magnify himself above every god, and shall speak marvellous things against the God of gods, and shall prosper till the indignation be accomplished: for that that is determined shall be done.

37. Neither shall he regard the God of his fathers, nor the desire of women, nor regard any god: for he shall magnify himself above all.

38. But in his estate shall he honour the God of forces: and a god whom his fathers knew not shall he honour with gold, and silver, and with precious stones, and pleasant things.

39. Thus shall he do in the most strong holds with a strange god, whom he shall acknowledge and increase with glory: and he shall cause them to rule over many, and shall divide the land for gain.

40. And at the time of the end shall the king of the south push at him: and the king of the north shall come against him like a whirlwind, with chariots, and with horsemen, and with many ships; and he shall enter into the countries, and shall overflow and pass over.

41. He shall enter also into the glorious land, and many countries shall be overthrown: but these shall escape out of his hand, even Edom, and Moab, and the chief of the children of Ammon.

42. He shall stretch forth his hand also upon the countries: and the land of Egypt shall not escape.

43. But he shall have power over the treasures of gold and of silver, and over all the precious things of Egypt: and the Libyans and the Ethiopians shall be at his steps.

44. But tidings out of the east and out of the north shall trouble him: therefore he shall go forth with great fury to destroy, and utterly to make away many.

45. And he shall plant the tabernacles of his palace between the seas in the glorious holy mountain; yet he shall come to his end, and none shall help him.

Think of the abomination of desolation in the sanctuary of strength the Church. Meditation. Pull me out of the net that they have laid privily for me: for thou art my strength. Into thine hand I commit my spirit: thou hast redeemed me, O Lord God of truth.

MAP OF TIME   40 BILLION A.D.+/-

CHAPTER 13 REVELATION COMES TRUE.

The sand of the sea is 40 billion years. The head that was wounded was a king who died and brought back to life in verse 14 and 15. Image means just that, a live image. A body brought back to life and inhabited by the angel the Beast. People were forced to worship him by a guy like Goebbels to Hitler- the false prophet who was also possessed by a frog. The false prophet was only possessed in the usual way. By the way he had no excuse because the same frog that possessed him is the same frog that possessed St. Paul (II Cor. 12.7, Galatians 4:14), but St. Paul defeated the demon.

The reason the false prophet had horns like a lamb meant that he was as meek as Jesus, but he spoke like a dragon, which means he lied like Satan. That's in verse13:11.

Revelation Chpt 13.

1. And I stood upon the sand of the sea, and saw a beast rise up out of the sea, having seven heads and ten horns, and upon his horns ten crowns, and upon his heads the name of blasphemy.
2. And the beast which I saw was like unto a leopard, and his feet were as the feet of a bear, and his mouth as the mouth of a lion: and the dragon gave him his power, and his seat, and great authority.
3. And I saw one of his heads as it were wounded to death; and his deadly wound was healed: and all the world wondered after the beast.
4. And they worshipped the dragon which gave power unto the beast: and they worshipped the beast, saying, Who is like unto the beast? who is able to make war with him?
5. And there was given unto him a mouth speaking great things and blasphemies; and power was given unto him to continue forty and two months.
6. And he opened his mouth in blasphemy against God, to blaspheme his name, and his tabernacle, and them that dwell in heaven.
7. And it was given unto him to make war with the saints, and to overcome them: and power was given him over all kindreds, and tongues, and nations.
8. And all that dwell upon the earth shall worship him, whose names are not written in the book of life of the Lamb slain from the foundation of the world.
9. If any man have an ear, let him hear.
10. He that leadeth into captivity shall go into captivity: he that killeth with the sword must be killed with the sword. Here is the patience and the faith of the saints.
11. And I beheld another beast coming up out of the earth; and he had two horns like a lamb, and he spake as a dragon.
12. And he exerciseth all the power of the first beast before him, and causeth the earth and them which dwell therein to worship the first beast, whose deadly wound was healed.
13. And he doeth great wonders, so that he maketh fire come down from heaven on the earth in the sight of men,
14. And deceiveth them that dwell on the earth by the means of those miracles which he had power to do in the sight of the beast; saying to them that dwell on the earth, that they should make an image to the beast, which had the wound by a sword, and did live.
15. And he had power to give life unto the image of the beast, that the image of the beast should both speak, and cause that as many as would not worship the image of the beast should be killed.
16. And he causeth all, both small and great, rich and poor, free and bond, to receive a mark in their right hand, or in their foreheads:
17. And that no man might buy or sell, save he that had the mark, or the name of the beast, or the number of his name.
18. Here is wisdom. Let him that hath understanding count the number of the beast: for it is the number of a man; and his number is Six hundred threescore and six.

Think how awful it was the that people worshipped the Beast. Meditation. How long shall I take counsel in my soul, having sorrow in my heart daily? how long shall mine enemy be exalted over me ?

MAP OF TIME   40 BILLION AD+/-

II THESSA. COMES TRUE.

II Thessalonians fits in this time period

II Thessa.2: 7-12.

7. For the mystery of iniquity doth already work: only he who now letteth will let, until he be taken out of the way.
8. And then shall that Wicked be revealed, whom the Lord shall consume with the spirit of his mouth, and shall destroy with the brightness of his coming:
9. Even him, whose coming is after the working of Satan with all power and signs and lying wonders,
10. And with all deceivableness of unrighteousness in them that perish; because they received not the love of the truth, that they might be saved.
11. And for this cause God shall send them strong delusion, that they should believe a lie:
12. That they all might be damned who believed not the truth, but had pleasure in unrighteousness.

Think of the Wicked one the Beast doing evil. Meditation. Be merciful unto me, O God for man would swallow me up; he fighting daily oppresseth me.

MAP OF TIME   40 BILLION AD+/-

I JOHN FITS IN THIS TIME PERIOD.

I John 2:18-19

18. Little children, it is the last time: and as ye have heard that antichrist shall come, even now are there many antichrists; whereby we know that it is the last time.
19. They went out from us, but they were not of us; for if they had been of us, they would no doubt have continued with us: but they went out, that they might be made manifest that they were not all of us.

I John 4:1-6

1. Beloved, believe not every spirit, but try the spirits whether they are of God: because many false prophets are gone out into the world.
2. Hereby know ye the Spirit of God: Every spirit that confesseth that Jesus Christ is come in the flesh is of God:
3. And every spirit that confesseth not that Jesus Christ is come in the flesh is not of God: and this is that spirit of antichrist, whereof ye have heard that it should come; and even now already is it in the world.
4. Ye are of God, little children, and have overcome them: because greater is he that is in you, than he that is in the world.
5. They are of the world: therefore speak they of the world, and the world heareth them.

6. We are of God: he that knoweth God heareth us; he that is not of God heareth not us. Hereby know we the spirit of truth, and the spirit of error.

Think of the many anti Christ's or people who hate Jesus go with Satan and their new religion. Meditation The Lord loveth the gates of Zion more than al the dwellings of Jacob.

MAP OF TIME   40 BILLION AD+/-

THE UNIVERSE WIDE CIVIL WAR IS FOUGHT WITH SPACESHIPS.

Ezekiel 38-39 talks about that great universe wide civil war 40 billion A.D.+/-. God really went all out to destroy the nation of Satan and the Beast. He was furious.

Ezekiel Chpt 38.

1. And the word of the Lord came unto me, saying,
2. Son of man, set thy face against Gog, the land of Magog, the chief prince of Meshech and Tubal, and prophesy against him,
3. And say, Thus saith the Lord God; Behold, I am against thee, O Gog, the chief prince of Meshech and Tubal:
4. And I will turn thee back, and put hooks into thy jaws, and I will bring thee forth, and all thine army, horses and horsemen, all of them clothed with all sorts of armour, even a great company with bucklers and shields, all of them handling swords:
5. Persia, Ethiopia, and Libya with them; all of them with shield and helmet:
6. Gomer, and all his bands; the house of Togarmah of the north quarters, and all his bands: and many people with thee.
7. Be thou prepared, and prepare for thyself, thou, and all thy company that are assembled unto thee, and be thou a guard unto them.
8. After many days thou shalt be visited: in the latter years thou shalt come into the land that is brought back from the sword, and is gathered out of many people, against the mountains of Israel, which have been always waste: but it is brought forth out of the nations, and they shall dwell safely all of them.
9. Thou shalt ascend and come like a storm, thou shalt be like a cloud to cover the land, thou, and all thy bands, and many people with thee.
10. Thus saith the Lord God; It shall also come to pass, that at the same time shall things come into thy mind, and thou shalt think an evil thought:
11. And thou shalt say, I will go up to the land of unwalled villages; I will go to them that are at rest, that dwell safely, all of them dwelling without walls, and having neither bars nor gates,
12. To take a spoil, and to take a prey; to turn thine hand upon the desolate places that are now inhabited, and upon the people that are gathered out of the nations, which have gotten cattle and goods, that dwell in the midst of the land.
13. Sheba, and Dedan, and the merchants of Tarshish, with all the young lions thereof, shall say unto thee, Art thou come to take a spoil? hast thou gathered thy company to take a prey? to carry away silver and gold, to take away cattle and goods, to take a great spoil?

14. Therefore, son of man, prophesy and say unto Gog, Thus saith the Lord God; In that day when My people of Israel dwelleth safely, shalt thou not know it?

15. And thou shalt come from thy place out of the north parts, thou, and many people with thee, all of them riding upon horses, a great company, and a mighty army:

16. And thou shalt come up against My people of Israel, as a cloud to cover the land; it shall be in the latter days, and I will bring thee against my land, that the heathen may know me, when I shall be sanctified in thee, O Gog, before their eyes.

17. Thus saith the Lord God; Art thou he of whom I have spoken in old time by my servants the prophets of Israel, which prophesied in those days many years that I would bring thee against them?

18. And it shall come to pass at the same time when Gog shall come against the land of Israel, saith the Lord God, that my fury shall come up in my face.

19. For in my jealousy and in the fire of my wrath have I spoken, surely in that day there shall be a great shaking in the land of Israel;

20. So that the fishes of the sea, and the fowls of the heaven, and the beasts of the field, and all creeping things that creep upon the earth, and all the men that are upon the face of the earth, shall shake at my presence, and the mountains shall be thrown down, and the steep places shall fall, and every wall shall fall to the ground.

21. And I will call for a sword against him throughout all my mountains, saith the Lord God: every man's sword shall be against his brother.

22. And I will plead against him with pestilence and with blood; and I will rain upon him, and upon his bands, and upon the many people that are with him, an overflowing rain, and great hailstones, fire, and brimstone.

23. Thus will I magnify myself, and sanctify myself; and I will be known in the eyes of many nations, and they shall know that I am the Lord.

Think of the great civil war between Christians and non Christians that was fought over the whole universe. Meditation. Why do the heathen rage, and the people imagine a vain thing? The kings of the earth set themselves, and the rulers take counsel together, against the Lord, and against His anointed, saying, Let us break their bands asunder, and cast away their cords from us.

MAP OF TIME   40 BILLION A.D +/-

PLAGUES FROM GOD .

God plagued Satan's nation marvelously. Read Revelation. But also Ezekiel.

Ezekiel Chpt 39.

1. Therefore, thou son of man, prophesy against Gog, and say, Thus saith the Lord God; Behold, I am against thee, O Gog, the chief prince of Meshech and Tubal:

2. And I will turn thee back, and leave but the sixth part of thee, and will cause thee to come up from the north parts, and will bring thee upon the mountains of Israel:

3. And I will smite thy bow out of thy left hand, and will cause thine arrows to fall out of thy right hand.

4. Thou shalt fall upon the mountains of Israel, thou, and all thy bands, and the people that

is with thee: I will give thee unto the ravenous birds of every sort, and to the beasts of the field to be devoured.

5. Thou shalt fall upon the open field: for I have spoken it, saith the Lord God.

6. And I will send a fire on Magog, and among them that dwell carelessly in the isles: and they shall know that I am the Lord.

7. So will I make my holy name known in the midst of my people Israel; and I will not let them pollute my holy name any more: and the heathen shall know that I am the Lord, the Holy One in Israel.

8. Behold, it is come, and it is done, saith the Lord God; this is the day whereof I have spoken.

9. And they that dwell in the cities of Israel shall go forth, and shall set on fire and burn the weapons, both the shields and the bucklers, the bows and the arrows, and the handstaves, and the spears, and they shall burn them with fire seven years:

10. So that they shall take no wood out of the field, neither cut down any out of the forests; for they shall burn the weapons with fire: and they shall spoil those that spoiled them, and rob those that robbed them, saith the Lord God.

11. And it shall come to pass in that day, that I will give unto Gog a place there of graves in Israel, the valley of the passengers on the east of the sea: and it shall stop the noses of the passengers: and there shall they bury Gog and all his multitude: and they shall call it the valley of Hamongog.

12. And seven months shall the house of Israel be burying of them, that they may cleanse the land.

13. Yea, all the people of the land shall bury them; and it shall be to them a renown the day that I shall be glorified, saith the Lord God.

14. And they shall sever out men of continual employment, passing through the land to bury with the passengers those that remain upon the face of the earth, to cleanse it: after the end of seven months shall they search.

15. And the passengers that pass through the land, when any seeth a man's bone, then shall he set up a sign by it, till the buriers have buried it in the valley of Hamongog.

16. And also the name of the city shall be Hamonah. Thus shall they cleanse the land.

17. And, thou son of man, thus saith the Lord God; Speak unto every feathered fowl, and to every beast of the field, assemble yourselves, and come; gather yourselves on every side to my sacrifice that I do sacrifice for you, even a great sacrifice upon the mountains of Israel, that ye may eat flesh, and drink blood.

18. Ye shall eat the flesh of the mighty, and drink the blood of the princes of the earth, of rams, of lambs, and of goats, of bullocks, all of them fatlings of Bashan.

19. And ye shall eat fat till ye be full, and drink blood till ye be drunken, of my sacrifice which I have sacrificed for you.

20. Thus ye shall be filled at my table with horses and chariots, with mighty men, and with all men of war, saith the Lord God.

21. And I will set my glory among the heathen, and all the heathen shall see my judgment that I have executed, and my hand that I have laid upon them.

22. So the house of Israel shall know that I am the Lord their God from that day and forward.

23. And the heathen shall know that the house of Israel went into captivity for their iniquity: because they trespassed against me, therefore hid I my face from them, and gave them into the hand of their enemies: so fell they all by the sword.

24. According to their uncleanness and according to their transgressions have I done unto them, and hid my face from them.

25. Therefore thus saith the Lord God; Now will I bring again the captivity of Jacob, and have mercy upon the whole house of Israel, and will be jealous for my holy name;

26. After that they have borne their shame, and all their trespasses whereby they have trespassed against me, when they dwelt safely in their land, and none made them afraid.

27. When I have brought them again from the people, and gathered them out of their enemies' lands, and am sanctified in them in the sight of many nations;

28. Then shall they know that I am the Lord their God, which caused them to be led into captivity among the heathen: but I have gathered them unto their own land, and have left none of them any more there.

29. Neither will I hide my face any more from them: for I have poured out my spirit upon the house of Israel, saith the Lord God.

Think of all the Plagues of Revelation from God's altar. Meditation. He that sitteth in the heavens shall laugh: the Lord shall have them in derision. Then shall He speak unto them in His wrath, and vex them in His sore displeasure

MAP OF TIME _____ 40 BILLION AD+/-

THE BEAST IS CAPTURED.

Revelation 19:11-21

11. And I saw heaven opened, and behold a white horse; and he that sat upon him was called Faithful and True, and in righteousness he doth judge and make war.

12. His eyes were as a flame of fire, and on his head were many crowns; and he had a name written, that no man knew, but he himself.

13. And he was clothed with a vesture dipped in blood: and his name is called The Word of God.

14. And the armies which were in heaven followed him upon white horses, clothed in fine linen, white and clean.

15. And out of his mouth goeth a sharp sword, that with it he should smite the nations: and he shall rule them with a rod of iron: and he treadeth the winepress of the fierceness and wrath of Almighty God.

16. And he hath on his vesture and on his thigh a name written, KING OF KINGS, AND LORD OF LORDS.

17. And I saw an angel standing in the sun; and he cried with a loud voice, saying to all the fowls that fly in the midst of heaven, Come and gather yourselves together unto the supper of the great God;

18. That ye may eat the flesh of kings, and the flesh of captains, and the flesh of mighty men, and the flesh of horses, and of them that sit on them, and the flesh of all men, both free and bond, both small and great.

19. And I saw the beast, and the kings of the earth, and their armies, gathered together to make war against him that sat on the horse, and against his army.

20. And the beast was taken, and with him the false prophet that wrought miracles before him, with which he deceived them that had received the mark of the beast, and them that worshipped his image. These both were cast alive into a lake of fire burning with brimstone.

21. And the remnant were slain with the sword of him that sat upon the horse, which sword proceeded out of his mouth: and all the fowls were filled with their flesh.

Think how glorious it is the Beast is captured by Jesus Christ. Meditation. Serve the Lord with fear, and rejoice with trembling. Kiss the Son, lest He be angry, and ye perish from the way, when His wrath is kindled but a little. Blessed are all they that put their trust in Him.

MAP OF TIME   40 BILLION AD+/-

THE BEAST IS THROWN INTO THE LAKE OF FIRE.

Revelation 20:10

10. And the devil that deceived them was cast into the lake of fire and brimstone, where the beast and the false prophet are, and shall be tormented day and night for ever and ever.

Think of the Beast being thrown into the Lake of fire the core of the collapsing universe. Meditation: Arise, O Lord; save me, O my God: for thou hast smitten all mine enemies upon the cheek bone; thou hast broken the teeth of the ungodly.

The End of the book the Beast.

CHAPTER FOUR
JESUS CHRIST IS LORD. KING OF KINGS AND LORD OF LORDS, ALMIGHTY GOD, THE GOD OF ISRAEL. THE CREATOR OF THE UNIVERSE, CREATOR OF INFINITE UNIVERSES AND WORSHIPPED IN INFINITE MULTIPLE UNIVERSES. MIGHTY IN BATTLE. KING OF GLORY.

The Lords Master Plan and History.

The Lord Jesus Christ is God. He created Satan. As a matter of fact Jesus existed with the Father before the world was created (John 17:5, 24)

John 17:4-5

4. I have glorified thee on the earth: I have finished the work which thou gavest me to do.
5. And now, O Father, glorify thou me with thine own self with the glory which I had with thee before the world was.

There was life before the big bang. Jesus had a "glory" before the world was. What is a "glory"- a glory is a kingdom. Who were in His kingdom before the big bang? Christians were His subjects. You and I.

John 17:24

24. Father, I will that they also, whom thou hast given me, be with me where I am; that they may behold my glory, which thou hast given me: for thou lovedst me before the foundation of the world.

Again Jesus repeats that He existed before the big bang

In John 17:5 we see that Jesus had a "glory" or a kingdom before the world was. Jesus was a King before the creation of the world. And every King has subjects. Who were Christ's subjects before the creation of the universe?

Well God asked a question to St. Job (38:4)

Job 38:4

4. Where wast thou when I laid the foundations of the earth? declare, if thou hast understanding.

Job must have been somewhere before the universe was created for God would not have asked him that question unless there was an answer. The answer lays in Job 18:20.

Job 18:20

20. They that come after him shall be astonied at his day, as they that went before were affrighted.

Actually in context

Job 18:5-20.

5. Yea, the light of the wicked shall be put out, and the spark of his fire shall not shine.
6. The light shall be dark in his tabernacle, and his candle shall be put out with him.
7. The steps of his strength shall be straitened, and his own counsel shall cast him down.
8. For he is cast into a net by his own feet, and he walketh upon a snare.
9. The gin shall take him by the heel, and the robber shall prevail against him.
10. The snare is laid for him in the ground, and a trap for him in the way.
11. Terrors shall make him afraid on every side, and shall drive him to his feet.
12. His strength shall be hungerbitten, and destruction shall be ready at his side.
13. It shall devour the strength of his skin: even the firstborn of death shall devour his strength.
14. His confidence shall be rooted out of his tabernacle, and it shall bring him to the king of terrors.
15. It shall dwell in his tabernacle, because it is none of his: brimstone shall be scattered upon his habitation.
16. His roots shall be dried up beneath, and above shall his branch be cut off.
17. His remembrance shall perish from the earth, and he shall have no name in the street.
18. He shall be driven from light into darkness, and chased out of the world.
19. He shall neither have son nor nephew among his people, nor any remaining in his dwellings.
20. They that come after him shall be astonied at his day, as they that went before were affrighted.

In context it starts to talk about the wicked and what will happen to them. Job 18:20 is a pivotal sentence in the Bible. It says "the good" existed before the wicked to be "affrighted" at what God was going to do to them- burn them forever in the fires of the Lake of fire-and the verse also says the good were "astonied"- astonished- after the wicked ceased to exist, for God burned them all.

Job 18:20

20. They that come after him shall be astonied at his day, as they that went before were affrighted.

So we have the good existing before the wicked to be "affrighted" and the good existing after the wicked to be "astonished" at their fate. The wicked- Satan and his demons were created right after the Big Bang. So the good existed before the Big Bang.

Putting John 17:5,24 and Job 38:4 and Job 18:20 together we see a picture emerging about what happened before the creation of the universe- before Gen 1:1- it was the fact that Jesus was a King and Job and Christians- the good were Christ's subjects before the Big Bang- the creation of the universe. Jesus had a "glory" before the world was. So Jesus and Christians existed before the Big Bang according to those verses.

Now Jesus in the past kingdom- lets call it - The Kingdom of the King of Glory kingdom-planned a great war with a creature He was going to create- a dragon who Jesus was first going to call " Lucifer" Jesus planned a war where His Christians would go to a place called earth- a stage where good and evil would be fought. Christ's Christians would be called "Sheep" and the opponents would be called "goats". The Sheep would volunteer to go to the earth to suffer death, pain, misery and poverty and He Jesus would go there and suffer a great painful death to save His Sheep from the dragon and show them how much He loved them.

Then Jesus would dissappear to heaven and His Sheep would fight the goats, demons and the dragon for about 2000 +/- years, then Jesus would return at a time called -The Second Coming of Jesus Christ. Jesus would rule the earth for a 1000 years or approximately 40 billion human years until the universe went into Blueshift. During that time Jesus was going to throw the dragon and a Beast into His dungeon called the Bottomless Pit.

Jesus also planned to let out the dragon and his demons and goats in a final battle where they would take over the universe and test His Christians in WWIII. Jesus would retreat to heaven, then He would return for the Third Coming of Jesus (chpt 19 Rev.) and totally destroy the dragon, Beast, demons , falseprophet and goats, by throwing them all into a Lake of fire or the core of the collapsing universe.

Jesus and His Sheep would loot and spoil all the goats and they would live in peace until the complete collapse of the universe. Then Jesus was going to judge everyone and He would give medals and rewards to His Sheep and they would live happily ever after.

That was Christ's plans even before the Big Bang, before He created His Christians in the kingdom of The King of Glory, in the past universe before we ever came to this earth to fight in the Invisible War. So approximately 100 Billion+/- years B.C. Jesus the King created His Sheep the Christians. The Wicked goats, demons and Satan were created after the Big Bang.

We Christians existed before the big bang with Jesus, and Jesus created Satan and his goats after the big bang. So we should not be worried about them being thrown into the fire.

THE NATIONS AS THEY WERE 100 BILLION YEARS AGO

Jesus created many nations and they all lived in peace and love. There was love
Joy, peace, longsuffering, gentleness, goodness, faith and people lived by the Spirit.
We were all Christians, white children would play with black children and the Chinese and Japanese, and Vietnamese would also play. There was no sorrow but there was righteousness, godliness, faith, love, patience, meekness and humility, for
No one ever died there. It was pure love, pure Christianity.
People were rich in good works, ready to distribute, willing to communicate.
Those were the sheep, the Christian sheep, but God had not created the goats who

Are covetous, boasters, proud, blasphemers, disobedient to parents, unthankful,
Unholy, without natural affection, trucebreakers, false accusers, incumbent, fierce,
Despisers of those that are good, traitors, high-minded, lovers of pleasures more
Then lovers of God. Ever learning and never able to come to the knowledge of the
Truth, being filled with all unrighteousness, fornicators, uncleaness, covetousness,
Maliciousness full of envy, murder, debate, deceit, malignity, whisperers backbiters,
Implacable, homosexuals, lesbians, adulterers, and such evil traits

We Christians a 100 billion years ago did not know about the goats and their leader Satan. We had love among us for Christ's only commandment was to love one another. There were celebrations of happiness and sacrifices of thanksgiving to God. Jesus chose our kings and queens and everyone did their public duty as kings and priests of God. There was no war among the nations and each nation did its best to help one another. The news was only good for only good things happened in Christ's kingdom. There was no hunger or disease for there was no sin yet. Men and women were equal for it was heaven. It was a land overflowing with righteousness and goodness and love. And when Jesus comes back again at the Second Coming, He will recreate the earth as it was a 100 billion years ago, before the Great Volunteering and the Invisible War.

Supporting the Church.

Kush as a nation supported the Footstool like all the other nations, the Church, and God rested His feet. Kush shall support the Church and provide Levites or priests to the Church of Jesus. Also all believers are the Church. We will give as we gave 10% of our GNP to the Footstool of God. That was the Blackraces purpose when they were created a 100 billion years ago and that will be the mission of the nation of Kush when Jesus comes back. This is the national purpose, the soul of Kush, the reason it was created, the reason it exists. Never let it go, let no man or politician deceive you. It would be a shame if the black race or Kush tried something different like Hitler, and God, The God of Israel got angry and wiped out, ceased to exist the black race. So don't upset God's feet and His Footstool. Always uphold the Church.

This is a warning to all the other nations too.

The Great Volunteering

After we were created we stayed in heaven or this universe for about 60 billion years. We had fun and we the nations played in peace with our King Jesus Christ. I think we became bored. For even people on earth today say that there is nothing to do in heaven except play harps. Well Jesus interrupted our eternal bliss 40 billion years ago and asked us if we wanted to go to war. War was a new concept to us, but Jesus explained it to us as good vs evil, light vs darkness, truth vs lies, spirit vs flesh, Christians vs nonchristians, and Jesus vs Satan. After a while we came to understand it and it was called " The Invisible War." It was to be fought on a battlefield called Earth, a stage where good fought evil. So Jesus took Volunteers for the war, and you and I volunteered to come to earth to suffer shame, poverty, sickness and death for Jesus. That was the Great Volunteering 40 billion years ago when this universe was in blueshift, before it had a big bang and the earth was created.

The Great Conference

After the nations volunteered Jesus our Shepherd called an international conference. Jesus had let us read the Bible (which had already been written trillions of years ago-God knows all things). Jesus called a conference of the nations and He explained to us what the evil foe Satan would do to us. That he would pit nation against nation, people against people. That peoples and nations would become enslaved and made extinct. That sin would cause disease to be rampant on earth. Jesus gave us a terrible picture of what was going to happen. And He asked us to volunteer for certain roles in the invisible war. So we had to decide what role we would take. The American Indians who were brave decided to suffer for Jesus, to be wiped out. The Egyptians, the Assyrians, the Mayans, the Aztecs, everyone volunteered to do something for Jesus. Kush, the Black race also volunteered to suffer. They volunteered to be enslaved for Jesus. To go hungry and be the worst of the human race. To lose their dignity and be hated. This was because they wanted to show Jesus how much they loved Him and were willing to suffer for Him. But those who suffered the most are the Jews. They took the brunt of Satan's fury. It's such a sad story I don't want to write more about it. But you can see what happened yourself. We all suffered tremendously. Every nation suffered Satans fury. Jesus will be back to save us. The main point here is that we all volunteered to suffer the way we did. The Blacks were not enslaved against their will, they volunteered for it.

So there is no shame to what happened, and we cant hate our oppressors, for we volunteered for it. We knew what was going to happen to us before we came here to battlefield earth. The Jews also and the Indian native Americans. Satan thought he was being original, but we fooled him, we outplayed him. Now he and his followers, nonchristians are going to be burned forever. We were affrighted to hear what Jesus was going to do to the wicked when He told us about it 40 billion years ago. Job 18:20.

The Book of Life.

At the Great Volunteering those who volunteered to come to earth had their names written in Christ's great book The Book of Life. This was so no sheep would be lost and no goat would be saved. That's where the Book of Life came from for those who are wondering. If you lived a 100 billion years ago, you will be saved. If you were created after the big bang with Satan you will be burned. This is what it meant when the Bible says Jesus can shut the door on you or keep it open. Jesus shut the door on Satan and his followers. Revelation 3:7 " And to the angel of the Church in Philadelphia write; These things saith He that is holy, He that is true, He that hath the key of David, He that openeth, and no man shutteth; and shutteth, and no man openeth;"

Revelation 20:15 " And whosoever was not found written in the Book of Life was cast into the lake of fire".

The nations escape to Heaven

After the Great Volunteering and the Great Conference and after the Book of Life was written 40 billion years ago the nations escaped to Heaven. The reason was because this universe was in blue shift and was collapsing. The entire universe became so small that it disappeared. The Bible says that todays present universe was created from things that cannot be seen. The worlds were created from things that do not appear. Look it up for yourself. Paul said it. Well scientists say the same thing. Actually Physicists should take note since they say the universe started with a singularity. The bible says the universe was created out of the unseen- as such a point-the invisible singularity. Hebrews 11:3 Through faith we understand that the worlds were framed by the word of God, so that things which are seen were not made of things which do appear." That disappearance happened to this universe in its past cycle. But what Iam saying is that the nations went to Heaven, and that's where Christians waited to come to earth to fight in the invisible war.

Christians existed before the Big Bang in another universe, then we came here to this universe with Jesus to fight in the invisible war against Satan, demons and antiChristian goats.

JESUS AND LIFE BEFORE THE BIG BANG

God has given me a gift- the gift of interpretation. I will now reveal to you the first seven chapters of Genesis. This is for Mother Church the bride of Christ. This is what Jesus revealed to me about the first seven chapters of Genesis. Jesus says the K.J.V. is the most accurate Bible in existence. It was the Holy Spirit that wrote the KJV.

God the Father, Jesus and the Holy Spirit existed forever past and they had no beginning. All Christians know that. But a long, long, long time ago approximately 100 billion years ago God and Jesus created Christians. Jesus created the Angels first- St. Michael and St. Gabriel and St. Anna a Cambodian Angel I met in Hadley Massachusetts. He created billions of Angels and divided them into their own nations (Isaiah 13:3-5) Then Jesus created human beings the Adamic nations. When we were created we just woke up into consciousness and Jesus gave each of us a secret name that no one else will know, but Jesus and you (Revelation 2:17)

All the nations loved each other and we lived among our big brothers the Angels. After about a few billion years of peace and love Jesus decided to spice up our lives. People have always told me that there was nothing to do in heaven except play harps. So Jesus decided to spice up our lives. He asked us if we wanted to go to war?

War was a new concept and game that we never played before. Now wait a minute- you ask where did I get the information that we lived 100 billion years ago. The Holy Spirit pieced it together for me. First lets look at certain verses in the Bible that point to us existing before the Big Bang. The first clue is John 17:24. It says that Jesus existed with the Father before the Big Bang which is 20 billion years ago.

John 17:24

24. Father, I will that they also, whom thou hast given me, be with me where I am; that they may behold my glory, which thou hast given me: for thou lovedst me before the foundation of the world.

Now the second clue is found in Job 38:4

Job 38:4

4. Where wast thou when I laid the foundations of the earth? declare, if thou hast understanding.

God asked Job a question that got me wondering – Where were we? Well there are two answers- we didn't exist or we existed. Now Jesus has always been a King and every king has subjects. Who were Christ's subjects before the Big Bang? You could say Christians or no one. We know that Lucifer and his angels were created after the Big Bang- before us right? Wrong, we Christians were created before Lucifer and his angels . Job 18:20 says so.

Job 18:20

20. They that come after him shall be astonied at his day, as they that went before were affrighted.

Actually it goes like this in context.
Job 18:5

5. Yea, the light of the wicked shall be put out, and the spark of his fire shall not shine.

Job 18:20

20. They that come after him shall be astonied at his day, as they that went before were affrighted.

Read from verse 5 to 20 to see the whole picture. Lets examine verse 20.

" They that come after the wicked shall be astonished" So that means that one day the wicked shall cease to exist and good people will exist after them. Why are they – the good- astonished? They are astonished because God threw the wicked into the Lake of fire forever in Revelation at the end. After that – after

Judgment day people were astonished at what God did to them. That also means we existed after this universe collapsed in 70 billion AD+/-. Life after the contraction of the universe for those physicists who believe the human race is going to be wiped out. Now lets go back and look at the other half of the sentence. "they that existed before the wicked were affrighted" So people existed before the wicked were created and when God told them what He was going to create wicked people and burn them forever- those people were affrighted. So we have people affrighted before the wicked were created and you have people astonished after God burnt the wicked in the fire forever. That means we the good existed before Satan and his angels were created and God gives us the hint in Job's question of where were you before the Big Bang. Answer we existed before the Big Bang. We existed with Jesus and we Christians were Christ's subjects.

Now for a clincher. Theologians in seminary school are taught that Genesis 1:1 does not start with " In the beginning" but what's its supposed to say is " In a beginning". That makes all the difference. This is not the first beginning. But if you piece together John 17:24, Job 38:4 and Job 18:20 you can see some light seeping in from before and beyond the Big Bang of the universe. We existed on the other side, for Satan was created on this side – the very first part of time after the Big Bang is called the "Morning" and those angels who were created then were called "morning stars"

Job 38:7

7. When the morning stars sang together, and all the sons of God shouted for joy?

Job 18:20 means Christians existed before the " morning stars". So that's that part of the puzzle- before the Big Bang. How many times has our universe gone into Big Bang and collapse cycle. I don't know, but now we know we existed on the other side- then it collapsed , then we now exist in this present expansion.

Job 38:4

4. Where wast thou when I laid the foundations of the earth? declare, if thou hast understanding.

Answer we were with Jesus. Now I said before we lived in peace in a past kingdom – lets call it The King of Glory Kingdom after Psalm 24 for the psalm was written in those days to be used at the Second Coming after the battle or the Invisible War or after the Chaos where Christ's kingdom was thrown into the wind and now at the Second Coming it is re-organized again. When Jesus returns to Jerusalem for the second time in our universe He re enters the gates of Jerusalem and the Psalm says.

Psalm 24

1. The earth is the Lord's, and the fulness thereof; the world, and they that dwell therein.
2. For he hath founded it upon the seas, and established it upon the floods.
3. Who shall ascend into the hill of the Lord? or who shall stand in his holy place?
4. He that hath clean hands, and a pure heart; who hath not lifted up his soul unto vanity, nor sworn deceitfully.
5. He shall receive the blessing from the Lord, and righteousness from the God of his salvation.
6. This is the generation of them that seek him, that seek thy face, O Jacob. Selah.
7. Lift up your heads, O ye gates; and be ye lift up, ye everlasting doors; and the King of glory shall come in.
8. Who is this King of glory? The Lord strong and mighty, the Lord mighty in battle.
9. Lift up your heads, O ye gates; even lift them up, ye everlasting doors; and the King of glory shall come in.
10. Who is this King of glory? The Lord of hosts, he is the King of glory. Selah.

Now after billions of years of living in peace in the kingdom of The King Of Glory-lets say 40 billion years ago. 40 billion years ago our present universe was in blue shift- Jesus asked us if we wanted to go to war. He explained that war was a struggle between opposites – we Christians against non Christians, good vs evil , Truth vs lies, love vs hate, light vs darkness, Jesus vs Satan. So a lot of us volunteered to serve in the Invisible War because we loved Jesus. Jesus had written the whole Bible in those days and we all read

it from Genesis to Revelation. God knows all things. We call 40 billion years ago the great volunteering. Now nothing in the Bible is written uselessly. Verse 24:4 of Psalm 24 is a warning to all Christians at the Second Coming not to have promised falsely to suffer for Jesus in the Great Volunteering.

Psalm 24:4

4. He that hath clean hands, and a pure heart; who hath not lifted up his soul unto vanity, nor sworn deceitfully.

You volunteered to come here to suffer. So after that universe collapsed it became a singularity. We escaped to a place above the heavens.

Psalm 148:4

Praise him, ye heavens of heavens, and ye waters that be above the heavens.

4. After a few million years or maybe less or probably more God told the universe to explode.

Isaiah 48:13

13. Mine hand also hath laid the foundation of the earth, and my right hand hath spanned the heavens: when I call unto them, they stand up together.

And Genesis 1:1 says

Genesis 1:1

In the beginning God created the heaven and the earth.

The Bible says it took more then just seven days to create the earth- it took Generations (Genesis 2:4)

GOD WANTS YOU TO BELIEVE IN GOD-GUIDED EVOLUTION.

Most Christians don't believe in Evolution because the Bible says it took God Seven days to create
the earth while scientists say it took million of years- (with dinosaurs etc). Well there is a sentence in the Bible that says it took God millions or billions of years to create the earth. Mainly it says much, much,
more then Seven days. This is what Christians believe Genesis 1:31, 2:1-2
Gen 1:31And God saw every thing that he had made, and, behold, it was very good. And the evening and the morning were the sixth day.

Gen 2:1-2

1. Thus the heavens and the earth were finished, and all the host of them.
2. And on the seventh day God ended his work which he had made; and he rested on the seventh day from all his work which he had made.

But this next sentence in Genesis says it took God much more then Seven days. It took "Generations". "Generations" could be eon's, era's, millions or billions of years. The key word is

"Generations".

Genesis 2:4

4. These are the generations of the heavens and of the earth when they were created, in the day that the Lord God made the earth and the heavens,
Not only does it say " Generations". It also says it took God "One Day" to create the heavens and the earth. So the Bible says "Seven days", "generations", and "One Day". Which is correct? What we know is that God's days are not human days. The scientists are correct when they say life was established on earth in 600+/- years- most likely 700 million years. We Christians believe in God guided Evolution. The scientists are only partially right. They know the time frame- but they say life is a mathematical probability and don't give God the glory. But the part God revealed in the past section on the Bible talking about the collapse of the universe –can that be a mathematical probability-the Bible saying that.? But going back Christians and Creationism- are partially right- they give God the Glory which is correct, but they don't know the time frame. "Generations" the Bible says. So Dinosaurs did exist.but God destroyed them because He created the earth for Adam. He wanted Adam to dominate the earth.
Remember God pronounced everything good when He created something on earth. Good for who? Now what happened in that Court case where the Evolutionists beat the Creationists because the

Creationists were stuck on Seven human days and the Evolutionists could prove things like dinosaurs and with Carbon dating? How could the Creationists not have read Genesis 2:4., "Generations"?

It was because Satan blinded them- by force. Satan was for the Evolutionists. That's Satan for you. But

to put things right- It took God millions of years in " God Guided Evolution". Now where did mankind

Adam –the finished product come to be finished.? 600-700 +/- million years of work ended 7000

years ago. All the people- cavemen, of all kinds etc are mentioned in Genesis 1:26-30

26. And God said, Let us make man in our image, after our likeness: and let them have dominion over the fish of the sea, and over the fowl of the air, and over the cattle, and over all the earth, and over every creeping thing that creepeth upon the earth.

27. So God created man in his own image, in the image of God created he him; male and female created he them.

28. And God blessed them, and God said unto them, Be fruitful, and multiply, and replenish the earth, and subdue it: and have dominion over the fish of the sea, and over the fowl of the air, and over every living thing that moveth upon the earth.

29. And God said, Behold, I have given you every herb bearing seed, which is upon the face of all the earth, and every tree, in the which is the fruit of a tree yielding seed; to you it shall be for meat.

30. And to every beast of the earth, and to every fowl of the air, and to every thing that creepeth upon the earth, wherein there is life, I have given every green herb for meat: and it was so.

31. And God saw every thing that he had made, and, behold, it was very good. And the evening and the morning were the sixth day.

The Adam product, the first Christian was finished in Genesis 2:7. Why is man created in Genesis 1:26 and Adam in Genesis 2:7 ?

Genesis 2:7 . And the Lord God formed man of the dust of the ground, and breathed into his nostrils the breath of life; and man became a living soul.

The verse "… formed man of the dust of the ground…" was first from dust, then to single cell, through monkeys, to Homosaipiens, to Adam product- took 600-700+/- millions of years.

Genesis 2:4. These are the generations of the heavens and of the earth when they were created, in the day that the Lord God made the earth and the heavens,

God Guided Evolution is correct- Intelligent design-(see what the Bible says about the Collapse of the Universe). Add the Word " generations" to Intelligent design vocabulary and you'll see " God Guided Evolution". Christians can reverse the Courts.

- Whatever happened to Darwin? Did he go to hell for making such a ruckus?. Well Darwin when he was dying recanted his theory of Evolution but scientists wont tell you that. My Pastor said he read a book written by some women who was at or close to Darwins death. Darwin as he was dying asked for the book of Hebrews to be read to him. Now they wont tell you that in school. Ask one of my Pastors at the Greater Congregation

Church in Lee or Lenox Mass.. How many people went to hell holding on to Darwin's partial truth.? He was right about the time scale, but Satan wont give God the glory.

Here we give God the Glory- if you were a little sympathetic to the Bible you can see Evolution and

Its sequence of events being layed out in Genesis 1:8-31. Lets just look at it a little because you should read all Seven and this book to completely comprehend the "Latter Rain or the Refreshing" That God gave the Church.

First scientists say the planet was covered by water at first- the primordial soup bowl, right? Then the land mass appeared.-The Bible says the same thing.

Genesis 1:9-10

9. And God said, Let the waters under the Heaven be gathered together unto one place, and let the dry land appear: and it was so.
10. And God called the dry land Earth; and the gathering together of the waters called he Seas: and God saw that it was good.

Then just as scientist say the Bible says- plants appeared. How many years we don't know- the Bible just tells us after the land appeared, God created grass and plants on the land.

Genesis 1:11-12

11. And God said, Let the earth bring forth grass, the herb yielding seed, and the fruit tree yielding fruit after his kind, whose seed is in itself, upon the earth: and it was so.
12. And the earth brought forth grass, and herb yielding seed after his kind, and the tree yielding fruit, whose seed was in itself, after his kind: and God saw that it was good.

One of the questions that should be in your head is how did Moses know the earth was first covered by water- the whole earth, since he didn't even know the earth was round. Where did he get his information? Then he accurately says just like the Evolutionists of 2005 agree, that animals appeared after the plants and not only that, life first started in the oceans or seas. Evolution says life came from the waters. The Bible says the same thing. The Evolutionists saying that life started in the Oceans and the Bible saying the same that life started in the waters is enough to convince me. It takes a little sympathy, Evolutionists and the Bible agree.

Genesis 1:20-22

20. And God said, Let the waters bring forth abundantly the moving creature that hath life, and fowl that may fly above the earth in the open firmament of heaven.
21. And God created great whales, and every living creature that moveth, which the waters brought forth abundantly, after their kind, and every winged fowl after his kind: and God saw that it was good.
22. And God blessed them, saying, Be fruitful, and multiply, and fill the waters in the seas, and let fowl multiply in the earth.

If you were just a little bit sympathetic, but that convinces anyone who is reasonable –that's what

Jesus means by saying be like children- (hold on to this little light-Satan and his three billion demons will erase it from your memory- you'll just forget) (Mathew 13: 1-23)

Now you see the whole picture of Evolution and the Bible.. But after the Bible and Evolutionists saying life came from the waters- the Bible fills in the story- land animals appeared after sea animals- or "fish walked" as Evolutionists say-We are just finding out how God created us. Read Genesis 1:23-25 to see what happened. But we stop with verse 26. God creates mankind- not Adam himself, but other men. Who are these men? Adam was created in Genesis 2:7. So we have other men created beside Adam in Gen 1:26. Read it for yourself. Those men in Genesis 1:26 are the monkeys to men or Human as we know them today tree. God then took a Man from Mankind and put him in the garden and called him –Adam. Read my books if you want or just be like children- a little sympathetic.

Intelligent Design –GOD GUDED EVOLUTION-with the Word " Generations" added to it is the answer.

JESUS

" Abraham saw Jesus and washed His feet"

The Jews can now believe in Jesus because He said the universe is going to collapse in the New Testament just as Isaiah and David said the same thing. This gives the New Testament authenticity because the Old Testament and the New Testament say the same thing.

Isaiah 28:12 " To whom He said, This is the rest wherewith ye may cause the weary to rest: and this is the refreshing: yet they would not hear."

This book is not new material for Christians and the Church. But Mom has not exhausted the things about Jesus. New material in this book is that it was Jesus who walked in the garden of Eden and cursed Adam and Eve, Jesus visited Abraham and Abraham washed His feet before He destroyed Sodom. Jesus also walked the earth as King Melchisedec and was the ruler of Salem. So He had practice as King ruling Salem now modern day Jerusalem. Jesus is also called the Eagle in Mt 24:28. Jesus is also the Moon in Revelation 12. Other then that the Church has almost exhausted Christ's name and history. But I will now tell the story of Jesus from before the big bang 100 billion B.C. to the end , past Judgment day 100 Billion A.D.

JESUS CHRIST IS LORD

JESUS CHRIST, LORD GOD, WORD OF GOD, LAMB OF GOD, DREADFUL SOVEREIGN, MIGHTY IN BATTLE, KING OF WARRIORS, THE ALMIGHTY GOD, THE EVERLASTING FATHER, THE PRINCE OF PEACE, THE KING OF GLORY, THE LORD OF HOSTS.

Who is the blessed and only Potentate, The King of kings, and Lord of lords. Who only hath immortality, dwelleth in the light which no man can approach unto. Whom no man hath seen, nor can see. To whom be honor and power everlasting. Amen.

JESUS _____ INFINITE PAST.

Jesus existed as God in the infinite past, Jesus is God. Jesus is just another name of God and He has no beginning. The Father, the Son and the Holy Spirit always existed and they are one. Jesus said He existed before the foundation of the world (the big bang) with God the Father. (John 17:24)

Think of the infinite past where Jesus has always existed as God the Father. Meditation. He bowed the heavens also, and came down: and darkness was under His feet. And He rode upon a Cherub, and did fly: yea, He did fly upon the wings of the wind.

JESUS _____ 100 BILLION B.C +/-

Then one day Jesus created His subjects, the Angels and Christians probably 100 billion years ago in the past phase of this expanding and collapsing universe. We all lived in peace with the Angels and Jesus was there on His throne so we could admire Him.

Colossians 1:15-16

15. Who is the image of the invisible God, the firstborn of every creature:
16. For by him were all things created, that are in heaven, and that are in earth, visible and invisible, whether they be thrones, or dominions, or principalities, or powers: all things were created by him, and for him:

John 17:5

5. And now, O Father, glorify thou me with thine own self with the glory which I had with thee before the world was.

Think of the Creation of Christians 100 billion B.C.+/- Meditation. He made darkness His secret place; His pavilion round about Him were dark waters and thick clouds of the skies.

JESUS   40 BILLION B.C +/-

Then one day after billions of years of peace Jesus decided to spice up our lives. He asked us Christians if we wanted to go to war. We didn't know what war was, but He explained it as a battle between us the good against the evil, night vs Day, Light vs darkness, Truth vs lies, Jesus against Satan and Christians against non Christians.

We all agreed and Jesus said He loved us so much that He was willing to die for us and we in turn volunteered to die, suffer shame and poverty for Jesus because we loved Him so much. Then Jesus told us that after we fought the wicked He was going to burn them forever and we were affrighted to hear such a thing. Also we were astonished at Gods punishment after the wicked were destroyed 100 billion A.D on Judgment day. So St. Job says.

Job 18:20

20. They that come after him shall be astonied at his day, as they that went before were affrighted.

The book of life was written in those days of the Great Volunteering, as we passed by Jesus and volunteered, our names were written in the book of life, that way we wont be lost. No sheep would be lost and goat would be saved.

Think of the Great Volunteering where we volunteered to serve Jesus on a battlefield or stage called earth. Meditation. Who shall ascend into the hill of the Lord? Or who shall stand in His holy place? He that hath clean hands, and a pure heart; who hath not lifted up his soul unto vanity, nor sworn deceitfully.

JESUS   20 BILLION BC +/-

THE BIG BANG

After the Great Volunteering we all went up above the heavens, that universe collapsed. Then after a ew years probably millions there was another big bang and the Bible says.

Genesis 1:1

1. In the beginning God created the heaven and the earth.
Jesus commanded the universe to explode as Isaiah says.

Isaiah 48:13

13. Mine hand also hath laid the foundation of the earth, and my right hand hath spanned the heavens: when I call unto them, they stand up together.

Think of the big bang. Meditation. At the brightness that was before Him His thick clouds passed, hail stones and coals of fire.

JESUS   20 BILLION BC+/-

After the big bang Jesus created Lucifer and all of his angels. Our good Angels who had been created before were brought down from above the heavens and mixed with Lucifer's angels. Only Jesus knew who was a goat and who was a sheep. Lucifer was given the task of ruling the Angels as high priest, prophet and governor of God. Things went well for a long time and St. Job mentions such a time in Job 38:7.

Job 38:7

7. When the morning stars sang together, and all the sons of God shouted for joy?

Then one day Lucifer who was created a perfect angel started to strong arm the other Angels for their jewels or heavenly things. Ezekiel records what Jesus had to say about those days in Ezekiel 28:11-15

The king of Tyre is Lucifer.

Ezekiel 28:11-15

11. Moreover the word of the Lord came unto me, saying,
12. Son of man, take up a lamentation upon the king of Tyrus, and say unto him, thus saith the Lord God; Thou sealest up the sum, full of wisdom, and perfect in beauty.
13. Thou hast been in Eden the garden of God; every precious stone was thy covering, the sardius, topaz, and the diamond, the Beryl, the onyx, and the jasper, the sapphire, the emerald, and the carbuncle, and gold: the workmanship of thy tabrets and of thy pipes was prepared in thee in the day that thou wast created.
14. Thou art the anointed cherub that covereth; and I have set thee so: thou wast upon the holy mountain of God; thou hast walked up and down in the midst of the stones of fire.
15. Thou wast perfect in thy ways from the day that thou wast created, till iniquity was found in thee.

Jesus said Lucifer was wheeling and dealing so much that he started to use violence against the other Angels and thus defiling himself. This was terrible, for Lucifer was God's clothing, the covering Cherub. Today Jesus Christ is God's garment which means High Priest. But when Lucifer was fired by Jesus he did not repent as his wise head told him to, but he decided to fight God. He did this because of pride and the fact that he thought he was too beautiful to be shamed.

Ezekiel 28:16-17

16. By the multitude of thy merchandise they have filled the midst of thee with violence, and thou hast sinned: therefore I will cast thee as profane out of the mountain of God: and I will destroy thee, O covering cherub, from the midst of the stones of fire.

17. Thine heart was lifted up because of thy beauty, thou hast corrupted thy wisdom by reason of thy brightness: I will cast thee to the ground, I will lay thee before kings, that they may behold thee.

Lucifer also defiled his church's that he had in heaven and God decided to destroy him for good.

Ezekiel 28:18-19

18. Thou hast defiled thy sanctuaries by the multitude of thine iniquities, by the iniquity of thy traffick; therefore will I bring forth a fire from the midst of thee, it shall devour thee, and I will bring thee to ashes upon the earth in the sight of all them that behold thee.

19. All they that know thee among the people shall be astonished at thee: thou shalt be a terror, and never shalt thou be any more.

A fire or anger would come out of Lucifer at his end that he would turn into a dragon. A dragon is a person who wants to destroy the whole human race. He would fall from highpriest, prophet and governor of Angels to Serpent, to Satan to devil to dragon and St. Michael and St. Gabriel who knew Lucifer at the beginning would be astonished at his end.

So Lucifer rebelled and he tried to get the other Angels to rebel against God. He used lies and confusion to do this. He was the wisest creature that God ever made so he used his powers to bring chaos and darkness to heaven such the Genesis 1:2 says.

Genesis 1:2

2. And the earth was without form, and void; and darkness was upon the face of the deep. And the Spirit of God moved upon the face of the waters.

" Waters" means " political circles" of Angels and "deep" means the "political ocean of heaven".

Then God said " Let there be Light". He did not mean let there be photons because Angels and God can see in the day and night alike (Psalms). What God meant was let there be Jesus, for Jesus is the Light of John 1:1-9

Genesis 1:3

3. And God said, Let there be light: and there was light.

Jesus appeared in heaven and He rallied all the good Angels to Him. The Angels called Him "The Truth" for any Angel who wanted "Truth" went to Him. He attracted all the Truthful Angels to Him and Lucifer attracted all the children of lies and pride to him. God divided the good Angels from the bad angels and Genesis 1:4 says.

Genesis 1:4

4. And God saw the light, that it was good: and God divided the light from the darkness.

There was a battle between Jesus and Lucifer the very first day. Jesus is called Morning or DAY, and Lucifer is called evening or night. Morning fought evening the very first day and Genesis 1:5 says.

Genesis 1:5

5. And God called the light Day, and the darkness he called Night. And the evening and the morning were the first day.

Then God put a barrier between the politics of heaven and earth. " Waters" means " Politics" and the politics of heaven don't mix with the politics of the earth. That's why no one ever comes back from heaven and the only way to get there is by death.

Genesis 1:6-8

6. And God said, Let there be a firmament in the midst of the waters, and let it divide the waters from the waters.
7. And God made the firmament, and divided the waters which were under the firmament from the waters which were above the firmament: and it was so.
8. And God called the firmament Heaven. And the evening and the morning were the second day.

There was a battle between Morning and evening the second day. Then the nonsymbolic creation of the earth began. It took God 600 million years to go from Genesis 1:9 to 31. 600 million years divided into seven parts or days. Time was accelerated, for the Angels in heaven did not have to wait 600 million years for the earth to be created for the battle to continue between Jesus and Lucifer. We call this time "evolution", but it is actually " God guided evolution" and God favored Adam.

Think of the creation of Lucifer and Adam . Meditation. Then the channels of waters were seen, and the foundations of the world were discovered at thy rebuke, O Lord, at the blast of the breath of thy nostrils.

JESUS   7000 BC+/-

LORD GOD

Jesus is the Lord God of Genesis Chpt 3. It was He who walked in the garden and talked to Adam and Eve. It was Jesus who cursed Adam, Eve and Lucifer the serpent. Jesus is also called the "Tree of Life" for only God has two Cherubims surrounding Him.

Psalm 99:1

1. The Lord reigneth; let the people tremble: he sitteth between the Cherubims; let the earth be moved.

The tree of life is stationed on the east side of the garden of Eden. If Jesus is going to be stationed in Jerusalem when He comes back at the Second Coming, then Jerusalem is the east side of the garden of Eden. As you know the garden of Eden was in Israel. Now you know where the east side of it is.

Think of the Lord God Jesus talking to Adam and Eve. Meditation. The Lord also will be a refuge for the oppressed, a refuge in times of trouble.

JESUS   7000BC-6000BC+/-

THE FLOOD.

It was Jesus who told Noah to build the Ark and it was Jesus who brought the flood to destroy the known earth because Satan and his demons had sex with humans. Satan and his angels were visible in those days as men, but after the flood Jesus turned them invisible so they cant commit fornication with human beings. They have been invisible ever since.

Think of the flood brought about by Jesus. Meditation. And He shall judge the world in righteousness, He shall minister judgment to the people in uprightness.

JESUS   2166B.C+/-

MELCHISEDEC

King Melchisedec was Jesus Christ. Jesus used to visit the earth once in a while and He practiced or enjoyed being a King. He created a city called Salem and was a King there. That same city, that is in that same spot is called Jerusalem today.

Jesus practiced being King there. Who says that Melchisedec was Jesus? St. Paul through the Holy Spirit said so, he said.

Hebrews 7:1-3

1. For this Melchisedec, king of Salem, priest of the most high God, who met Abraham returning from the slaughter of the kings, and blessed him;
2. To whom also Abraham gave a tenth part of all; first being by interpretation King of righteousness, and after that also King of Salem, which is, King of peace;
3. Without father, without mother, without descent, having neither beginning of days, nor end of life; but made like unto the Son of God; abideth a priest continually.

Only Jesus who is God, is without father, without mother, without descent, having neither beginning of days, nor end of life; but made like unto the Son of God;..."

Only Jesus has those attributes. So King Melchisedec was God or Jesus. Abraham saw and talked to Jesus as Jesus said in the book of John (Iam). Jesus had the office of HighPriest, King and prophet of God when He was in Salem. Now that we know Jesus was on earth before His rebirth with Mary-who was His treasurers, who were His soldiers. Was He always meek? What kind of King was Jesus? A lot of questions are unanswered. Jesus ruled the Canaanites as their King, then He destroyed them

93

with Joshua because they didn't hear or adhere to His gospel, but as King He was the King of the Canaanites of Salem long before He was King over Israel.

Think of King Jesus in Salem. Meditation. In Judah is God known: His name is great in Israel. In Salem also is His tabernacle and His dwelling place in Zion.

JESUS   2166 B.C+/-, 2BC+/-

I AM

Jesus said He existed before Abraham and that Abraham had seen Him.

John 8:56-58

56. Your father Abraham rejoiced to see my day: and he saw it, and was glad.
57. Then said the Jews unto him, Thou art not yet fifty years old, and hast thou seen Abraham?
58. Jesus said unto them, Verily, verily, I say unto you, Before Abraham was, I am.

Think of Jesus talking to the Jews and telling them He met Abraham. Meditation. My flesh and my heart faileth: but God is the strength of my heart, and my portion for ever.

JESUS   2166 BC+/-

LORD

Lord is another name for God, and the Lord visited Abraham while he was in his tent. Abraham saw the Lord from afar off with the two Cherubim Angels and recognized Him. This only means that he had seen Him before and that was when Jesus was Melchisedec. So Jesus visited Abraham and talked with him. Then Jesus told Abraham that He was going to destroy Sodom, but Abraham pleaded for some of the people there. Abraham knew that Jesus was God because he called Him "the judge of the whole earth" in Genesis 18:25. After Abraham washed the feet of Jesus, Christ left and went back to heaven and brought fire on Sodom while His Cherubim Angels went and saved Lot.

Jesus later on in history returned Abraham's kindness by washing Abraham's children's feet, His disciples. He also instituted the washing of feet to all His followers in the New Testament as a Church does today in Atlanta Georgia on a hill near the capital dome.

Think of Abraham washing Jesus' feet. Meditation. But it is good for me to draw near to God: I have put my trust in the Lord God, that I may declare all thy works.

JESUS   2166-1876 BC+/-

JACOB WRESTLES WITH JESUS

Jacob wrestled with Jesus and Jesus named Jacob Israel.

Genesis 32:24-28

24. And Jacob was left alone; and there wrestled a man with him until the breaking of the day.

25. And when he saw that he prevailed not against him, he touched the hollow of his thigh; and the hollow of Jacob's thigh was out of joint, as he wrestled with him.

26. And he said, Let me go, for the day breaketh. And he said, I will not let thee go, except thou bless me.

27. And he said unto him, What is thy name? And he said, Jacob.

28. And he said, Thy name shall be called no more Jacob, but Israel: for as a prince hast thou power with God and with men, and hast prevailed.

The reason today the Jews can believe in Jesus is because the New Testament talks about the collapse of the universe as does the Old Testament (Psalm 102, and Isaiah) That proves that Jesus gospel is authentic and is from God.

Think of Jesus wrestling with Jacob. Meditation. Whom have I in heaven but thee? And there is none upon earth that I desire beside thee.

JESUS   2166-1876 BC+/-

JACOB'S PROPHECY

Jacob prophesied that Jesus will come from the tribe of Judah and He shall be called Shiloh.

Genesis 49:9-10

9. Judah is a lion's whelp: from the prey, my son, thou art gone up: he stooped down, he couched as a lion, and as an old lion; who shall rouse him up?

10. The sceptre shall not depart from Judah, nor a lawgiver from between his feet, until Shiloh come; and unto him shall the gathering of the people be.

Think of Jacob on His death bed talking about Jesus. Meditation. For God is my King of old working salvation in the midst of the earth.

JESUS   1446 BC+/-

THE GOD OF ISRAEL

The God of Israel on Mt Sinai was Jesus Christ, for Moses said that he and the elders saw The God of Israel and that He had feet. Only Jesus has feet for the human form or the Image of God is Jesus.

Exodus 24:10

10. And they saw the God of Israel: and there was under his feet as it were a paved work of a sapphire stone, and as it were the body of heaven in his clearness.

Think of Jesus the God of Israel on Mt. Sinai. Meditation. Have respect unto the covenant: for the dark places of the earth are full of the habitations of cruelty.

JESUS   1050 BC+/-

THE GOD OF DAVID.

95

The God of David is Jesus Christ.

Think of David calling on The God of Israel. Meditation. Blessed be the Lord my strength, which teacheth my hands to war, and my fingers to fight.

<u>JESUS</u>   1050 BC+/-

PSALM 110

The Lords, God the Father and Jesus, sit side by side in heaven and this psalm is about the Second Coming of Jesus. The rod of His strength out of Zion is the Holy Spirit and it shall rule Christians who are among His enemies on earth as it is doing today. At the Second Coming Christians shall be willing to serve Jesus voluntarily. Also Jesus was crowned in the morning to history and He has the dew of His youth. That means He will never age past 33 years old and be rather youthful. The Lord will make sure He has the titles that He had as Melchisedec and at the Second Coming God shall destroy His enemies the kings of the earth. He shall drink up Satan's political barrier on earth (the brook) and He shall crown Jesus as ruler of the planet.

Psalm 110

1. The Lord said unto my Lord, Sit thou at my right hand, until I make thine enemies thy footstool.
2. The Lord shall send the rod of thy strength out of Zion: rule thou in the midst of thine enemies.
3. Thy people shall be willing in the day of thy power, in the beauties of holiness from the womb of the morning: thou hast the dew of thy youth.
4. The Lord hath sworn, and will not repent, Thou art a priest for ever after the order of Melchizedek.
5. The Lord at thy right hand shall strike through kings in the day of his wrath.
6. He shall judge among the heathen, he shall fill the places with the dead bodies; he shall wound the heads over many countries.
7. He shall drink of the brook in the way: therefore shall he lift up the head.

Think of the Lords in heaven. Meditation. Bow thy heavens, O Lord, and come down: touch the mountains and they shall smoke.

<u>JESUS</u>   2010 AD+/-

PSALM 72

Psalm 72 is about Christ's rule when He comes back at the Second Coming. The mountains are the nations.

Psalm 72

1. Give the king thy judgments, O God, and thy righteousness unto the king's son.
2. He shall judge thy people with righteousness, and thy poor with judgment.
3. The mountains shall bring peace to the people, and the little hills, by righteousness.

4. He shall judge the poor of the people, he shall save the children of the needy, and shall break in pieces the oppressor.
5. They shall fear thee as long as the sun and moon endure, throughout all generations.
6. He shall come down like rain upon the mown grass: as showers that water the earth.
7. In his days shall the righteous flourish; and abundance of peace so long as the moon endureth.
8. He shall have dominion also from sea to sea, and from the river unto the ends of the earth.
9. They that dwell in the wilderness shall bow before him; and his enemies shall lick the dust.
10. The kings of Tarshish and of the isles shall bring presents: the kings of Sheba and Seba shall offer gifts.
11. Yea, all kings shall fall down before him: all nations shall serve him.
12. For he shall deliver the needy when he crieth; the poor also, and him that hath no helper.
13. He shall spare the poor and needy, and shall save the souls of the needy.
14. He shall redeem their soul from deceit and violence: and precious shall their blood be in his sight.
15. And he shall live, and to him shall be given of the gold of Sheba: prayer also shall be made for him continually; and daily shall he be praised.
16. There shall be an handful of corn in the earth upon the top of the mountains; the fruit thereof shall shake like Lebanon: and they of the city shall flourish like grass of the earth.
17. His name shall endure for ever: his name shall be continued as long as the sun: and men shall be blessed in him: all nations shall call him blessed.
18. Blessed be the Lord God, the God of Israel, who only doeth wondrous things.
19. And blessed be his glorious name for ever: and let the whole earth be filled with his glory; Amen, and Amen.
20. The prayers of David the son of Jesse are ended.

Think of Jesus ruling the nations and taking care of the poor. Meditation. I will extol thee, my God, O King; and I will bless thy name for ever and ever.

<u>JESUS</u>   2010 AD +/-

PSALM 75

Psalm 75 is Christ's inauguration speech at the Second Coming. Jesus is the only one who is upholding good on earth today with Christianity, everyone else is barbaric. Only Christianity sets the moral standard on earth today. This is what Jesus said at His inauguration.

Psalm 75.

1. Unto thee, O God, do we give thanks, unto thee do we give thanks: for that thy name is near thy wondrous works declare.
2. When I shall receive the congregation I will judge uprightly.
3. The earth and all the inhabitants thereof are dissolved: I bear up the pillars of it. Selah.

4. I said unto the fools, Deal not foolishly: and to the wicked, Lift not up the horn:

5. Lift not up your horn on high: speak not with a stiff neck.

6. For promotion cometh neither from the east, nor from the west, nor from the south.

7. But God is the judge: he putteth down one, and setteth up another.

8. For in the hand of the Lord there is a cup, and the wine is red; it is full of mixture; and he poureth out of the same: but the dregs thereof, all the wicked of the earth shall wring them out, and drink them.

9. But I will declare for ever; I will sing praises to the God of Jacob.

10. All the horns of the wicked also will I cut off; but the horns of the righteous shall be exalted.

Think of Jesus at His inauguration reading Psalm 75 Meditation. Every day will I bless thee, and I will praise thy name for ever and ever.

<u>JESUS</u>   1050 BC+/-

PSALM 80

Psalm 80 mentions Jesus Specifically. In verse 17 Israel asks God to send Jesus quickly to save them, so that He could rule over Israel forever, that way they would never turn away from God forever.

Psalm 80

1. Give ear, O Shepherd of Israel, thou that leadest Joseph like a flock; thou that dwellest between the cherubims, shine forth.

2. Before Ephraim and Benjamin and Manasseh stir up thy strength, and come and save us.

3. Turn us again, O God, and cause thy face to shine; and we shall be saved.

4. O Lord God of hosts, how long wilt thou be angry against the prayer of thy people?

5. Thou feedest them with the bread of tears; and givest them tears to drink in great measure.

6. Thou makest us a strife unto our neighbours: and our enemies laugh among themselves.

7. Turn us again, O God of hosts, and cause thy face to shine; and we shall be saved.

8. Thou hast brought a vine out of Egypt: thou hast cast out the heathen, and planted it.

9. Thou preparedst room before it, and didst cause it to take deep root, and it filled the land.

10. The hills were covered with the shadow of it, and the boughs thereof were like the goodly cedars.

11. She sent out her boughs unto the sea, and her branches unto the river.

12. Why hast thou then broken down her hedges, so that all they which pass by the way do pluck her?

13. The boar out of the wood doth waste it, and the wild beast of the field doth devour it.

14. Return, we beseech thee, O God of hosts: look down from heaven, and behold, and visit this vine;

15. And the vineyard which thy right hand hath planted, and the branch that thou madest strong for thyself.

16. It is burned with fire, it is cut down: they perish at the rebuke of thy countenance.

17. Let thy hand be upon the man of thy right hand, upon the son of man whom thou madest strong for thyself.
18. So will not we go back from thee: quicken us, and we will call upon thy name.
19. Turn us again, O Lord God of hosts, cause thy face to shine; and we shall be saved.

Jesus is also called the Arrow. Where did Jesus come from to destroy Satan? He came from God's quiver of Arrows.

Isaiah 49:1-2

1. Listen, O isles, unto me; and hearken, ye people, from far; The Lord hath called me from the womb; from the bowels of my mother hath he made mention of my name.
2. And he hath made my mouth like a sharp sword; in the shadow of his hand hath he hid me, and made me a Polished shaft; in his quiver hath he hid me;

Think of Jesus The Arrow of God. Meditation. One generation shall praise thy works to another, and shall declare thy greatness.

JESUS   1050 BC+/-

PSALM 45

Psalm 45 is the marriage song between the Church the Queen and Jesus the King. Verse 10 says that the Church should forget their fathers house or their nationality for the Church is an international Church called Zion. Verse 16 says that the Church is over State and that in the future she determines who will be the kings and rulers of the nations.

Psalm 45

1. My heart is inditing a good matter: I speak of the things which I have made touching the king: my tongue is the pen of a ready writer.
2. Thou art fairer than the children of men: grace is poured into thy lips: therefore God hath blessed thee for ever.
3. Gird thy sword upon thy thigh, O most mighty, with thy glory and thy majesty.
4. And in thy majesty ride prosperously because of truth and meekness and righteousness; and thy right hand shall teach thee terrible things.
5. Thine arrows are sharp in the heart of the king's enemies; whereby the people fall under thee.
6. Thy throne, O God, is for ever and ever: the sceptre of thy kingdom is a right sceptre.
7. Thou lovest righteousness, and hatest wickedness: therefore God, thy God, hath anointed thee with the oil of gladness above thy fellows.
8. All thy garments smell of myrrh, and aloes, and cassia, out of the ivory palaces, whereby they have made thee glad.
9. Kings' daughters were among thy honourable women: upon thy right hand did stand the queen in gold of Ophir.
10. Hearken, O daughter, and consider, and incline thine ear; forget also thine own people, and thy father's house;

11. So shall the king greatly desire thy beauty: for he is thy Lord; and worship thou him.
12. And the daughter of Tyre shall be there with a gift; even the rich among the people shall intreat thy favour.
13. The king's daughter is all glorious within: her clothing is of wrought gold.
14. She shall be brought unto the king in raiment of needlework: the virgins her companions that follow her shall be brought unto thee.
15. With gladness and rejoicing shall they be brought: they shall enter into the king's palace.
16. Instead of thy fathers shall be thy children, whom thou mayest make princes in all the earth.
17. I will make thy name to be remembered in all generations: therefore shall the people praise thee for ever and ever.

Think how beautiful it is that the King and Queen married. Meditation. The Lord is gracious, and full of compassion; slow to anger, and of great mercy.

JESUS   2010 AD+/-

THE KING OF GLORY.

Psalm 24 is a special psalm. It is about the Second Coming when Jesus who abandoned Jerusalem 40 billion years ago re-enters its recreation on earth 2010 AD +/-. The battle between Him and Satan is over and He is the winner. He is The King of Glory, Mighty in battle. Verse 24:4 talks about the Great Volunteering and that only those Christians who kept their promises to suffer without complaint shall stand in God's kingdom of Holy place. Psalm 24 was already written 100 billion years ago to be used in our generation.

Psalm 24

1. The earth is the Lord's, and the fulness thereof; the world, and they that dwell therein.
2. For he hath founded it upon the seas, and established it upon the floods.
3. Who shall ascend into the hill of the Lord? or who shall stand in his holy place?
4. He that hath clean hands, and a pure heart; who hath not lifted up his soul unto vanity, nor sworn deceitfully.
5. He shall receive the blessing from the Lord, and righteousness from the God of his salvation.
6. This is the generation of them that seek him, that seek thy face, O Jacob. Selah.
7. Lift up your heads, O ye gates; and be ye lift up, ye everlasting doors; and the King of glory shall come in.
8. Who is this King of glory? The Lord strong and mighty, the Lord mighty in battle.
9. Lift up your heads, O ye gates; even lift them up, ye everlasting doors; and the King of glory shall come in.
10. Who is this King of glory? The Lord of hosts, he is the King of glory. Selah.

Think of Jesus King of Glory Mighty in battle. Meditation. The Lord is good to all: and His tender mercies are over all His works.

JESUS   790 BC+/-

THE EVERLASTING FATHER

God calls Jesus "God" and The Almighty God, for if "The Everlasting Father" is Almighty God and Jesus is The Everlasting Father as Isaiah 9:6 says , then Jesus is "Almighty God".

Isaiah 9:6

6. For unto us a child is born, unto us a son is given: and the government shall be upon his shoulder: and his name shall be called Wonderful, Counseller, The mighty God, the everlasting Father, The Prince of Peace.

Think of Jesus as the Father. Meditation. All thy works shall praise thee, O Lord; and thy saints shall bless thee.

JESUS   790 BC+/-

THE LORD OF HOSTS.

Jesus is The Lord of Hosts of Israel.

Think of Jesus as The Lord of Hosts in heaven, King of Angels. Meditation. They shall speak of the glory of thy kingdom, and talk of thy power;

JESUS   00AD+/-

JESUS DIED FOR OUR SINS.

Jesus died for our sins and it was prophesied that one day we would offer up His soul for sin as the Church does nowadays.

Isaiah 53:10 "….. When thou shalt make His soul an offering for sin…."

That means the Church today is on the right track for that prophecy has come true.

Isaiah 53 is about Christ's passion on the Cross.

Isaiah 53

1. Who hath believed our report? and to whom is the arm of the Lord revealed?
2. For he shall grow up before him as a tender plant, and as a root out of a dry ground: he hath no form nor comeliness; and when we shall see him, there is no beauty that we should desire him.
3. He is despised and rejected of men; a man of sorrows, and acquainted with grief: and we hid as it were our faces from him; he was despised, and we esteemed him not.
4. Surely he hath borne our griefs, and carried our sorrows: yet we did esteem him stricken, smitten of God, and afflicted.
5. But he was wounded for our transgressions, he was bruised for our iniquities: the chastisement of our peace was upon him; and with his stripes we are healed.
6. All we like sheep have gone astray; we have turned every one to his own way; and the Lord hath laid on him the iniquity of us all.
7. He was oppressed, and he was afflicted, yet he opened not his mouth: he is brought as a lamb to the slaughter, and as a sheep before her shearers is dumb, so he openeth not his mouth.

8. He was taken from prison and from judgment: and who shall declare his generation? for he was cut off out of the land of the living: for the transgression of my people was he stricken.
9. And he made his grave with the wicked, and with the rich in his death; because he had done no violence, neither was any deceit in his mouth.
10. Yet it pleased the Lord to bruise him; he hath put him to grief: when thou shalt make his soul an offering for sin, he shall see his seed, he shall prolong his days, and the pleasure of the Lord shall prosper in his hand.
11. He shall see of the travail of his soul, and shall be satisfied: by his knowledge shall my righteous servant justify many; for he shall bear their iniquities.
12. Therefore will I divide him a portion with the great, and he shall divide the spoil with the strong; because he hath poured out his soul unto death: and he was numbered with the transgressors; and he bare the sin of many, and made intercession for the transgressors.

Think of Jesus at the cross date before Pilate. Meditation. Thy kingdom is an everlasting kingdom, and thy dominion endureth throughout all generations.

JESUS   790BC-2000AD+/-

THE GRAPES OF WRATH.

Jesus trode the grapes of wrath in Isaiah and Revelation, thus as being also the Moon stained His robe red.

Isaiah 63:1-7

1. Who is this that cometh from Edom, with dyed garments from Bozrah? this that is glorious in his apparel, travelling in the greatness of his strength? I that speak in righteousness, mighty to save.
2. Wherefore art thou red in thine apparel, and thy garments like him that treadeth in the winefat?
3. I have trodden the winepress alone; and of the people there was none with me: for I will tread them in mine anger, and trample them in my fury; and their blood shall be sprinkled upon my garments, and I will stain all my raiment.
4. For the day of vengeance is in mine heart, and the year of my redeemed is come.
5. And I looked, and there was none to help; and I wondered that there was none to uphold: therefore mine own arm brought salvation unto me; and my fury, it upheld me.
6. And I will tread down the people in mine anger, and make them drunk in my fury, and I will bring down their strength to the earth.
7. I will mention the lovingkindnesses of the Lord, and the praises of the Lord, according to all that the Lord hath bestowed on us, and the great goodness toward the house of Israel, which he hath bestowed on them according to his mercies, and according to the multitude of his lovingkindnesses.

Revelation 14:18-20

18. And another angel came out from the altar, which had power over fire; and cried with a loud cry to him that had the sharp sickle, saying, Thrust in thy sharp sickle, and gather the clusters of the vine of the earth; for her grapes are fully ripe.

19. And the angel thrust in his sickle into the earth, and gathered the vine of the earth, and cast it into the great winepress of the wrath of God.

20. And the winepress was trodden without the city, and blood came out of the winepress, even unto the horse bridles, by the space of a thousand and six hundred furlongs.

Think of Jesus treading the grapes of wrath. Meditation. The Lord upholdeth all that fall, and raiseth up all those that be bowed down.

JESUS   INFINITY PAST-INFINITY FOREVER.

JESUS HAS A THRONE.

In Ezekiel 1:26 we see Jesus sitting on His throne as a Man.

Ezekiel Chpt 1

1. Now it came to pass in the thirtieth year, in the fourth month, in the fifth day of the month, as I was among the captives by the river of Chebar, that the heavens were opened, and I saw visions of God.

2. In the fifth day of the month, which was the fifth year of king Jehoiachin's captivity,

3. The word of the Lord came expressly unto Ezekiel the priest, the son of Buzi, in the land of the Chaldeans by the river Chebar; and the hand of the Lord was there upon him.

4. And I looked, and, behold, a whirlwind came out of the north, a great cloud, and a fire infolding itself, and a brightness was about it, and out of the midst thereof as the colour of amber, out of the midst of the fire.

5. Also out of the midst thereof came the likeness of four living creatures. And this was their appearance; they had the likeness of a man.

6. And every one had four faces, and every one had four wings.

7. And their feet were straight feet; and the sole of their feet was like the sole of a calf's foot: and they sparkled like the colour of burnished brass.

8. And they had the hands of a man under their wings on their four sides; and they four had their faces and their wings.

9. Their wings were joined one to another; they turned not when they went; they went every one straight forward.

10. As for the likeness of their faces, they four had the face of a man, and the face of a lion, on the right side: and they four had the face of an ox on the left side; they four also had the face of an eagle.

11. Thus were their faces: and their wings were stretched upward; two wings of every one were joined one to another, and two covered their bodies.

12. And they went every one straight forward: whither the spirit was to go, they went; and they turned not when they went.

13. As for the likeness of the living creatures, their appearance was like burning coals of fire, and like the appearance of lamps: it went up and down among the living creatures; and the fire was bright, and out of the fire went forth lightning.

14. And the living creatures ran and returned as the appearance of a flash of lightning.

15. Now as I beheld the living creatures, behold one wheel upon the earth by the living creatures, with his four faces.

16. The appearance of the wheels and their work was like unto the colour of a beryl: and they four had one likeness: and their appearance and their work was as it were a wheel in the middle of a wheel.

17. When they went, they went upon their four sides: and they turned not when they went.

18. As for their rings, they were so high that they were dreadful; and their rings were full of eyes round about them four.

19. And when the living creatures went, the wheels went by them: and when the living creatures were lifted up from the earth, the wheels were lifted up.

20. Whithersoever the spirit was to go, they went, thither was their spirit to go; and the wheels were lifted up over against them: for the spirit of the living creature was in the wheels.

21. When those went, these went; and when those stood, these stood; and when those were lifted up from the earth, the wheels were lifted up over against them: for the spirit of the living creature was in the wheels.

22. And the likeness of the firmament upon the heads of the living creature was as the colour of the terrible crystal, stretched forth over their heads above.

23. And under the firmament were their wings straight, the one toward the other: every one had two, which covered on this side, and every one had two, which covered on that side, their bodies.

24. And when they went, I heard the noise of their wings, like the noise of great waters, as the voice of the almighty, the voice of speech, as the noise of an host: when they stood, they let down their wings.

25. And there was a voice from the firmament that was over their heads, when they stood, and had let down their wings.

26. And above the firmament that was over their heads was the likeness of a throne, as the appearance of a sapphire stone: and upon the likeness of the throne was the likeness as the appearance of a man above upon it.

27. And I saw as the colour of amber, as the appearance of fire round about within it, from the appearance of his loins even upward, and from the appearance of his loins even downward, I saw as it were the appearance of fire, and it had brightness round about.

28. As the appearance of the bow that is in the cloud in the day of rain, so was the appearance of the brightness round about. This was the appearance of the likeness of the glory of the Lord. And when I saw it, I fell upon my face, and I heard a voice of one that spake.

Think of Christ sitting on His throne. Meditation. The eyes of all wait upon thee; and thou givest them their meat in due season.

JESUS   INFINITY PAST-INFINITY FOREVER.

JESUS ON HIS THRONE.

In Revelation we see Christ on His throne again, same as Ezekiel's with a little modification.

Revelation 4

1. After this I looked, and, behold, a door was opened in heaven: and the first voice which I heard was as it were of a trumpet talking with me; which said, Come up hither, and I will shew thee things which must be hereafter.
2. And immediately I was in the spirit: and, behold, a throne was set in heaven, and one sat on the throne.
3. And he that sat was to look upon like a jasper and a sardine stone: and there was a rainbow round about the throne, in sight like unto an emerald.
4. And round about the throne were four and twenty seats: and upon the seats I saw four and twenty elders sitting, clothed in white raiment; and they had on their heads crowns of gold.
5. And out of the throne proceeded lightnings and thunderings and voices: and there were seven lamps of fire burning before the throne, which are the seven Spirits of God.
6. And before the throne there was a sea of glass like unto crystal: and in the midst of the throne, and round about the throne, were four beasts full of eyes before and behind.
7. And the first beast was like a lion, and the second beast like a calf, and the third beast had a face as a man, and the fourth beast was like a flying eagle.
8. And the four beasts had each of them six wings about him; and they were full of eyes within: and they rest not day and night, saying, Holy, holy, holy, Lord God Almighty, which was, and is, and is to come.
9. And when those beasts give glory and honour and thanks to him that sat on the throne, who liveth for ever and ever,
10. The four and twenty elders fall down before him that sat on the throne, and worship him that liveth for ever and ever, and cast their crowns before the throne, saying,
11. Thou art worthy, O Lord, to receive glory and honour and power: for thou hast created all things, and for thy pleasure they are and were created.

Think of the Elders near Christ's Throne. Meditation. Thou openest thine hand, and satisfiest the desire of every living thing.

JESUS   INFINITY PAST- INFINITY FOREVER.

ANCIENT OF DAYS

Jesus is the Ancient of Days of Daniel.

Daniel 7:9-10

9. I beheld till the thrones were cast down, and the ancient of days did sit, whose garment was white as snow, and the hair of his head like the pure wool: his throne was like the fiery flame, and his wheels as burning fire.
10. A fiery stream issued and came forth from before him: thousand thousands ministered unto him, and ten thousand times ten thousand stood before him: the judgment was set, and the books were opened.

The verse is repeated in Revelation.

Revelation 1:13-16

13. And in the midst of the seven candlesticks one like unto the Son of man, clothed with a garment down to the foot, and girt about the paps with a golden girdle.
14. His head and his hairs were white like wool, as white as snow; and his eyes were as a flame of fire;
15. And his feet like unto fine brass, as if they burned in a furnace; and his voice as the sound of many waters.
16. And he had in his right hand seven stars: and out of his mouth went a sharp twoedged sword: and his countenance was as the sun shineth in his strength.

Think of the Ancient of Days with hair as white as wool. Meditation. The Lord is righteous in all His ways, and Holy in all His works.

JESUS   536 B.C +/-

ONE

Jesus is also called "One" instead of "Trinity".

Zechariah 14:9

9. And the Lord shall be king over all the earth: in that day shall there be one Lord, and his name one.

Think of Jesus King over all the earth and called "One" for He One with God. Meditation. The Lord is nigh unto all them that call upon Him, to all that call upon Him in truth.

JESUS   INFINITY PAST-INFINITY FUTURE.

SON OF GOD.

Jesus is the Son of God.
Think of Jesus as the Son of God. Meditation. He will fulfil the desire of them that fear Him: He also will hear their cry, and will save them.

JESUS   1050 BC+/-

SON OF DAVID

Jesus is the Son of David.
Think of Jesus as the Son of David according to the flesh. Meditation. The Lord preserveth all them that love Him; but all the wicked will He destroy.

JESUS   33 BC+/-

SON OF JOSEPH

Jesus is the Son of Joseph

Think of Joseph playing with his Son Jesus. Meditation. My mouth shall speak the praise of the Lord: and let all flesh bless His holy name forever and ever.

JESUS   30 BC+/-

SON OF MARY

Jesus is the Son of Mary. The Catholics love this title the most.
Think of Mary suckling Jesus. Meditation. Praise ye the Lord. Praise the Lord, O my soul.

JESUS   100 BILLION BC- INFINITY

SON OF MAN

Jesus is the Son of Man. The Protestants love this title the most.
Think of The Son of Man on the cross. Meditation. The Lord is righteous in all His ways, and holy in all His works.

JESUS   INFINITY-INFINITY

THE IMAGE OF GOD.

Jesus is the image of God.

Colossians 1:15

15. Who is the image of the invisible God, the firstborn of every creature:

John 14:9 "… he that hath seen Me hath seen the Father…"
Think of Jesus as the Father, and the Father came to earth and we nailed Him to the cross. Meditation. It is a good thing to give thanks unto the Lord, and sing praises unto thy name, O Most High.

JESUS   00AD+/-

THE VINE

Jesus is the vine and we Christians are the branches.

John 15

1. I am the true vine, and my Father is the husbandman.
2. Every branch in me that beareth not fruit he taketh away: and every branch that beareth fruit, he purgeth it, that it may bring forth more fruit.
3. Now ye are clean through the word which I have spoken unto you.
4. Abide in me, and I in you. As the branch cannot bear fruit of itself, except it abide in the vine; no more can ye, except ye abide in me.
5. I am the vine, ye are the branches: He that abideth in me, and I in him, the same bringeth forth much fruit: for without me ye can do nothing.

6. If a man abide not in me, he is cast forth as a branch, and is withered; and men gather them, and cast them into the fire, and they are burned.

7. If ye abide in me, and my words abide in you, ye shall ask what ye will, and it shall be done unto you.

8. Herein is my Father glorified, that ye bear much fruit; so shall ye be my disciples.

9. As the Father hath loved me, so have I loved you: continue ye in my love.

10. If ye keep my commandments, ye shall abide in my love; even as I have kept my Father's commandments, and abide in his love.

11. These things have I spoken unto you, that my joy might remain in you, and that your joy might be full.

12. This is my commandment, That ye love one another, as I have loved you.

13. Greater love hath no man than this, that a man lay down his life for his friends.

14. Ye are my friends, if ye do whatsoever I command you.

15. Henceforth I call you not servants; for the servant knoweth not what his lord doeth: but I have called you friends; for all things that I have heard of my Father I have made known unto you.

16. Ye have not chosen me, but I have chosen you, and ordained you, that ye should go and bring forth fruit, and that your fruit should remain: that whatsoever ye shall ask of the Father in my name, he may give it you.

17. These things I command you, that ye love one another.

18. If the world hate you, ye know that it hated me before it hated you.

19. If ye were of the world, the world would love his own: but because ye are not of the world, but I have chosen you out of the world, therefore the world hateth you.

20. Remember the word that I said unto you, The servant is not greater than his lord. If they have persecuted me, they will also persecute you; if they have kept my saying, they will keep yours also.

21. But all these things will they do unto you for my name's sake, because they know not him that sent me.

22. If I had not come and spoken unto them, they had not had sin: but now they have no cloke for their sin.

23. He that hateth me hateth my Father also.

24. If I had not done among them the works which none other man did, they had not had sin: but now have they both seen and hated both me and my Father.

25. But this cometh to pass, that the word might be fulfilled that is written in their law, They hated me without a cause.

26. But when the Comforter is come, whom I will send unto you from the Father, even the Spirit of truth, which proceedeth from the Father, he shall testify of me:

27. And ye also shall bear witness, because ye have been with me from the beginning.

Think of Jesus as the Vine and we Christians as the branches. Meditation. I will say of the Lord, He is my refuge and my fortress: my God; in Him will I trust.

JESUS   00 AD+/-

CHAPTER 17 JOHN

Chapter 17 John is very important for we find out that Jesus existed before the big bang in verse 17:24 and verse 17:5

John chpt 17

1. These words spake Jesus, and lifted up his eyes to heaven, and said, Father, the hour is come; glorify thy Son, that thy Son also may glorify thee:
2. As thou hast given him power over all flesh, that he should give eternal life to as many as thou hast given him.
3. And this is life eternal, that they might know thee the only true God, and Jesus Christ, whom thou hast sent.
4. I have glorified thee on the earth: I have finished the work which thou gavest me to do.
5. And now, O Father, glorify thou me with thine own self with the glory which I had with thee before the world was.
6. I have manifested thy name unto the men which thou gavest me out of the world: thine they were, and thou gavest them me; and they have kept thy word.
7. Now they have known that all things whatsoever thou hast given me are of thee.
8. For I have given unto them the words which thou gavest me; and they have received them, and have known surely that I came out from thee, and they have believed that thou didst send me.
9. I pray for them: I pray not for the world, but for them which thou hast given me; for they are thine.
10. And all mine are thine, and thine are mine; and I am glorified in them.
11. And now I am no more in the world, but these are in the world, and I come to thee. Holy Father, keep through thine own name those whom thou hast given me, that they may be one, as we are.
12. While I was with them in the world, I kept them in thy name: those that thou gavest me I have kept, and none of them is lost, but the son of perdition; that the scripture might be fulfilled.
13. And now come I to thee; and these things I speak in the world, that they might have my joy fulfilled in themselves.
14. I have given them thy word; and the world hath hated them, because they are not of the world, even as I am not of the world.
15. I pray not that thou shouldest take them out of the world, but that thou shouldest keep them from the evil.
16. They are not of the world, even as I am not of the world.
17. Sanctify them through thy truth: thy word is truth.
18. As thou hast sent me into the world, even so have I also sent them into the world.
19. And for their sakes I sanctify myself, that they also might be sanctified through the truth.
20. Neither pray I for these alone, but for them also which shall believe on me through their word;
21. That they all may be one; as thou, Father, art in me, and I in thee, that they also may be one in us: that the world may believe that thou hast sent me.
22. And the glory which thou gavest me I have given them; that they may be one, even as we are one:

23. I in them, and thou in me, that they may be made perfect in one; and that the world may know that thou hast sent me, and hast loved them, as thou hast loved me.

24. Father, I will that they also, whom thou hast given me, be with me where I am; that they may behold my glory, which thou hast given me: for thou lovedst me before the foundation of the world.

25. O righteous Father, the world hath not known thee: but I have known thee, and these have known that thou hast sent me.

26. And I have declared unto them thy name, and will declare it: that the love wherewith thou hast loved me may be in them, and I in them.

Think of Jesus with the Father before the big bang. Meditation. O Lord God of hosts, hear my prayer: give ear, O God of Jacob.

JESUS   00AD+/-

THE LAMB OF GOD.

Jesus is the Lamb of God which was sacrificed for our sins.

John 1:29

29. The next day John seeth Jesus coming unto him, and saith, Behold the Lamb of God, which taketh away the sin of the world.

When Jesus was being sacrificed on the cross and said "My God, My God" He was saying psalm 22 word for word. And the reason Jesus was born from a virgin is so He could not have original sin passed down from Adam to all people.

Think of the lamb of God without sin. Meditation. But thou art holy, O thou that inhabitest the praises of Israel.

JESUS   1984-INFINITY.

EAGLE

Jesus is the Eagle of Mathew 24:28, Satan is the other eagle.

Mathew 24:28

28. For wheresoever the carcase is, there will the eagles be gathered together.

DAYSTAR

Jesus is also called Daystar for only Jesus is to arise in your heart and not Lucifer or Satan.

II Peter 1:19

19. We have also a more sure word of prophecy; whereunto ye do well that ye take heed, as unto a light that shineth in a dark place, until the day dawn, and the day star arise in your hearts:

Some theologians have made a profound mistake by calling Satan the Day Star. But as you see in II Peter the Day Star is another name of Jesus.

Think of the Eagle Jesus Christ. Meditation. The Lord hear thee in the day of trouble; the name of the God of Jacob defend thee.

JESUS   10 AD+/-

JESUS IS THE MOST POTENTATE.

I Timothy 6:15-16

15. Which in his times he shall shew, who is the blessed and only Potentate, the King of kings, and Lord of Lords;
16. Who only hath immortality, dwelling in the light which no man can approach unto; whom no man hath seen, nor can see: to whom be honour and power everlasting. Amen.

Think of the Most Potentate Jesus Christ. Meditation. Send thee help from the sanctuary, and strengthen thee out of Zion.

JESUS   00 AD+/- - INFINITY

THE LION OF JUDAH

Jesus Christ is The Lion of Judah.

Revelation 5:5

5. And one of the elders saith unto me, Weep not: behold, the Lion of the tribe of Juda, the Root of David, hath prevailed to open the book, and to loose the seven seals thereof.

Think of Jesus not only as the Lamb of God but also as the Lion of Judah. Meditation. We will rejoice in thy salvation, and in the name of our God we will set up our banners: the Lord fulfil all thy petitions.

JESUS   2010 AD+/-

THE MOON.

In Revelation 12:1 the Woman is the Church, the twelve stars are the Apostles and just as a man in love with a woman is under the feet of His wife- Jesus the Moon is under the feet of His wife the Church.

Revelation 12:1

1. And there appeared a great wonder in heaven; a woman clothed with the sun, and the moon under her feet, and upon her head a crown of twelve stars:

The " Sun" is God the Father.

Think of Jesus the Moon in love with the Church. Meditation. Our fathers trusted in thee, and were delivered: they trusted in thee, and were not confounded.

JESUS   00 AD+/-

THE CHILD

Jesus is the Child of Revelation Chpt 12:5

Revelation 12:5.

5. And she brought forth a man child, who was to rule all nations with a rod of iron: and her child was caught up unto God, and to his throne.

Jesus was taken up to heaven at the Ascension and the Angels have fought His battle ever since. Think of the Ascension of Jesus. Meditation. The fear of the Lord is clean, enduring forever: the judgments of the Lord are true and righteous altogether.

JESUS   INFINITY.

THE WORD OF GOD.

Jesus is the Word and The Word of God.

John 1:1

1. In the beginning was the Word, and the Word was with God, and the Word was God.

Revelation 19:13-14

13. And he was clothed with a vesture dipped in blood: and his name is called The Word of God.
14. And the armies which were in heaven followed him upon white horses, clothed in fine linen, white and clean.

Those two verses add up to Jesus being God the Creator.

Think of the Word of God on a white horse. Meditation. How long wilt thou forget me, O Lord? Forever? How long wilt thou hide thy face from me?

JESUS   2010 AD+/-

KING OF kings, LORD OF lords.

Revelation 19:16

16. And he hath on his vesture and on his thigh a name written, KING OF KINGS, AND LORD OF LORDS.

Think of Jesus as The King of kings and Lord of lords . Meditation. But I have trusted in thy mercy; my heart shall rejoice in thy salvation.

<u>JESUS</u>   <u>300 BILLION AD +/-</u>

INFINITE SPIRIT

Psalm 148:4-6

4. Praise him, ye heavens of heavens, and ye waters that be above the heavens.
5. Let them praise the name of the Lord: for he commanded, and they were created.
6. He hath also stablished them for ever and ever: he hath made a decree which shall not pass.

Jesus is worshipped in other universes, "waters" above and outside the heavens. Jesus is worshipped in millions, billions, trillions and infinite other universes by infinite Alien Christian brethren throughout infinity. Jesus fills all infinity. Jesus is worshipped also in other infinite dimensions besides the infinite third dimension. This is the Great Glory He was talking about in the New Testament. Infinite Glory. The humble carpenter is worshipped throughout infinity for He is God. Infinite Spirit. Ancient of Days.

Think of Jesus having different bodies for our Alien Brethren but one Spirit that fills all infinity. Also Jesus will lead us, His sheep through the wilderness of time forever.There is about a googolplex of us human sheep in our kraal of a googolplex universes. Jesus has personally given everyone of us a secret name as His personal sheep. We were the only sinners throughout infinity and Jesus suffered great pain to save us. Meditation Psalms 23

1. The Lord is my shepherd; I shall not want.
2. He maketh me to lie down in green pastures: he leadeth me beside the still waters.
3. He restoreth my soul: he leadeth me in the paths of righteousness for his name's sake.
4. Yea, though I walk through the valley of the shadow of death, I will fear no evil: for thou art with me; thy rod and thy staff they comfort me.
5. Thou preparest a table before me in the presence of mine enemies: thou anointest my head with oil; my cup Runneth over.
6. Surely goodness and mercy shall follow me all the days of my life: and I will dwell in the house of the Lord for ever.

The end of book Jesus.

CHAPTER FIVE
MY DEALINGS WITH SATAN AND THE ANTICHRIST ANGEL AT THE PRESECOND COMING BATTLE (2000 AD+/-.)

MAGNIFICENT EAGLE JESUS

Mathew 24:28 "For wheresoever the carcase is, there will the eagles be gathered together."

Eagle : Jesus

. eagle : Satan

Carcase: A born again Christian who is dead to the world of Satan. Gospel of Paul in Romans, crucified in Him, crucified our flesh, but our spirit lives. This person is supposed to welcome Jesus at the Second Coming. The Eagle Jesus is protecting and guiding him, while the eagle Satan is trying to confuse or kill

him. This is Chpt 12 Revelation, the battle, the Invisible war. As you read this book realize you are living in the end times.

This is a story about how I heard the same voices that Mohammed heard in the wilderness. Fortunately for me I also had the Holy Spirit of Jesus Christ to help me in deciphering the voices of these alien beings.

For I was targeted for destruction by the Beast Angel and Satan and his demons. As you read the book it will not make any sense to you until the end where I beat my captors and stopped WWIII from the earth as Jesus prophesied with His help I would.

Unknowing to me The God of Israel had given me a gift when I was born. I was to be the Melek of Kush and the messenger of Isaiah 14 and the Carcase of Mt 24:28. As also the Melek of Kush who beheld Satan and defiled his brightness I am not here to boast, Iam here to reveal the dark secrets of the Invisible War and what Angels do to men. For the same Anti Christ angel that talked to Mohammed also talked to me and tried to make me a modern day prophet, but Jesus saved me. The worst that happened to me was I killed someone and I was pronounced insane after I told the Judge my story.

All my life I had been attacked by the dragon with dreams and near death experiences but The God of Israel saved me from all my troubles like He saved King David from all his troubles. Satan visited me many times in my life, I can pinpoint two occasions one in 1968 when I was about 7 years old and another time when I went to Africa from the U.S.A. same year. As I said I escaped my captors for Jesus saved me, Iam deemed an insane man hearing voices, but had Mohammed lived in my times and the voices came to him he would have been deemed insane like Iam, but with the help of Satan and the anti Christ they made an antiChristian religion called Islam and a billion people believe in the great lie. Satan offered me his power and the Beast offered me great military prowess like he offered Hitler and Mohammed. It was a narrow escape indeed. For God also had His intentions of a Roughwind, but He "stayeth" His Roughwind in the day of the east wind. So in my story we have demons given me dreams and directions and Jesus the Holy Spirit given me directions.

As for me all I have to say about me was I was a warrior, the very gunho of the 82nd Airborne, my goal in life was to become a mercenary in Cambodia then after a two year hitch a soldier of SWAPO.

For life. Fighting was in my blood and I consider myself the very best. My long term goal was to unite Africa into one nation or die trying. My mother Africa had borne me and had called me to battle. Unknowing to me I had another Mother. Mother Church the bride of Christ and it is she who would claim my life in the end. As if it was nothing The God of Israel also made me Melek, (prophet and Messenger of Isaiah and of Kush) just for serving Him against Satan, the Beast and their frog demons. In Mathew 24:28 the two Eagles are Jesus and the eagle Satan.

Iam the dead body that they fought over, dead to the world of Satan as Paul preached in Romans.

Matthew 24:28 " For wheresoever the carcase is, there will the eagles be gathered together"

Magnificent Eagle Jesus
As an Eagle protects her young
So does the Lord protect me.
He teaches me how to fly
Until my wings become strong
Over the battlefield I hover
To drink the blood of the slain
Armageddon is history
The Carcase I remain.
The Lord is mighty in Battle.
Magnificent Eagle is His name.

As I said the story doesn't make sense for my body was being contested by confusing and very stupid demons, insane Satan ,abomination poltergeist the Beast and Jesus the King. Satan tried to explain it to me by publishing and making me read the Secret Wars by Marvel comics for Doom was my idol. I was only a child and Isaiah says even though I played with the serpent in his hole I would never be bitten – Jesus explained it to me as being the Carcase of Mt 24:28 and I was born to welcome Him at the Second Coming. Here is the confusing story.

This is the story of my life, and the story of the Carcase of Mt 24:28
A long, long, long time ago about 40 billion years go, I stood in line in the Great Volunteering. We had been created by Jesus 100 billion years ago but 40 billion B.C. the Lord was recruiting an Army of His Christians to come and fight in the invisible war on battlefield earth in our times.

I was young in those days being a few billion years old, but I loved Jesus and He had asked us to come to the stage called earth where good and evil was to be played out , to die and suffer shame for Him. It was going to be a battle between Truth and lies, good Vs evil, love Vs hate, Christians Vs non Christians and Christ against Satan. As you've probably read in my books this was called the Great Volunteering where we all volunteered to come to earth to show our love for Jesus.

When I reached the Lord He gave me a small but great part in the war. My job was to welcome the Lord at the Second Coming and become the architect for it. I was to be the Carcase of Mt. 24:28, the child of Isaiah 11:8 who played in Satan's hole and never got bit, Jesus is the other Child who led the world. Also I was a messenger of Isaiah 14:31-32- flooded the world with the gospel of the foundation of the earth Habakkuk 3:13. Also I was to swallow the flood of Satan (political dictation) and be the earth of Revelation 12:15-17. I was also to be the king who beheld Satan in Ezekiel 28:17

and defiled his brightness, and another part I wont reveal until it happens- but the Lord also told me my gospel is mentioned in Is 18:3, 27:3 or my destruction of the U,S,.S.R. in Is 27:8 would not be believed by the Church. The Lord told me in Is 28:5-12, it is I who is weaned from the breast who sitteth in judgment that has been given strength from the Lord to turn the battle at the gate when Satan almost broke Christianity with communism, Islam, lust of the flesh, viols, pomp in movies and science. The Church is at risk of destruction for Jesus has not shown up and Satan is destroying the Church with the pedophile scandal and Islam. He would have used communism – but I took that away from him.

Well Jesus explained all these things to me 40 billion years ago and I was amazed at the role that He gave me. To be the Carcase of Mt 24:28 . He also told me that when He comes back I would be taken in chains to Jerusalem to declare that God is really The God of Israel. (Is 45:14) and all I would have to take there is the vessels of the Lord (Is 52:11-12)

So I thanked the Great Lord Jesus Christ 40 billion years ago and told Him I loved Him and that I would do my utmost best and that I would trust Him- even in death. We as Christians disappeared into the heavens when that universe collapsed.. Then there was the Big Bang as Jesus told the universe to expand again.

In the days of Daniel 2700 years ago it was the time for Jesus to declare His plan of redemption for Adam. The Invisible War had been going on for some time. Lucifer had been created and Satan had fallen from grace as you've read in my books. 2700 years ago Jesus played with His toy Satan and made a deal with him. He told him that He Jesus will come down to earth and that He would sow the Light with His ministry. Satan would get a chance to kill Him and that he Satan should try to fight the expansion of Christianity until the end. But if he failed to stop Christianity's expansion, he Satan still had one more chance to destroy the whole thing, all he had to do was convert one man to his side or kill him, or deceive him and he Satan could win the entire war. That man was to be called the Carcase and Jesus the Eagle and Satan the other eagle would hover over the body and fight for him.

Carcase in Mt 24:28 or body in Luke means born again Christian – a person who is dead to the world of Satan crucified his flesh in Jesus according to the gospel of Paul in Romans. All true Christians are Carcases.

Matthew 24:28 "For wheresoever the carcase is, there will the eagles be gathered together"

Throughout history Satan has been fantasizing about the Carcase. One of the most fantastic lies was when in world war II he told his nation of demons that the end had come and that Hitler was the Carcase. Satan rallied his nation of demons to fight like they never had done before. Satan tried to tell his demons that WWII was Revelation 13-20 come true. He orchestrated the economic blockade against the Jews

Like Chpt 13 talked about. Because Jesus had told Satan that the Carcase would be homeless, he made Hitler into a tramp. Because the Carcase would be an artist, he made Hitler study art. Because the Carcase would go to prison, he put Hitler in prison, all to deceive his nation of demons. And to stop the nation of Israel rebirth in the last days as Jesus said it would, Satan and his demons decided to kill off all the Jews in the world. That was why WWII was fought. It came to the point that the wounded and defeated German troops from the Eastern front were denied access to transportation by train back to Germany just so the trains could be used to carry the Jews to be killed in camps by the S.S. The destruction of the Jews was more important then the survival of Germany. Satan played up Germanys glories in vast parades. Because the Banner of Jesus would be white, black and red Satan made Hitlers flag the same colors and when I decided as the Carcase to change from white to yellow- present day Germany's colors are red, yellow and black, he hit all bases, my room for maneuver is limited. Just as not Beast Hitler had a false prophet- Satan made Goebbels into the second beast and Satan and his nation fought. They fought harder then they ever fought before for the demons thought that this war was the end battle- Armageddon . Satan would possess the French Generals and make them do dumb things and the AntiChrist would possess the German Generals to do brilliant maneuvers. The German soldiers were possessed by demons to fight like berserkers. But the opposing armies would be possessed to be afraid and run and be confused. This was how the Eastern front was fought. The Russians weren't stupid, they had supernatural forces fighting against them. This went on until the God of Israel decided to fight back. Who bumped Japan into the U.S.? It was the Lord for no man could have made such a blunder. And who made Hitler declare war on the U.S- Jesus did to Satan's destruction. And you know Einstein was a Jew- so the Angels fought for the Jews. You know the rest of the story of WWII.

When Satan failed he switched over to the U.S.S.R. and he told his demons that he had lied to them, that WWIII wasn't yet. So they were relieved and had Satan in great awe for lying to them like that. When Stalin tried to kill off the Jews by sending them to the Gulag, God killed him. (see book Gulag Archipelago page 92 by Aleksandr I. Solzhenitsyn) Harper & Row , publishers..

So God has been fighting for the Jews throughout history even though Satan has been trying to bring hate against them by host nations stereotyping them. Why were the Jews more economically and culturally stable then the people they were held captive by ? It is because the Lord helped them (Bible) ,

To continue after WWII the colonial powers were weaker and with Vietnam as an example into what could happen worldwide , Africa was released from their grip. Satan toyed with Nkurumah and his Inner circle stint (My invention) even to Idi Amin and many other people who were to be the Carcase to demons. Satan just kept lying to them until today they don't know who is who. But a core of demons at the top know.

But one day I think before WWII my grandfather who was a pagan Maasai went into his coffee plot to till the ground with a hand held hoe. (things had happened to the Maasai due to Satan- that's another story)

One day my grandfather Mella was tilling the ground and as he worked an Angel in white appeared to him.

He was as bright as lightening he said and the Angel called out to him and called him- Lotegeluaki ! Lotegeluaki ! Lotegeluaki !- three times. My grandfather perceived it was an Angel and that was his new name. So the Holy Spirit led my grandfather to become a Christian- a Lutheran. The next day my grandfather said he worked in the corn plot behind his boma or kraal and a presence , a whirlwind type presence flew to him, and he said it was Satan. My grandfather threw a clog of dirt at him and the presence flew down the small valley down away from the cornfield.

I was born on August 24/1961 and I didn't know all these things or what life Jesus had in store for me as all Christians are born into. I had no recollection that I (as all Christians) have lived before and I didn't remember volunteering for the invisible war.

I have no major recollections about my childhood except I was born premature, but I ate a lot so I grew up normal. My father became a Lutheran minister and was invited to the U.S.A. and in 1967-68 I ended up in Minnesota (St. Paul) in a house on Lutheran seminary grounds.

One thing did happen though that had an impact on Satan later in life. I met my third grade girlfriend.

One day in the winter all the girls in my class decided to chase me. I was the only black boy in the class and for some reason about 12 girls chased me across the playground. That evening I ended up with one of them and went to her house instead of going home to play with her toys. When her parents came home they were surprised to see a little black boy playing with their daughter. They asked me my name and once determined they called my dad who came to pick me up. Fortunately her dad was a Lutheran minister and my dad was a Lutheran minister also and the families hit it off.

Another thing that happened at the house on Lutheran seminary grounds was that I met Satan. I went out to play astronaut one day . It was during the time or era when men were going to the moon and I as many children did, played astronaut. I went outside with my fantasies and I felt a presence. It was Satan and he told me that I should play soldier and that at 7-8 years old I should emulate Mao, Stalin and Hitler and that I should start planning on how to conquer Africa. So from then on I watched "Combat" on T.V. and my standard of people or peer group was Stalin, Hitler and Mao. I planned my life from 18 years old and on, on what I should do and how I should start my career of taking over Africa. I never knew that The God of Israel had made me Melek of Kush.

Unfortunately adultery destroyed my family. An epidemic that was plaguing the U.S.A. So my father sent the family back to Tanzania. I ended up in Germany on the way back at a friends house. I went out to play riding a tricycle and I met a column of tanks rolling down the street. I never knew that I would participate in Reforger with the 82nd Airborne in Germany when I grew up.

After about a month later when I was in Tanzania a terrifying thing happened to me as I was sleeping in my grandmothers hut. As I slept I had a dream that I was being chased by a gigantic green dragon. I ran and ran and I soiled my pants in my terror . I woke up in the middle of the night and went outside of my grandmas hut (a feat in Africa being so young and having terrors like leopards outside) and I buried the German leather folk shorts I was wearing. The dragon flew away and went down out back down the valley of my grandfathers corn field and disappeared.

Then after a few years I started to have dreams of the U.S.A.. One time I dreamed that I was walking down a path and all the brush around me was all serpents and snakes, but as long as I stayed on the path I was safe. I dreamed of the U.S.A. often and I knew I was going to return there again. In 1971-72 I dreamed of the green house where I killed Cindy or Terra. I dreamed of Honey Pot.

My father came and took us from Tanzania, but Satan tried to stop him from that, actually three days after we left, the border between Kenya and Tanzania was closed as Tanzania became more communist.

We lived in Rochester Minnesota and moved to Kasson Minnesota but Satan never bothered me there.

He waited until I got to Milwaukee. I went to college at the University of Wisconsin and that's where all the fun started. For example I had many dreams and I couldn't figure out why all my dreams were in green. I wasn't doing good in college. I was too young and I wanted to socialize (party) – something my parents never let me do (a mistake by them) and I had broached the subject of me joining the Army first, but they never listened. So I partied in college and I was on the verge of flunking out my first year. With the prospect of getting a bad report card one day Satan visited me during summer vacation. It was three days or so before my 18th birthday and I was upstairs in my room. Satan asked me a question " What are you going to do to live forever "? Satan had been visiting me in Church and had eroded my confidence in Christianity for a month before this question. Fleetingly Christianity was shoved out of the way. So my first thought was I was going to study physics and find a way , but my second thought was I was going to take over a country and cultivate a group of scientists to work on the problem.

(Stalin's last project). So I came up with a plan where I would join the Army , then go to Cambodia and fight for Polpot (for some reason Satan told me he was a great guy) then once I got combat experience – go fight for SWAPO (a completely different environment – desert versus Jungle) and command a battalion- breakaway from SWAPO – march north to Rwanda and Burundi- knock out both countries and start pulling off coupe de tats throughout Africa in a secret service war. Build a gigantic army and attack South Africa.

Once that was done the rest of Africa would be easy. (hook or crook). (Later on when Satan lost to Jesus he took vengeance on the people of Rwanda and Burundi. He also created or souped up Cambodia's dilemma for me.)

So the next day – three days before my 18th birthday I left home on my quest and I wasn't coming home until I did it. Join the army and go to Cambodia where Satan was going to torture me at Angkor prison temple . That was his secret plan for seducing me to Cambodia.

When I joined the Army I realized the reason why all my dreams were in green. When I got to AIT San Antonio I knew where all the bathrooms were in the building like I had been there before. That's when I realized I could see the future. I was so proud of myself. I thought I was so intelligent that I could see the future- actually I was so stupid- I never attributed it to God.

Then I went to jump school and even though jumping was terrifying I jumped anyway and got accustomed to it. I really never knew what I signed up for. I wanted to go Special forces but I wasn't a citizen so the 82nd was the next best thing my recruiter told me. When I got to the 82nd the very first two weeks they put me in Recon school. I thought I was going to stay there for the rest of my tour.- winter recon- but three days before the school ended I was told I could terminate so I did. When I got back to base I was told I had to finish the course, so I was sent back that summer and I finished it. I didn't count it as a failure – its just that I got double recon- winter and summer recon. I was super gunho because I knew I was going to Cambodia and become a mercenary.

In my last years in the Army Satan visited me a lot. We planned not only on how I was going to take over Africa, but we planned on how we were going to take over the planet. I was possessed not knowing.

I was going to wield Africa as a weapon and take over the planet earth. I planned on being the first to kill 100 million people and the first to conquer the planet. Then that's when the problem started. What was the human race going to do afterwards ? How and where should I lead the human race?. First I wanted the humans to discover time travel, then if I succeeded they were going to come back in time and take me into the future. I was sure I succeeded for I was super gunho. I believed in myself. (Actually Satan believed in himself and was very confident). Being possessed I had the same feeling of invincibility. Just like the evil guys in the cartoons- super heroes. I was crazy. So I knew I won, but why did not I come from the future to give myself encouragement.? Also I did not know that Satan had told his demon nation that he was going to come back from the future to fight for them at the Second Coming. That's where the concept of the Terminator came from. Even the last episode of Star Trek the next generation had the same concept. It was from Satan. But I planned on things the human race was going to do under my guidance. I was going to unleash a program and a course for the human race. We were going to get rid of hunger, and Christianity and we were going to replace it with psychiatry. Everyone had to see a therapist every week. (God actually made me see a psychiatrist for 17 years) I was going to nuke Israel for starters and conquer time travel. Only the good people would be saved or sent into the future by a council of judges. But after planning for 3 million years we ran out of things for the human race to do. On one of the pieces of papers I was planning on I wrote on the side (without me knowing it)- " So this is the plan to fight God". But only three years later after I got out of the Army and was rereading my notes did I discover what I wrote. I was a Christian by then, actually possessed by demons who I didn't know were in me.

One day we paratroopers medics were laying around drunk in the hall ways of our barracks. That day I had read in Time Magazine about a submarine called the Trident. She was a great ship and I realized that that was my ticket to unite Africa. If I stole that sub I could have everything. So I asked my fellow paratroopers if they wanted to be mercenaries, and most said yes. So I brought up the possibility of stealing the Trident, but they thought I was crazy. Some saw the possibilities. I kept quiet about that after that since I was going to Cambodia to fight for Polpot and Satan was going to torture me at Angkor by the gods of the Cambodians.

So I E.cho T.ango S.uitcased out of the Army. But before I went to Cambodia I had been yearning for my third grade girlfriend and I decided that I would travel to the North East and try to meet her there. It was the only thing stopping me from Cambodia- a monkey wrench in Satan plans of torturing me at Angkor.

She really saved my life and God noted it in Isaiah 14:31. I missed my "appointed time" or marriage date. So I decided to study physics at U.Mass for a while until I found her and if I couldn't find her I would go to Cambodia.

I lived in Northampton or Leeds, never can tell the difference, and I had a dream. I saw myself in a Calculus class taught by a young female professor and when I really did go to school at U.Mass I ended up in the same class as I dreamed. The walls were the same, the desks, chairs and I had seen my professor in my dream. So I thought I was really intelligent. What a fool I was.

I worked at a Hess gas station and one night Satan gypped me out of a 20 dollar bill. He came to me and I served a customer in a trance. I gave him free gas and twenty dollars. He said thank you for the free gas and the money and left. I got fired the next morning. Then that night I had a dream that I was working at Powertest and the next two days or so I applied there and got a job. That's when I remembered the dream and I was awed. Now the place was not called Powertest by Satan for no reason, for my life would be fought over by Jesus and Satan at this gas station. There was going to be a powertest between Jesus and Satan. Jesus won, but it's a long story.

One day as I worked in the gas station mini mart I met Sharon the owner of the green house in Honey Pot. She drove me down to her house in my van and we became friends. It was a great ranch and she let me live there. I respected her as my mother and I enjoyed the horses she had there. I didn't believe in riding horses for I thought it wasn't fair for the horse, I'd rather walk with the horse, but anyway I stayed there the summer of 1984. I soon realized I couldn't afford school and I was too proud to apply for financial aid. I decided I had to find a paying job, so I went to New England Tractor-Trailer school. I wanted to drive tractor-trailers after watching Mad Max in the Road warrior movie. I played my cards and I concentrated on getting my license and I finally got it. But I did not tell my employer of the gas station, a good man who was Jewish (Bacon) that I was about to make my move to a higher paying job.

Three days before I went to my new job in Springfield MA as a truck driver (two Jewish brothers owned the company and were my bosses) a girl Janet met me and the chemistry was right. So I planned to date her the night before I started on my new job to celebrate. Three days before that I had a dream that I was in a jail cell. The lights were bright and I noted the cracks in the wall. But I didn't think much of it. So the day of the date (July 18th 84) I parked in front of Forbes Library and waited for Janet. I had a joint and a bottle of wine and I planned on going to a motel. So I waited and waited. I decided to put a dime in the parking meter just in case something happened. Well not long afterwards, about three minutes later a State police cruiser pulled up and for absolutely no reason came after me. He pulled out his gun and told me to get out of my blue van. He looked through my van and found a knife- a British commando double-edged knife that was with my National Guard equipment. It was on my dashboard but it was my combat knife for the Mass National Guard. He decided to take me in for that. When I was in the backseat of the cruiser he asked me if I had any other illegal thing in my van and since I didn't know how to lie I told him I had a joint in my ashtray- so they got me for that also. As we were about to leave the scene- after the tow truck took my van- my girl showed up. She looked distressed when she saw what was happening. So that was Satan after me. I never knew that I wasn't supposed to meet girls. It was written in the Bible. The Beast in Daniel was supposed to hate women and love power. But in the Army as a paratrooper Satan let me visit prostitutes, but to fall in love was a no, no .

I ended up in the same cell that I had dreamed about, the light, the cracks in the wall, I had seen all this three days before in my dream. I got a lawyer, who I still owe $300 to, and got out the next morning and I tried to get to my job in Springfield as quickly as possible. I got my van out and as I was going south Satan destroyed my van. The engine just seized up on the highway. I said goodbye to my new job. I got it towed back to Northampton with triple A and I went back to my gas station job like nothing had happened.

I asked the good Israelite man for $200 to buy a new engine and he gave it to me. After work I walked down to Honey pot for some reason. When I got there in my invincibility of being a paratrooper I decided not to go back to the bridge but swim the Connecticut river and jump across the highway to a Northampton dealership. I had swam the river before more then once without any problems, but on that day Satan was out to get me. I jumped into the water and as I started to swim out twenty feet out I started to feel weak, then all my energy was drained out of me. I started to flounder, then I started to drown. I kicked off my shoes, but I went down anyway. I said to myself -paratroopers don't panic, paratroopers never panic, so I came up again. Then I went down, came up again for the last time and I looked up at the sky for the last time. I could see that there was a clear bubble around me as I went down for the last time. My hand was the only thing above water and I said " God help me", and incredibly I was propelled across the river to the other side onto some rocks. I was drained and all I could do was hug the rocks. I was exhausted and drained. For some reason Sharon and her family were watching and they started to applause and clap when I reached the other side. When I finally got up I said " God I owe You one". I took two steps and I forgot about God

I finally got an engine in my van. I owe it to my National Guard buddies- Willy and another guy. They put it together one night at the Armory in Leeds. I went back to work at the gas station but fall and winter was coming so I had to make my move. One day I decided I would go to New Haven and look for a tractor-trailer job. For the gas to get there I left a whole gas station full of gas and I took some gas from a broken down van my friend let me. I didn't know how to steal. It was brown and dirty but I didn't know it was going to clog up my van. I also didn't take my weeks pay. I was too honest for my own good.

For if I had filled up my van with good gas and taken my weeks pay I wouldn't be here writing this story.

New Haven actually West Haven was a nightmare. I drove down and surely my gas line clogged up. I threw away the filter and in West Haven my carburetor clogged up. I ended up on the beach on the Atlantic Ocean – at the place where the English were supposed to have landed. That week was my worst week and I parked behind an Italian restaurant for a week. I was lonely hungry and dispirited. I tried to get into the VA hospital around the corner for food. I even had an accident where I used poison oak to wipe my ass and I was scheduled to have surgery with some female surgeon but I never showed up. For alcohol addiction I had to have relatives and support in the city to get in. So I wandered around that area for a whole week picking up dimes to buy coffee. Then in my van I had a terrible dream. In my dream I was walking proudly on sandy ground in my blue jeans and jungle boots. Then I heard a mighty voice saying " Behold- the seat of the African nations" and I looked and a man in a tan suit was sitting on it. I looked forward, for the African nations was not all that I was interested in. Then the mighty voice said " Behold – the seat of the European nations" – and it was an empty seat. The seats were black   and looked like a two person sofa. So I looked back and I began to wonder about the guy who was sitting on the African nations seat. First I looked at his black shoes and each foot was as big as a football goal. So I started to look up and up and up and finally I saw his face. He turned to look at me, he had dreadlocks and his eyes were glowing with no pupils, and he looked at me and it was me. So in shock I started to run from that place. I tried to get up out of that dream and I had a seizure as I was trying to wake up . I kept being pulled back into the dream. I struggled between two worlds.

After that I was afraid to go to sleep. That was a daytime dream, but the next day I went to the beach and on the pier I started to hear Black Sabbath Iron Man and in a daze I imagined I was in a rockinroll band. On stage we had a gigantic dragon. That stayed with me for a while. The next day as I walked down the streets terrified I saw in a window a sign that said " God loves you" and I felt a feeling of love enter me. I didn't know that that was Satan, but I felt comforted. The reason I say that is because I completely distrust the origin of all the miracles that happened to me throughout my ordeal or story.

I decided that the best thing I should do is go back to Massachusetts and play the lottery for I had this feeling that I would win. So I sold my van for $50.oo to a guy from Nigeria in the Connecticut National Guard and I hitchiked north to Northampton . I had failed in New Haven.

But unfortunately for me Gerald Dean Ferraro the presidential candidate was in Amherst when I hit town. I looked like a Vietnam vet or some terrorist for I was dressed up in semi military uniform-fieldpants and field Jacket. The secret service took notice and an old man who better fit in North Carolina instead of the college crowd in Northampton started to follow me. So I hid from him. I had a death wish. Before long I had a platoon of guys following me. So I stayed away from Amherst that day. I went to sleep on the bikepath in September, it was Indian summer. But in my head I started to hear voices- actually they were lectures. Some person (it was the antichrist) started to lecture me in my father's voice. Satan thought that when God spoke to you He would do it in your father's voice. These lectures were about Africa and they were annoying as I tried to sleep, and I never remembered what they were about, I just caught the tail end of them as I woke up.

I got a job at powertest again and I kept having this fantasy about being a sniper and shooting someone. That was Satan trying to set me up. The Secret Service parked their car across the street from the gas station but they never came to kill me.

That year I had met Cindy and she said she was a friend of Sharon and that she needed a place to sleep with her boyfriend. She asked if she could sleep in Honeypot for now I was the official caretaker of the place. Sharon and her man had gone to the fairs around the country with their horses. This was in 1984.

I had a dream that I was climbing a mountain one night. The next night I climbed the rest of the cliff and when I got to the top- crawled on my hands and knees over the top, I saw Jesus standing there and I touched His toe and power as lightning went through me and I said. " I shall serve thee sweet Jesus" and I felt the taste of honey on my lips. I woke up and I could still taste the honey on my lips as I licked them.

Then a few days later I had another dream. I was coiled up in this huge snake and Satan told me " Stan, I won't play with you anymore if you keep talking to God". A few days later I was introduced to the invisible war. As I went to the outhouse I picked up a marvel comic I had bought and it was called "The Secret war" I read it and guess who won out of that epic battle of superheroes. My idol Doom won. I knew that that was not possible and that's when it dawned on me that someone out there was manipulating the entire

Planet just for me. That's when my small head began to suspect something.

One day as I lay beside Cindy I saw three frogs come out of her abdomen, hover over me and disappear into my chest. That's when I really started to hear voices in the day time- awake. A clacky witchy voice asked me if I wanted Satanic powers and I said "No". I was given a birds eye view of the Connecticut river where I was at and I was asked if I wanted to have the power to see things. (You'd think it was the Lord of the rings) But I got up and walked outside. I forgot about them after that.

The Secret Service was still watching me and to encourage the executioners the Terminator movie was playing that week. What really convinced me I was being hunted was that one day after working a night shift a broken down Datsun that had been parked all night across the street followed me to Honey pot.

It had blue State out of State plates and as I was on the embankment it stopped and a blackman in a suit got out of the passenger side . He took out a rifle and shook it at me, then laughing he got back in the broken down Datsun and it turned around and left. That was the last I saw of the Secret Service.

But that was not the end of my troubles, for "The Killing fields" was playing and Satan started to use Satanic Cults to destroy me.

On Dec 3rd I decided to go to Cambodia. I packed my bags and I decided to hitchhike to Texas to meet a mercenary friend of mine. I thought maybe I could get him to go with me. But I only got as far as the highway. It was too cold to hitchhike so I returned to Hadley. A few days later as I was trying to make sense of my world (it had gotten cold) I walked to Honey pot and halfway I stood looking at a tree. I wondered if the trees were gigantic antennas to God. I wondered if they funneled our prayers to God. That's when I started to feel two dots in my chest and one of these warm glowing dots in my chest said- It was God and the other warm tangible glowing dot was Jesus. Jesus was so meek and I felt a love in my stomach or abdomen. (supposed to be raptured)

Then I felt a third person in the middle of my chest, and I asked them who it was. I was told it was a demon or angel. I talked to God and He was the God of the Bible. I was so happy to talk to God that on the third day I vowed to Christianize the whole world for Him by the edge of the sword. (82nd Airborne Madness or Mohammed madness) Yes for Jesus I decided in this end war that I would give Him a soldiers ultimate gift. A thirty million man paratrooper jump around the world and take out the planet in 24 hours. I would amass an army of 30 million paratroopers and millions of airplanes and in one bold day put them in the air and have the final jump. In three months I intended to finish mopping up. But first I must steal the Trident and finish Ronald Reagan who I came to believe that he was the beast. (Satan's deceit) by giving him six letters in his first, second and last name. So that was my vow to The God of Israel.

Now you have to realize that this was Armageddon. The dots inside of me was not God, it was the demons. The silent person who I had not discovered yet was the Holy Spirit , Jesus and the True God of Israel. It was to be as confusing to me as possible as Satan the eagle with his demons inside me and Jesus the Eagle and the Holy Spirit fought for me.

As I said the Secret Service left me and Satan tried to kill me and lead me at the same time. My doctors call this stage my psychotic time, since Satan had created psychology from Mesmer's seances to break my faith. He wasn't about to lose this battle. My faith has been tested for 15 years by psychologists and psychiatrists trying to brainwash me, but the Holy Spirit prevailed. Sharon had told me in a trance that I wasn't going to win and that the deck was stacked. The movie Terminator was played out and the Secret Service for some reason decided not to execute me. So now was the time of the "killing fields". I was already in Cambodia.

Concerning the Satanic cult- One day as I was working in the gas station- talking to false God and false Jesus the dots in my chest a bunch of kids came up to me, about three girls and two boys- all about 12 years old or so, came up to me and told me that Cindy was a Satanist and was running a cult. I didn't think much of it but I decided to put her with the enemy.

I also had doubts about these voices and I decided to go to the VA and have the doctors examine me.

I was still in the National guard and I was a Vet. I should of got disability, but the doctors couldn't convince me that God and Jesus were not real.

In February of 1985 I decided to quit smoking for I thought Jesus did not want me to smoke. I went out into the woods to live and purify myself. I had taken Cindy's blanket and I went out to the banks of the Connecticut river to hideout. God had changed the weather for me. It was warm in February. I was always hiding for some reason, I think I was crazy. As I lay in the woods, Michael the ArchAngel visited me. He was a young man dressed in a light gray jacket or wool jacket and was wearing some slacks I cant remember the color. He just walked over to where I was hiding in the woods and stood outside a circle I had made. He just stood there and looked out toward the Connecticut river and that's when I trusted in Gods protecting Angels. I felt so protected by God that I just dozed off. I should have went over to the Angel and asked him what was happening in my life, but I was an idiot. I dozed off and I dreamed that this guy from Jamaica a priest of the Rastafarians was chasing me. I ran and I jumped across a fence but he stuck to me like a monkey on my back. I woke up and Michael was gone. The next day I met the Rasta man on the bus to Amherst. Satan had sent him to me. He said his name was Harold and he knew I was the AA 82nd man. I never met this guy before in my life. Then on the bus he started to chant as he sat beside me. He told me to come to Jamaica and he gave me his phone number. This was my lead by Satan to go to Jamaica and be worshipped as Jesus Christ by dope smoking madmen. He even wrote AA Rasta on the door to the toilet I used in the psych building where I usually slept.

I also had a dream in the psychology building at U.Mass . When Gorbachev was still in England before he came to power, three days before he came to power I saw him hitchiking in the rain in Hadley. When I went to work that day Cindy pulled up in her tan car. Her son was with her. Her son got out of the car in a trance and came into the minimarket. He gave me a Hitler salute as if he was drugged and told me that my father was waiting for me in Cindy's car. I looked out but it was drizzly (real spooky stuff) . That child really got me to kill his mother for that spooky stuff. I was scared after that.

Three days later I looked in Time magazine and I saw my father Gorbachev was the leader of the U.S.S.R.. That's when I started to see the awesome powers of Satan. The Angels also kept their vigil of me in the psychology building and that was our headquarters. The doors to the psych building would mysteriously be open to me and they would stay at the doors of the place at night , even the roof or skyroof door someone stayed there. I never talked to them. But one day I took the bus to work (they were free) and I noticed that in the last few days a Cambodian girl in a black beret would get out and run or sometimes briskly walk in front of me as if she led the way. Now I knew I was the only one to stop at that stop, there was nothing between the bridge into Northampton to the gas station that any student would stop for. She would get out and run in front of me and walk down past Coolidge bridge to Northampton.

I just went to the gas station. Well one day I ran up to her , and I knew she was an Angel out to protect me, so I asked her, her name, and she said she wouldn't tell me. I asked her why, and she said because I would ruin it. So I left off talking to her. I guess it is a custom of Angels not to tell their names. Even in Samson days to today they don't tell their names. There are at least 7 billion Angels in heaven and we only know the names of two of them. I guess they don't want us to worship them. So I called her Anna, for she looked like my aunt Anna. One day I will build a shrine to her and name a Church after her. God really showed me that I should love Cambodian people and that really pricked my heart. But after that she stopped jumping off the bus , actually that's when all the Angels or Angel students at U.Mass disappeared.

One other incident with the Angels. I used to go to the U.Mass Chapel to pray. I would pray for long hours and I just wanted to know what God wanted me to do. Then one day as I sat alone in the Chapel a young man went up to the Altar or place where the Bible was displayed . I watched him as he turned the pages. Then he stopped and in a loud strong voice he read to me Jeremiah 1:4-10. This is what he said or read.

4:Then the word of the Lord came unto me, saying 5 Before I formed thee in the belly, I knew thee; and before thou camest forth out of the womb I sanctified thee, and I ordained thee a prophet unto the nations. 6 Then said I, Ah, Lord God! Behold, I cannot speak: for I am a child.7 But the Lord said unto me, Say not, I am a child: for thou shalt go to all that I shall send thee, and whatsoever I command thee thou shalt speak.8 Be not afraid of their faces: for I am with thee to deliver thee, saith the Lord.9 Then the Lord put forth his hand, and touched my mouth. And the Lord said unto me, Behold, I have put my words in thy mouth 10 See, I have this day set thee over the nations and over the kingdoms, to root out, and to pull down, and to destroy, and to throw down, to build, and to plant."

I thought that he was an Angel , which he really was now that I see the whole picture of what happened to me. But anyway two days later when I went back to pray at the Chapel alone – a loud voice came out of the Altar and said. " I don't want to hear anymore words" – telling me to beat it and don't come to pray here anymore. I was really hurt that God would treat me so shabbily . Now that I look at it I know that the voice was from Satan. It was the invisible war and Satan and Jesus were hovering over me and Satan wanted me to be confused. I was getting these conflicting things. It took me a long while, when I was at BSH to figure that something's were from Satan and something's were from Jesus. The Angel was from Jesus and the voice was from Satan. Thus Mathew 24:28 was taking place and I was the Carcase or body of Luke 17:37.

That week as I worked , still raining in Hadley Cindy pulled up in her car and a gold limo with New York plates pulled up also and parked for gas. Cindy wasn't parked for gas. The two cars just stayed outside for a half hour. To this day I think that woman put a contract on me, or her demons did. After a while 5 black kids around 12-14 yrs old got out of the limo and came into the gas station. They huddled in the back of the store , then they all shuffled in a cluster and came to the counter. They had a rolled up newspaper but I noticed nothing amiss. They bought nothing as they just stared at me at the counter.

One of them had a crooked arm and they were all wearing Egyptian gold jewelry. I noticed nothing amiss and I smiled at them. They didn't spend much time or money in the gas station and they walked out around the corner outside where I couldn't see them. Then a few minutes later all of a sudden they ran to the limo and the limo took off. A customer walked in and said- " I just saw those kids beating an Uzi submachine gun against the wall and when they saw me they ran in the limo." So I thanked the Lord for the Uzi must have jammed.

I was in awe of the Lord from then on, for that's what those children had in the rolled up newspaper., I think

The next morning my shift reliever Carl who was an hour late came in and told me that he had a dream.

He said " Stan, I just had a dream that there were 18 bullet holes on the wall and you were in the back dead". Then he said the cash register was open but no money was taken. So I decided to quit. It was a Sunday and I walked to U.Mass to sleep. As I walked I heard voices saying in earnest " do you believe in Jesus" about four or five times. It was icy and drizzling out. I walked to U.Mass for the busses didn't run that early in the morning on Sunday. Midway I was stuck between a guard rail and the road. A blue station wagon pulled off the road and came to hit me, but I was teleported off the road close to the grass. That's when I believed in Jesus. The driver pulled off to a donut shop near a bank in the mall parking lot. I walked into the donut shop and nobody stood up to shoot me. I couldn't tell who the driver was of the blue station wagon so I left and walked away to U.Mass.

The next week I heard a voice in the commons cafeteria shout out " Somebody better check their mail box" so I went and did and my VEAP refund had come in. The money I was going to use to go to Cambodia- about 2000$.. I had a lot of weird things happen to me at U.Mass. One day a female student walked up to me and asked me if I was working on my project (to steal the trident and take over the world)

I didn't even know her. Also there was a group of people who followed me knowing that I had something to do with the Second Coming. It is amazing how I kept all this secret- That's why the disciples asked the Lord "Where" for it was going to be a secret and Jesus answered " Wheresover the Carcase is the eagles would be gathered together". I don't know if I would have gotten into more trouble had this been a public battle but it was trouble enough. Another time I asked the Lord what was going on and He led me to the bookstore in the commons. I found a stack of books called the Invisible war. I bought one and when I realized what it was I went back to the stack for more books and I found the whole stack of books gone. That was in three minutes of time. So I took the VEAP money and I planned to escape from Hadley and Satan's Cults.

I decided to flee to Lebanon New Hampshire. I looked on the map of New England traced south to throw off any demons watching, then quickly decided to go North to Lebanon. I never knew that they lived inside of you, so there is no geographical escape. I bought a car, wrote and attached false plates and drove north. As I drove north I drove past my exit to mislead anyone following. As I pulled off the next exit another car pulled off the road with me. I looked to see who it was and it was a woman . She looked at me and her eyes glowed like light bulbs. There were no pupils, just lights. So I drove to the southward ramp of the highway. A car just pulled out in front of me and ran interference by driving fast in front of me. I couldn't match his speed so I drove slowly behind him. This was all of Satan's miracles, these miracles were designed to dupe me. Jesus was still silent.

I got an apartment in Lebanon. Before I got my apartment the cops in Vermont stopped me and made me get Vermont plates. When I got the apartment, three Russians moved in with me. A girl and two young men. They were Satan's people. Slavic Mongolian in features. The girl put a gigantic picture of a demon or ork on her door opposite mine.

I had a dream about them. I had a dream that I was standing in front of a river. Someone shot three arrows into the river and Gorbachev, Reagan and Senior Bush were following hard on my heels, chasing me and this woman who was supposed to be Africa but I thought the woman was Jessica in the Dune series.

Across the river I watched as all types of African animals stampeded into the jungle. Then we crossed the river. This is just a stupid demon dream but the end is important. I saw three snakes hanging in a tree behind me and a evil voice said " these are the evil spirits that are chasing you". Then one of the snakes uncoiled off the tree and chased me. I ran and ran to my room jumped into my bed but it crawled up to me quickly and bit me. I woke up with the pain on my left hand above my thumb. I woke up and I could swear I was bit. From then on I had a very painful time reading the Bible. It took me 14 days to read it but it was very painful. I actually had to stop reading the psalms and skip them until the end. I guess demons can make it very spiritually painful to read the Bible and that's why a lot of people have a hard time reading it, yet they can read a 1000 page novel just like that.

One day after a month I decided to escape again and go to Canada. Nevertheless I dreamed of going to Canada beforehand. But I just got on the bus and took off to northern Quebec.

I must tell you of a temptation I had when I first arrived in New Hampshire. It was on a hill behind the McDonalds on the border between New Hampshire and Vermont. I ended up making a hootch on top of a hill I called Beersheba, behind the McDonalds.

On the hill I was told by someone that I was Jesus Christ. I had made a campfire on the hill and someone was out to lie to me. At first I was taken aback. I didn't want to be Jesus Christ, it felt so yucky.

I wanted to be a soldier, a machine gunner, not Jesus Christ. And that's what I decided I was, a soldier.

So my temptation or the tempter left. So anyway after living in the apartment for a few months and working at the Wendy's at the bus stop (there is also a burger king there and Mc Donalds) I decided to go to Quebec to escape the demons for I perceived they found me in Lebanon, NH. So I just got up and left Lebanon and went to Quebec. I met an Italian chic on the bus who was visiting Canada from Italy.

We hit it off but I was a bum so I had to leave her. One thing I noted about Canada was the further north you went the more blasted the trees looked, like some cold wind had shrunk all the trees. But anyway I got to the Hudson ? river in the middle of July . It was warm, and it was going to get colder from then on. So after looking around the Hudson river I decided to go back south to North Carolina to see if my friends would help me. So I hitchiked south. I met a farmer near the U.S border in Canada south of Toronto and he asked me to stay with him. I helped him with his vegetable garden and cattle. He was very nice to me and I told him that I would visit him again- probably in May of the next year. I hitchiked to North Carolina and I found out my friend had left Ft.Bragg so I hitchiked to Rutland VT. I lived outside near the train tracks on an abandoned factory and I got a job at Filenes. Then as it got colder I got a room in an apartment . One day I went looking for a job at a construction site repairing a road, but I walked through another construction site building a road and a overpass. They just stopped me and gave me a job as a flag man. Now actually I wasn't right in my head, talking to the glowing dots in my chest (seemed like I was talking to myself). I almost got people killed for my mind was not on the job. As I worked on the road underneath the uncompleted overpass I had a daylight vision.

A bright light , not a photonic light but a very bright spiritual light shown around and over me. My partner couldn't see it, but I could feel the light. I looked at myself and I said, look at me. I was good and I haven't killed anyone like Satan. Satan looked like a murderous monster killing people all over the world. But that light was engineered by Satan, playing with me for I was about to kill someone. After the light, a few days later I decided to go back to Massachusetts and play the lottery. I knew that since I was with God I would win and start on my jihad or Roughwind against Reagan and Gorbachev.

I got back to Hadley and I got a job at Powertest. This was in 1985, I worked there for some time. Nothing crazy happened except that I had gone in full circle in my escape of Satan, but I was highly possessed. Then one day I decided I had enough faith to win the lottery. I knew all I had to do was believe and I would win and since I was convinced I was going to win I decided to pack my bags or rucksack and leave town with the ticket. So that night at work I packed my backpack and this time I took $150 as my pay for the week. Just before I closed up at 11:00 PM Cindy showed up. I was surprised at how she always knew that something important was about to happen in my life. She told me that she would wait for me in Honey Pot . She wanted to sleep there because she didn't have any place to go. So I said okay. When she left I toyed with the idea of killing her as a favor to God. I was memorizing Chpt 24 Isaiah- a very terrible Chpt to memorize. Its about death and destruction from the Lord. But as I packed I decided against killing Cindy. On my way to Honey Pot the idea came to me again and one of the dots in my chest began to glow, so I realized that God wanted me to kill her. The corn was only knee high and I remembered recon school. I got off the road and decided to pull off a raid on Honey Pot. When I got there I decided against it. So I let her sleep in one of the rooms near the kitchen. I packed my rucksack taking certain books for the journey. Then Cindy got up and she said she had butterflies in her stomach . That set me off. So this demon master knew I had planned to kill her. How did she know. Her demons must have told her . I still had the glow in my chest, so I decided to kill her. I never killed anyone before so I went looking around for an axe or a spear or anything. I found a knife and I dispatched her as she tried to enter her car. I really didn't want to do it, but I felt I had to do it so God could trust me. Paratrooper medics weren't supposed to kill people but I had declared war on the place and I was on my way to steal the Trident.

Now something happened that was really scary. After I killed her I thought to myself that I should bury her under the house. Two seconds later a husky voice from above, not my fathers voice said " Bury her under the house". That was supposed to be God, but it was P.P- the antiChrist. I call him P.P.- Poltergeist the modern day Philistine. But now looking back, the anti Christ and Satan's demons were there, but I never felt Satan who was probably there. Also it seemed to me that the forces of Satan were in disarray by the time lag in the voice and repeating what I had thought of myself- bury her under the house. I guess they were surprised I actually killed her. But that unit- Satan's forces were unprepared.

To this day I cant understand why God- the real God didn't interfere and give me some kind of sign that I was being misled. It would have spared the woman's life. Eventually I really did pray for her soul and my soul that the Lord accept us both into heaven because we were both victims of Satan. Whether she was a Satanist – that's open for conjecture, I mean with her son spooking me with his trance and the children saying she was running a cult and the Bible saying you should kill witch's and Satanist, I think it was a real tragedy. I could justify myself and say she was a Satanist or take the Judge's position in court that I was psychotic and hearing voices, but that's not true also. I was as sane as sane could be. It was Satan and supernatural forces that brought about this tragedy. For example the week I was supposed to leave Bridgewater State Hospital Satan tried to muddy the political waters by killing a woman in Bridgewater called Zapp. How I could I live with her death for my sake . How about all the Cambodians and the people the demons of Satan killed in Rwanda and Burundi for vengeance against me. Where was God in all these cases ? It really hurts me for my life is not worthy for even the least of the children killed in Rwanda or Cambodia, let alone these two women.

The next morning after I had buried her under the house I took her car to U.Mass and I slept in the commons. I lost the lottery, so I decided maybe God wanted me to get my friends involved first before He could give me money. So I drove down to Ft. Bragg and I ended up on Sicily DZ parked near the bleachers. After contemplating my next move. I went to my old unit and I couldn't find anyone I knew there. So I went to the Papa Juliet training area. I was in cammies like everyone else on base, but I had no headgear or boots. Nobody noticed me

I went into the woods in my old training area and I found a company of infantry training. I decided to steal a m-16 or a m-60. I just walked into the middle of their camp and I couldn't find an m-16, but I did find someone's MRE's or lunch so I took that and I walked out of the camp away from Ft. Bragg. After a few hundred yards I realized a flank of troops chasing me. But God was with me. I ran and I found a water duct underneath the road and I ducked under it , crawled to the other side of the road and doubled back .

I went and watched the company train or melee as I ate the guys lunch. They were all cherry's to me. I had already had my tour of duty in the 82nd. But I decided I was still in danger so I went back to my car. That night I decided if I was going to get some m-16's I would have to get them from recon base camp. So I drove out to the area. Taped up the tail lights of the blue Voltaire car I had from Cindy, drove slowly to within a 1000 yards of base camp. I had a knife and my plan was to go through the tents as the men slept and steal their m-16's. Also I was going to knife the lot of them as they slept. So I walked to the camp around 12:30 AM, I jumped over the concentino into the camp. Fortunately or unfortunately for me they kept guard duty. Something we never did when I went through. The guard saw me and he started to smile as he walked toward me with his backpack radio. He must of thought I was an instructor prowling at night or some guy trying to bring in booze to the camp, but he was smiling as he walked toward me. That's when I decided I shouldn't kill this guy. I felt sick to my stomach. I really felt like I didn't want to kill again. I felt sorry for the guy. What's this poor soldier got to do with my war? So I jumped out of the perimeter out of the concentino wire and left.

A friend of mine I met in my old unit was in another unit. He just flunked out of delta team and he gave me $300.oo to go back to Massachusetts. I still owe him, he wanted to join the French foreign legion, but he didn't want to join my killer sheep unit. That's what he called it, after I told him my plans. He was interested but I didn't have any money to show him.

So I drove back to U.Mass and I left the car in the parking lot. Satan really wanted the cops to find me, for I left my I.D and a book on how to make explosives in the car. I wanted to be chased it seemed. He was working to kill me and was leading me at the same time. But I was on a mission from God. I asked the Lord to bring Cindy back to life but the dots couldn't do that. So I was confused about the capabilities of my God.

After staying in Mass and seeing that nothing happened to me I left the State. As I was leaving town Cindy's daughter Chris saw me and she called the cops and told them I had killed her mother. How did she know? Satan must have told her- the cult. That's when I came to believe that the whole cult was family related. The Northampton police questioned me and I lied. They let me go and I hitchiked home to my parents. My quest to take over Africa and never come home until it was done failed. Things beyond my control – supernatural forces and the invisible war had decided my fate. My parents took one look at me and decided I was insane, so they put me in the VA hospital. First my father took me to see a psychiatrist in a hospital. She was an Indian lady from India and she told me that I should get a lobotomy. It would be painless and I only had to stay in the hospital for three days. Since I used to be a medic I knew what a lobotomy was so I kindly refused. I never told my parents what I had done. I ended up in Tomah VA for the winter of 86-87 and I never told the doctors. The medication never helped the voices, for one day the spring of 87 God or god- the dots in my chest came to me and in a very kind and pleading voice said " Come and help us". The kings in 40 billion AD better watch themselves when these demons are unleashed on them. They will use anything, any trick in the book, to use you. So I left Tomah and hitchiked to Texas where my merc friend was supposed to be. I ended up in sublime Texas and I met his wife. She in turn drove me to Augusta Georgia. He had re-enlisted in a leg unit and was a 91 Charlie at the hospital on the base there. He also was living with another girl which caused much distress when I showed up with his wife. They worked it out and she left with most of his guns, reassurance that he would come home.

I slept there and the next day when he went to work, I decided to take one of his guns- a mossberg 12 guage shotgun and rob a gun store I saw in the yellow pages. I was going to kill people from now on, this was Cambodia to me and I was going to rob banks and get the money that way. Wasn't God with me.?

I went to the gun store. I had the gun in a green army laundry bag. I layed it on the counter of the gun store and just as I was about to blow away the old man who owned the store, the dots in my chest blinked. So I stopped squeezing the trigger and I left. God wasn't willing. If I had killed that man I probably would have killed his whole family, for it was a family run gunstore which he ran in his house. The cops would have had a shoot out with me or I would have ended up in Angola prison on death row. Those two acts of cowardice by Satan and his demons, destroying the U.S.S.R on the rumor of stealing the Trident and this gunstore blinking incident made them lose the whole war. They are cowards.

They had a chance to kill me , but pure cowardice by demons and Satan destroyed them at Armageddon. For the world would not have had the easy problem of Osama bin laden but he could have used the U.S.S.R in the last days to nuke the world or produce distress. But they are cowards. They failed. They had their chance.

I hitchiked to Atlanta and I stayed there as a bum for the summer of 87 fed by Mother Church. The Atlanta Church's fed its poor. Iam really grateful to my Mother for that. They even washed your feet at one of the Church's. I started to have visions again around Dec 6th, I was tried of visions. I was a soldier and all I got was visions. I wanted guns, troops, money and God was unable to provide me with it. So I decided this was no God. He couldn't do anything. I was angry, so I decided to leave God and turn myself in. Once I decided that the visions increased, Satan's last desperate attempt to salvage WWIII.. I saw visions of the universe collapsing, I saw my friends appear and disappear in front of me. I even saw Noah appear and disappear so I can tell my fellow Hamites I saw Noah. I decided to commit suicide but as I climbed on the overpass near Peachstreet I decided against it. I would turn myself in.

I went to the police the first time and I got cold feet. Then that night on Dec 7th I called the police from a store and they came and picked me up. I was taken to a precinct and my records tell the story. But what the records don't tell was that the detective tried to kick me out of the police station and let me go. But I was in rebellion against God who had told me to fight Him earlier in another incident on the streets of Atlanta. He told me (the antiChrist) told me that in order to fulfill my mission of serving God I had to fight Him and that was His will. He told me to "advance" and fight. But I decided against it, against God's orders. This shows Iam smarter then the whole house of Satan. Anyway at the precinct Satan was there and the detective gave me one last chance. He told me to hit the road for he thought I was just trying to get a free ride to Mass. I wasn't on the computer and I could have walked on that basis and washed my hands of the whole thing but I was mad. I begged him to take me in, and he said he couldn't hold me on anything.

He asked me if I had any vehicle violations and I told him I had attached plates once and had unpaid tickets, so he held me on that until he could check out my story. It was the only way he could keep me since I wasn't on the computer. The Hadley police tried to find the body that night but there was a blizzard that night. But the next day they found it where I had told them it was. Three days later the State troopers came to Atlanta to pick me up. I ended up in a cell J-23 I think in Hampshire county jail. Then God let Satan take over me so much – the dots were given more power such that I was a lunatic. The demons had told me I was going to be shot and I would come back to life, then start the war. Just like the Beast in Chpt 13 Revelation. So I was afraid when they came to take me to Bridgewater State Hospital. The psychiatrist at the jail thought I was a nut talking to the dots and laughing to myself all the time.

I ended up at B.S.H in the Maxi's my first night and I decided to fast. The next morning I saw a vision of Jesus (it was a demon vision) and told me to fast. I cant understand why I always had the good ideas and they came after. I think they are just stupid. So I fasted for seven days. The next day after the Maxis I ended up on B-2 unit and had my first fight fasting. Some idiot called Flash tried to pick on me. But all the fun started at BSH. I reread the Bible. One of those early days as I was sitting in the side room I thought to myself. You know, all this time Ive been hearing three voices and three dots, it must be those demons from Cindy. Incredibly a patient who was laying on the floor next to me got up and started screaming-" the genius, the genius! Then I heard two voices in me saying " fool" a gruff voice, then another voice said "fool". So I called them "gruff" "Pipsqueak" and "no name". The smallest was pipsqueak, he probably was the demon Paul had as his temptation because as I saw him enter me from Cindy he looked tattered up a wounded demon. So thats where the term- pieces of shit- comes from. From then on I eyed the dots as my enemies and I turned to the real God of Israel in heaven. I read Psalm 142 and worshipped Him. Also I found out I was supposed to be the falseprophet, to my distress. They tried to convince me that's who I was and I refused and stayed closer to the real Jesus in heaven. That's when He Jesus started to reveal to me the secrets of the Bible, that Daniel had deceived Satan and that WWIII was really 40 billion years away. I also found out I was the Carcase. I started to write books. I wrote 23 books or booklets in all my time at BSH.

I published some and threw away the rest. Actually some I asked the Lord to bring back typed when He comes back at the Second Coming.

I told the doctors my story- the truth but they did not believe me. They thought that I was hearing voices and a war was fought between the doctors and I. They tried to brainwash me that I didn't have any demons. Demons don't exist and there is no God or supernatural forces. Satan had cultivated psychology for Armageddon for he wasn't about to lose this battle. The Holy Spirit fought and won.

On the other hand I started to play with my new found toys, that's what I called Satan , P.P and the demons. In the name of Jesus I put them in the toilet and made them eat feces and commit homosexual acts in the toilet full of feces. Since Satan didn't want me to have girls I had my vengeance.

I could have got out earlier if I pressed it with some of my social workers but I decided to stay in BSH for the rest of my life. I wanted to spend my life at BSH until Jesus came back. But I had some really kind Doctors- Doctor Wollhiem and Dr Brower and Di White the social worker and they coaxed me out of my shell or world and in the year 2000 I started the process of leaving BSH. Dr. Brower was Catholic and Dr Wollhiem was an Israelite and DR.Brower told me I shouldnt tell the doctors I heard demons. I should tell the priest that, but when it came to doctors I should tell them the scientific version of things. Before you can get out of BSH you have to admit to three things.

1. You have a mental illness 2. The medication is helping you and 3. You will continue to take your meds when you get out. That's the ticket out of there and if you have faith in God and you think your sane and the Meds don't work, you'll never get out of there and that's what Satan thought. But I outsmarted him or God outsmarted him for He wanted me to get out and publish His books about the Foundation of the world.

So in the end I was able to separate religion and psychology and got out. Satan didn't want me out and he fought. The week I was to go to court he killed that women Zap in Bridgewater to pollute the political air. As I said before Satan has done a lot of evil things in my name in the Invisible War. It distresses me to see people killed for my sake. The people in Rwanda, Burundi and Cambodia died for Jesus. Satan killed them for vengeance against Jesus Christ winning in the Invisible War. But God fought in this manner. He locked me up for 17 years, so that I wouldn't do anything stupid like enter politics where 1/3 of the angels were waiting to use me like Hitler. Do nothing was Gods strategy. This is because Satan and his nation were expecting a great war at the end of time, a great Jihad to take over the world. They wore themselves out preparing for that end war that John and Daniel deceived Satan about . John and Daniel did not put a 40 billion year pause between Chpt 12 Revelation and Chpt 13 Revelation and in Daniel between 11:28 and verse 11:29. They also lost the U.S.S.R. in their panic. Even though Satan put his heads in power they were useless- Andropov, Reagan, Bush I, BushII, Clinton and Gorbachev and Putin. Those are all of Satans head in Chpt 12 Revelation.

I ended up in Parkview Hospital in Springfield, complying with those three things the doctors wanted. I really don't know if Resperdol works against demons, but it made me realize that medication didn't work on me or on many people hearing voices, because most are hearing the voices of fallen angels. But I do attribute that med to making me realize its hopeless and my doctor at BSH Dr. Tannenbaum said he had been working as a psychiatrist since the Korean war and I was the first person he had ever heard get cured from hearing voices.

It never cured me, after taking it I realized I wasn't hearing voices, or not at least the random voices of a diseased mind the doctors were saying. I wasn't hearing random voices but I was hearing fallen angels. So I told them I stopped hearing voices and they attributed it to Risperidal and since for 12 years I had been telling them the truth and they would rather want me to tell them I had a malfunction in my head I told them it was true the Meds got rid of my voices. The scientific version. But even today I still got the dots in my chest, not voices in my head, so I wasn't lying to the docs, but I guess God wont get rid of them until I finish writing all my books. They always give me faith that God exists, so they serve a useful purpose in the Invisible War or as Satan calls it The Secret Wars of Marvel comics. Exorcisms do work, but Satan banned them for even the Church is embarrassed to do them. We think its stupid, but Jesus did them all the time. He wasn't stupid.

Well anyway I got out and I had a dream – this time with the real Lord. He said " feed the sheep". God has spoken to me only about three times throughout my ordeal or actually four or five. He is usually the smallest voice of love that I can discern , also He talks to me in cartoon language. So I published my book – " What the Bible says about the collapse of the universe, life before the big bang, the 200 billion year history of Christianity- the invisible war". *Now Titled " Christians existed before the Big Bang and will exist after the collapse of this universe" . Dr Angfang recommended that my meds be increased when I told him about my book. Risperdal causes me to have insomnia but its supposed to be my miracle drug.

My second book , Book II of what the Bible says about the collapse of the universe will be published in January 2004. They intend to recommit me in January and probably out into the world in the beginning of Summer, but I think Jesus will come back very soon and has been waiting for me to type this book.

Written 29/sept/03 Typed 23/Oct/03.

This is a summary of my life, all that I remember of the swahili language.
Mungu ni pendo, Apenda watu,
Mungu ni pendo, ani penda.
Sikilizeni, furaha yangu, Mungu nipendo, anipenda.

Nikapotea, katika thambi,
Nikawa mtumwa wa shetani, Sikilizeni furaha yangu
Mungu ni pendo, anipenda.

Akaja Yesu Kunikoboya
Yeye Kanipa, Uhuru yangu.
Sikilizeni, furaha yangu,
Mungu nipendo, anipenda

Ndio ye sasa, namtumikia
Mwokozi wangu, Yesus Kristos.
Sikilizeni, furaha yangu, Mungu Nipendo
Anipenda.

WWIII IS 40 BILLION YEARS FROM NOW.

The Second Coming is in my lifetime.

MYTH NO# 1. There is a rapture where Christians are going to dissappear and go to heaven while some great war takes place here on earth.

TRUTH: 1/3 of the human race will die . 2.3 billion people will die - the wicked- and we will burn their bodies in the streets. Their souls -the wicked souls will all be escorted to hell by the Angels, but Christians will remain on earth. The "taken" are the bad people- not the good. Satan confused Christians and the Church.

MYTH NO#2. WWIII is before the Second Coming or the return of Jesus where the AntiChrist will take over and get rid of all Bibles and Christians and Jews.- Then Jesus will come down and destroy the AntiChrist in our lifetime.

TRUTH: WWIII is after the 1000 year reign of Christ, after the return of Christ at the Second Coming. The 1000 Christ years is actually about 40 billion human years when the universe will be in Blueshift. WWIII is really an intergalactic war fought in space ships. Thats when the Lake of fire existed. The Lake of fire is the core of this collapsing universe for Jesus said " Heaven and earth will pass away..." Thats about the time WWIII will be fought with Gog and Magog. So relax. Those left behind series of books are pure idiocy and are the false prophecy of today. Chpt 1-12 Revelation is about our times. Chpt 13- 20 Revelation is in 40 billion years. There is a 40 billion year pause or interval between Chpt 12 and Chpt 13 Revelation just like there was a long-pause (Probably millions of years) between Gen 1:1 and Gen 1:2.

Read my books.

Book I. Christians existed before the big bang and will exist after the collapse of this universe.

Boo II. What the Bible says about the collapse of the universe.

Book III. Jesus Christ is Lord and is worshipped in infinte multiple universes- throughout infinity.

Book IV. The Holy Bible. " The Refreshing".

Book V. The Second Coming of Jesus Christ. The Return of the King.

Book VI. Intergalactic Jesus Christ Superstar.

Book VII. Africa: The Intergalactic Federation of African Tribes.

By Stanley O Lotegeluaki. Amazon.com. Barnes & Noble.com, Authorhouse.com
WWIII is in 40 billion AD.

Christianity is superior to Islam, Buddhism , Hinduism, Communism and the religion of Science for the Bible spoke of the collapse of the universe and that the universe is closed thousands of years ago in king David's time, Isaiah's time, Matthew, Mark, Luke, II Peter, I Corinthians and Revelation all say the universe is going to collapse, but science is just finding out today by sending inquiring satellites into space. Most astronomers believe the universe is closed and will collapse into itself (World Book Encyclopedia 1988). Science and the Bible agree for once proving the Bible is Truth. But then the Bible spoke of the collapse of the universe first thousands of years ago before science.

Before we start on the next book I must tell you how I found out that WWIII is 40 billion years from now. It took a little physics and our knowledge that the universe is now expanding and that one day it will contract. Its contraction phase is called blue shift. Well we know the passages in the

Bible that say the universe will contract and collapse. But did you know there is a verse that says this universe's burning core once it collapses will be used to burn the wicked ? Well II Peter 3:7 says so.

II Peter 3:7

> 7. But the heavens and the earth, which are now, by the same word are kept in store, reserved unto fire against the day of judgment and perdition of ungodly men.

Ungodly men will be burned in the Lake of fire. Now when will the Lake of fire exist ? A physicist will tell you it will come to exist in blue shift or once blue shift starts. That's in about 30-50 billion years from now. So the Lake of fire will definitely exist in 40 billion AD.

Now for the deduction. The false prophet was a man and he only could have only lived for 60 to 100 years, and he was thrown into the Lake of fire. So the Lake of fire existed in his days and the false prophet existed in the days when the universe was collapsing and had a fiery core- the Lake of fire. The only time that could happen is between 30-50 billion AD. So WWIII must have been 40 billion AD+/-. The false prophet and the lake of fire co-existed. They existed in the same time frame. That will happen in about 40 billion years from now- in Blueshift. That means all the chapters where the falseprophet is mentioned in the book of Revelation is 40 billion years from now. Chapters 13-20 Revelations. That whole war is not in our times, but Jesus will be back in my lifetime and our generation. WWIII is after the 1000 year reign of Christ. 1000 Christ years = 40 billion human years.

Read my books.
Book I. Christians existed before the big bang and will exist after the collapse of this universe.
Boo II. What the Bible says about the collapse of the universe.
Book III. Jesus Christ is Lord and is worshipped in infinte multiple universes- throughout infinity.
Book IV. The Holy Bible. " The Refreshing".
Book V. The Second Coming of Jesus Christ. The Return of the King.
Book VI. Intergalactic Jesus Christ Superstar.
Book VII. Africa: The Intergalactic Federation of African Tribes.

By Stanley O Lotegeluaki. Amazon.com, Barnes & Noble.com, Authorhouse.com

My name is Stanley O Lotegeluaki and Jesus sent me to feed His Church that is trapped by Science, Politics and Satan. These are the last days and this prophecy is coming true.
The "woman" is the Church.
Revelation 12:14" And to the woman were given two wings of a great eagle, that she might fly into the wilderness, into her place, where she is nourished for a time, and times, and half a time, from the face of the serpent"
Isaiah 25:6-8" And in this mountain shall the Lord of hosts make unto all people a feast of fat things, a feast of wines on the lees, of fat things full of marrow, of wines on the lees well refined.
7: And He will destroy in this mountain the face of the covering cast over all people, and the vail that is spread over all nations.8:He will swallow up death in victory; and the Lord God will wipe away tears from off all faces; and the rebuke of His people shall He take away from off all the earth: for the Lord hath spoken it."
I am the Messenger of Isaiah 14.

THE PSYCHOLOGY OF DEMONS (NAMELY FROGS)-that's if psychology is a science-poetic justice.

Of all the people the three frogs of Revelation possessed ,only two people on earth realized who these alien creatures were in their body. Paul was buffeted by one frog and I was possessed and buffeted by three frogs. I have lived with them unknowingly all my life and was shown by God what they looked like in 1984 when they came out of Cindy's abdomen and went into my chest, but I came to fully realize them in me my first year at BSH.

Now it would be a shame to the world and scientists if I did not do a study on these creatures that are still in my chest today 26/5/04. For sciences sake I better do at least an observation of these creatures we call fallen angels. It seems to me that the only thing these demons can say to me must be first allowed by God. God filters what they say to the human race. Not even one word can come from that world to this world without God's permission. This is why I find them rather stupid and they speak like fools most of the time. If Satan was allowed to speak his mind the world would be in trouble, so Satan and these frogs speak in songs, novels and movies. Now when I first was possessed , when they came to me from Cindy's chest they looked like little men about thumbsize, but with frog skins. One of them , the one who was supposed to babysit me while the others stayed in the background I call pipsqueak had a body that was tattered. Paul must have injured this frog. His head and shoulders were intact but the rest of his body was in pieces. Because Satan did not want me to make fun of them and hurt their feelings- he invented the term –pieces of shit-. Also to prepare for this day for they were told by God what would happen to them- the swear word by people in the late 70's and early 80's was "eat shit and die". This was common among a lot of people who were demon possessed and I heard it a lot. But these demons have been eating feces from the day I discovered them in BSH to today 2004. So actually they do eat feces and die for Jesus will soon come back to take over.

When they first entered me, they acted like witch's or to convey themselves as we would imagine them in the movies. But the movies are a recent phenomena and we have to realize that these creatures have lived for thousands of years. Their fingers and feet have webs- Satan was trying to convey them in his movie HellBoy. Now these creatures are very intelligent when it comes time to deceive you. At first they lectured me in my sleep, and I would wake up hearing the tail end of their speech. But the voice I heard was of the antiChrist in my early lectures. The frogs even gave me dreams of going to lectures in heaven. Anyway

The main thing I have come to believe about these creatures is that they are stupid, by not making sense when I ask them questions. The very first thing I asked these demons was to give me information on the Roman empire. I realized I could learn a lot of history from these creatures. But I couldn't get a straight answer from them. Also I expected to make scientific breakthroughs using them as a think tank. But they are very stupid. Satan with his vast mind and 1/3 of the angels have not even made one scientific breakthrough in the thousands of years they have been here.(Insert March 26 2005. As I read over did you know that 1/3 of all the angels including the brilliant Satan and the Beast were behind the U.S.S.R's military might, but the Scientists and technicians in the U.S.A beat them all in technology ? The U.S.A beat the U.S.S.R in the cold wars scientific race even though Satan and 1/3 – three billion angels were behind the U.S.S.R.- Satan had to resort to stealing technology) As a matter of fact I find them as a retardant to the advance of science. The human race could have been to the moon and back in the days of Egypt had they not had to spend their mental resources on worshiping these creatures. What was the use of all the efforts of the pyramids and temples? But anyway I have discovered that these creatures are geniuses when it comes to fantasy and the making of fantasy. Boy can they make up stories. Today in novels they excel , demons possessed writers like Stephen King and Koontz write like they are possessed, and they actually are. Isaac Asimov was also demon possessed to make up stories for Satan. The most damaging demon written book I can think of is the Dune series. (BeneGessarait) No one can make up fantasies and write books like Satan and his demons. Also in movies he is excellent. Like the Star War series was the work of Satan the Cherub.

Science fiction is the great lie that God does not exist and the recent drive to exalt secret services. That it is good to lie, kill, cheat, commit fornication and do abominable works in the name of the secret service work. That is the great achievement of Satan recently. If you really want to know or hear Satan speaking listen to the words in Pink Floyd – Shine on you crazy diamond. That is Satan speaking about himself as a cherub, speaking about his own history . Diamond is one of his clothes, also when he says he rode on the steel breeze he is talking about riding on the "political wind" for wind means "politics" in the Bible. When he says that he cried for the moon, that means that he tried to be God or tried to get what Jesus Christ has when he rebelled against God. Also in the 80's deep purple had an album where Satan spoke- about being a warrior who flew over a thousand oceans. "thousand oceans" means the "political sea" and that he has flown over a thousand political seas throughout history.

Its not hard to find Satan at music stores. If the album pictures look like demons that's what it is. But that's only the tip of the iceberg, for example Pink Floyd does not sound Satanic or ever indulged. They were just demon possessed. Led Zep is really snake music for no human could have imagined certain songs. But this is supposed to be a scientific examination of frogs. I told you what they look like but it's the internal mechanism that's important. My first conclusion of these frogs is that they have been psychologically twisted by Satan. They were designed by Satan to give "o" sex and eat feces at Armageddon. Satan started them on eating feces when the Moslems were in North Africa, when people used to eat the feces and drink the urine of the clergy. These demons were responsible. But the main thing is that Satan twisted them. Now Satan knew that frogs are female secret parts without the body just as a snake is a mans secret thing without the body. But I noticed that these frogs had a penis. So they are half women and half men. And they are twisted that way. They have been struggling for an identity ever since the days of Moses.(twisted sister) If the number of men who cross dress or have transsexual operations is an indication of how many frog demons are out there , then that's how many frogs are out there. But the caterpillar demons are in the public eye as fairies with wings. As you know a caterpillar becomes a butterfly- so the caterpillar demons see themselves as butterflies with human bodies.

That's what fairies are all about. Also the lepurcauns in Europe. Since at Armageddon I was calling my demons farts because farts come out screaming and are foul, Satan has made people say " God bless you" when you sneeze trying to convince me that demons come out of you that way instead of farts. So that's what all that was about. But as a scientist I should carefully examine these creatures. First I told you what they look like, and I told you they are twisted psychologically like "twisted sister"- (that's what all that was about). What other examination could I make without dissecting these frogs or demons? Well I have prayed that Jesus breaks all there bones, and I prayed to the God of Israel to make there brains into feces and I call them "shit for brains".   I have prayed to God to do all kinds of things to them so they don't look anatomically correct or the same when I first saw them.

At first pipsqueak as a demon was my friend for I asked Jesus to forgive him. That's what "ghostbusters" was all about. But he conspired to destroy me as psalm 35 says so I made him my enemy and now I know why God wont forgive them. For a time I couldn't get pipsqueak to admit or understand that he was going to burn in the fire, and he acted like he never heard of it, but one day he said " I don't want to be cooked". So I understood that he and other demons understood what was to happen to them.

First Pipsqueak would always say that he was "equal to Jesus", but after I explained to him that

Jesus was God he dissented. It took a long time, about 12 years. So they are very stupid or just plain stubborn. But to the scientists I have observed that every evil thing that the Bible says, these demons have pursued to increase. I asked them why and they said- namely pipsqueak that " he conquers the evil ", by doing it to excess, until it feels good. Also these demons speak a language called "falsehood". Sometimes yes means no or vice versa. So when the demon says "yes" he means "no". But sometimes it means "yes". So what I do is I judge every word they say and decide on it myself. I usually punish them if they lie. Woe to you if you make a biblical mistake in doctrine for these demons will compound your error- like the Protestant error about the rapture, some theologians saying that Christians will be taken to heaven before the Second Coming and others will stay on earth to experience Chpt13-19 Revelation. Satan confused Christians. It is not the good who are taken it is the bad who will be escorted to hell and Jesus will come down from the sky like as He left in the book of Acts. Proverbs 10:30 says so. The Bible is a puzzle that fits together. Look at the left behind series books designed to spook Christians. The guy who wrote them does not realize that there is a 40 billion year pause between chpt 12 Revelation and Chpt 13 Revelation. Now it has people confused, and Satan is compounding the error in doctrine. But there is a school of theologians who are pre Tribulationists and they have been outshouted by the postTribulationists. Satan is also a child molester and he is foaming out his own shame with what he has done. The book of Jude says they foam out their own shame. This they do- if you can understand what that means you will understand much. To foam out your own shame is to put whats in you on other people. If you are a homosexual, you accuse others of being gay when they are not.

Jude1:13 " Raging waves of the sea, foaming out their own shame, wandering stars, to whom is reserved the blackness of darkness forever"

"stars" means "angels" and "sea" means the "political sea".

How much shame do they foam out? Its is very great . Jesus said to possess ye your own soul. That means guard yourself from seeing, hearing, reading, wicked things. I heard things my poor soul was almost destroyed- so I wont repeat them so other peoples souls wont be destroyed.

Do you know the personality of Hellboy- that's what Satan's demeanor is like. Actually that confidence and trying to make things funny all the time is Satan's personality. He always acts confident even in deep trouble. But he is a cold blooded murderer and would destroy the human race. Actually in that movie Satan looked beaten and wasn't even really trying. But it was an attempt to tell his demons the reason the world was not destroyed was because he refused to destroy the human race, not that the carcase destroyed his plans. He always acts like he plays with me, but I know that this snake who I have put in a toilet in Lagos Nigeria is trying to kill me.

I could go on, but knowing they speak " falsehood" you get the idea. One more thing, do you remember the day the city of San Francisco started to use tax money to help city officials to become trans-sexuals. Well the night before I had prayed that Satan become a women and have womens parts – so that's what all that was about. Also Satan made that movie " Queen of the damned" and killed that girl for no reason.

He is a real piece of shit. My conclusion about these frogs and the nation of Satan's legend to leave behind is –THEY WERE COWARDLY IN BATTLE, BUT BRAVE TO COMMIT LEWDNESS IN THE TOILET.

This was due to the fact that they gave up the U.S.S.R , and in that Augusta gun store, but Satan was brave enough and his frogs to give each other strange sex. But these frogs , toys God gave me to play with at Armageddon , or I call them , the shit eating , TOILET DWELLING gods of Egypt. Toilet dwellers. People are fascinated with frogs in the West. They put them in gardens as Toadstools, frog statues, Kermit the frog on TV, Frog dolls, there everywhere. They are just the fertility gods of

Egypt. One last thing to finish the surgery I am doing on the patient the frogs, there is some real feces from demons. Do you know why people say " Bull Shit" all the time in the U.S.A. ? It is because demons knew that they would eat human feces at Armageddon from the Carcase who put all 3 billion demons in the toilets of the world in the name of Jesus. So to fool the humans- or to get in a word edge wise, people said " Bull Shit" to believe its not human feces they are eating.. Your demon possessed when you say those things, Or now you can guess why people used to say " eat shit and die !" That's because at Armageddon demons ate feces and died- were thrown into the bottomless pit. Jesus will be here soon. So that is what I think of the psychology of frogs and Satan at Armageddon. A scientific conclusion is that they are stupid, fools, intelligent to make up evil, lovers of their own selves, legends in their own minds, covetous, boasters, proud, blasphemers, disobedient, unthankful, unholy, without natural affection, trucebreakers, false accusers, incontinent, fierce, despisers of those that are good, traitors, heady, highminded, lovers of pleasures more than lovers of God, and having false godliness, lesbians and homosexuals. That is the true psychological makeup of demons.

Note: Ever since I put Satan in the toilet I can tell whenever he visits me. He smells like feces. So if one day you are talking (world leaders) and you smell a foul odor, and you feel very confident like on cocaine, or feel very angry all of a sudden (especially when you think of the Jews or Christians) or you feel all of a sudden depressed- strong emotions with the smell of feces- that's Satan visiting you. This is the same Satan who visited the leaders of the city of Atlanta in Georgia and told them to hurt the poor people on the street just because I mentioned in my books that Mother Church takes care of the poor there and washes their feet as Jesus said to do.

THE POLITICAL SITUATION THAT MOTHER CHURCH AND JESUS CHRIST HAD AT THE SECOND COMING.

Satan has been preparing for the Second Coming for many years, hundreds of years ago he and his demons had read the Bible and were also told by God what was going to happen to them in the end. So Satan had no illusions about the Second Coming. That they would live in the toilets of the earth and die eating feces. Satan had to find a lie, not only for the Church, but he had also to decieve his demons- even though they all knew the truth from God. Thats why when they met Jesus a long time ago, they asked Him if He had come to torment them before the time- the Second Coming.

So they knew that they would live until the time. The Church was easy to decieve and once the Church was decieved with those left behind series books and Rapture and Tribulations- the Church could decieve Satans demons for him. They believed their own lie. Also Jesus gave Satan all the necessary tools to decieve his nation by scrambling Revelations and making it look like their was going to be a war at the end where they the demons and the antChrist would get rid of the Church for a moment, ruling the earth and showing to the good Angels that Satan was a significant factor and could beat God. They knew the truth, that there was no such war, but that they would stay in the toilets of the earth and eat feces, yet they lied to themselves that the Carcase would take over the world for them and fight Christ . As a matter of fact (plan A) they wanted the Carcase to win the whole world in a war against the U.S.S.R and then they would kill him and have the antiChrist live in him and fight Jesus when He came down at the Second Coming. (Plan B) was kill the Carcase so he couldnt welcome Christ and (plan C) was to destroy the U.S.S.R. so the Christians would not have a rallying point- making God into a liar because He said their was going to be a war- thus breaking scripture an impossibility. (plan D) was put Ronald Wilson Reagan in power because he had six lettters in his three names, wound him like when they shot him,and his wound healed, make him bring fire down from heaven to the earth like when the shuttle craft beamed a laser down to earth in Reagans star wars program. Also Russia was to have the symbol of the bear and Gorbachev to have a patch on his forehead like the mark of the Beast on his forehead. The U.S. having the sign of an eagle and Russia the sign of a bear and both the C.I.A. and the K.G.B. were to kill Christians- (When the Carcase rallyed the Christians against both goverments by stealing the Trident Submarine)- but all that failed and theC.I.A. and K.G.B. ended up killing Moslems when God turned the secret services to kill off Satans religion. God turned the sword against Satans people- also God neutralized Iraq, Iran, Syria, Libya, Egypt, Afgantian, Tunisia, and Yemen by having the U.S.A. wage war against them- saving the trouble for Israel. Thats what really happened in the end instead of Satans dream of sicing the Secret Services against the Christians.

So is God a liar when He said in Chpt 24 Mathew there was going to be a war? No, because He inserted Mt. 24:28 and Is. 27:8 and Mt. 13:36-42 especially Mt 13:27-30. I asked Jesus if I could go out and kill all the tares in WWIII and He said no. All those verses say Jesus will come in peace. Mt 24:28 says the Carcase will determine how Jesus will come- in peace or war. Mt 24:27-30 says I would ask the Lord Jesus if I could kill all the tares on earth before He came back with WWIII (probably 500 million dead casualties) and Jesus said no. Is 27:8 says God "stayeth" His "Roughwind" - (political storm) against the "East wind" or communism. "wind" means "politics" and "stayeth" means stop.

So what happened at Armageddon part one ? Satan and his forces wore themselves out waiting for the war (ever see those Rock Albums saying Brave new World in the 1980's or DIO something about Holy Divers) - they were put in the toilets of the earth and they fought The God of Israel by eating feces and commiting homosexuals acts in the toilets full of feces. Thats what happened at the Second Coming.

Satan did do somethings- instead of the great war where the human race was in Jeopardy- there was Cambodia, Rwanda, Burundi, Ethiopia, Somalia, Sudan, Congo, Bosnia, Kosovo, the Arab uprising and Spring, the tea party where the U.S. was taken to the Right by racist-poor hating people and now to the left with "occupy wallstreet"

What is Satan going to do next- time is running out- today is Oct/10/2011. Satan has only a few options left- thats if he has any. God put him in a bind. The war did not work out, killing the Carcase did not work out, and not only that the Carcase published books of Life before the Big Bang, and life after the collapse of the Universe. Satan has been knocked out by Jesus and is just laying on the ground, you can hear the count in the background. What will he do?

He boasted in that song by "Queen" - "we will rock you"- that he would not be a loser before the whole human race.

Isaiah 31: 4. For thus hath the Lord spoken unto me, Like as the lion and the young lion roaring on his prey, when a multitude of shepherds is called forth against him, he will not be afraid of their voice, nor abase himself for the noise of them: so shall the Lord of hosts come down to fight for mount Zion, and for the hill thereof.

5. As birds flying, so will the Lord of hosts defend Jerusalem; defending also he will deliver it; and passing over he will preserve it.

SATAN

I met Satan numerous of times. I talked to him in a bookstore in Atlanta. I just looked into the bookcase and a purple fire came out of it and Satan started to rant and rave. He said that it wasn't fair that God had held him back from his true potential, he could have taken over the world. He said "his capabilities were awesome…." And so on. Then he said " go out side , God is waiting for you". So I went outside. Another time I remember I had a dream I was coiled up inside a gigantic snake, I was only a child and Satan told me "Stan, if you keep talking to God I wont play with you anymore." But now I have been possessed by frogs since 1984 and its now 2007. I talk to them like I talk to people, but God has made Satan , the Beast Angel, three frogs and the Bugs into my toys.

I talked about Satans history in my books, so read them to grasp this creatures history. Satan is Leviathan in Chpt 41 Job and God talks about His creation. Without Christ's hedge Satan can kill you or make a fool out of you or turn you into a homosexual- something like that. He is very deadly and is the wisest creature God has made in this universe.

But Satan has weaknesses. His strength is his weakness because God loves the weak and hates the strong. God loves the humble but hates the proud. So Satan is on the opposite side of God's love. He is under God's wrath and that's fatal. That's good for us humans because we are weak- so God loves us and all we have to do is humble ourselves and ask God's help and we defeat Satan every time. I have outlined the history of Satan and his failed life in my books. Read them if Satan lets you- ask God to help you. As you know I am the Porter to the sheepfold and Satan has attacked me. Let me tell you what Satan has been doing recently in the political sea. We go back to the time Bush Senior was campaigning for the office when he talked about Reagan's voodoo economics-those days. Satan had also put Andropov in office in the U.S.S.R. What Satan wanted to do was have a C.I.A. president run the West and a K.G.B. premier run the East. That way there would be a secret service war. Satan was trying to create the animal talked about in Revelation 13. Satan wanted to put Christians in the middle of this animal- with the feet of a bear and the mouth of a lion. Christians were to be secretly killed off worldwide. That was the plan with Andropov and Bush Senior. But the end had come and Satan wanted the prophecy of Revelation 13 come true. He doesn't realize its supposed to happen by itself. So he put Reagan in power because he had six letters in all three of his names. And because the Carcase was planning to destroy the U.S.S.R.- he put Gorbachev in power because he looked like he had a patch or the mark of the Beast on his head. That scenario came and went where the carcase decided to steal the Trident submarine and rally the Christians against the U.S.S.R. The C.I.A. and the K.G.B. would have murdered Christians like they are murdering Moslems today.

But Satan destroyed the U.S.S.R and the war was deleted. Satan tried to make God into a liar but Is 27:8 says God "stayeth" His Roughwind in the day of the "eastwind".

Now I have some shameful things to say about myself-it is the reason I did not want to reveal certain information about this war. My idol's used to be "Spock" and "Clint Eastwood". And Satan unashamedly made it a point by electing " Clinton" into office He wanted to show all of heaven and the Angels in heaven my sin. It's like the battle for St. Job. That's the only reason he was elected-the name "Clinton". I am ashamed to reveal it, but its so stupid. I don't want to reveal it. So Bush senior was elected because he was C.I.A Director , Andropov because he was K.G.B. Director, Reagan because he six letters in all three of his names, Gorbachev because he had a patch on his head. Clinton because of Clint Eastwood. Isn't Satan stupid? To go on you can guess why Bush II and Putin were elected. Satan couldn't put Bush Senior in power, so he put his Son in power to carry on the secret service war (we saw it worldwide)- thank God it's not against Christians. Satan put Putin in power to replace Andropov. Satan thinks he has safely crossed the bridge of the 1970's & 80's. Chernobyl was Revelation 16:10-11. What's next- Satan might groom a black man to take over the U.S.A. because I wrote in my book " No black man will ever be elected in the U.S.A. as president"- since blacks are going home to Africa. Or Satan might try to extend the "Seven heads" by putting Jeb Bush in power or another Clinton. All I got to say is watch out. Michael has already thrown Satan out of heaven and these books are the nourishment for the Church in the last 3.1/2 years.

The Ten problems of Satan

These are Satan's problems today.

(1) Christians and our good Angels existed before the big bang (Habukkuk 3:13) and he and his goats were created after the big bang. How can he tell the other Angels, "brethren, join my side against God". He can't, he and his angels are goats and demons- they are aliens- they were created after the big bang.

(2) The story of Genesis chpt 1-7 that I revealed.

(3) The flood- He and his demons were made invisible so they wont have sex with sheep or humans.

(4) Moses turned them into bugs- Actually God did in Exodus 12:12. This is a great Revelation in my books. Satan knows the humans now know what they look like.

(5) Jesus destroyed him at the cross. Read the Bible. Fatal.

(6) No war at the Second coming- U.S.S.R. lost. They expected the war and thought Revelation 13-20 was in our times.

(7) 40 billion years of being burned in the bottomless pit. That's a real problem- they only thought it was a 1000 human years punishment, but it's a 1000 Christ years- 40 billion years. Could you imagine being burned for 40 billion years?.

(8) After 40 billion years in the fire, a small stint probably 400-2000 year season of being let out to do a war-then Eternity in the Lake of fire- the collapsed core of this universe- fiery core where billions of galaxies are smashed together, fire brimstone, stars etc . Very hot.

(9) God promised to keep them there forever.

(10) Christ's infinite Glory of being worshipped by multiple universes. Jealousy for Satan for he wanted the worship of men and Angels and nailed lowly Jesus to the cross. Now Jesus whom he hates is worshipped by men and Angels and infinite universes in infinite dimensions- Infinite glory forever and ever.

It was the Church that condemned Satan to the Lake of fire forever. We shall judge angels. (New Testament). Also note- Satan never went to hell as he said he would go there to rule, but when he visited hell at the Second Coming , he was beaten senseless by the inhabitants of hell and kicked out of hell. Then he was thrown into the bottomless pit. Isaiah chpt 14 tells the story.

142

CHAPTER SIX
APPENDIX B

Appendix B,

The life and times of a Latino Queen.

If you took every atom in the universe and wrote a zero on its back, then took all the zero's and lined them up in front of the number 1- that number would not even represent a googolplex. You cant write out the number googolplex as a number because there is not enough room in the universe to write it out.

If that is the case of just writing out the number- what is a googolplex? I cant imagine it, but there are other numbers larger then a googolplex like "Grahams number". But to come to the conclusion that the human race has a googolplex universes as its home forever is an amazing conclusion. I had made the mistake in my other books of saying there was a googolplex atoms in our universe, but that is not true, there is about a googol atoms in the universe, a minor mistake, but now the human race has a googolplex universes to live in. To come to that conclusion a whole host of concepts have to be explained. How did I come to this end of the human story? It was a mistake, I thought that there was a googolplex atoms in our universe, but actually there is a googol or less atoms. I also said there was as many people as there are atoms in the universe due to Abrahams blessing- that really is a googol, but I had said each would recieve their own universe or mansion, so I said the human race had a googol universes. Unforutnately and really fortunately for us I made the mistake of saying there was a googolplex universes available for the human race. God can do anything so my mistake can stand, God will provide us with a googolplex universes for our Kraal if we ask Him. I expect those scienctists and mathematicians that represent the nations to approach Jesus to ask Him for a suitable amount of universes. I think a googolplex is quite much, but it is possible. We can ask for more later. But to be humble when I said a googolplex I meant googol. So I stand corrected in my work. But "WOW a googolplex universes for the human race?" or a googol? "Wow" Jesus is truly amazing!

It started a very long, long, long time ago. Actually it was in the infinite past for Jesus and the Father and the Holy Ghost have no beginning. They are the only ones in physics who have no beginnings. They have created an infinite number of beings before the human race was created. We were created a 100 billion years ago in the past phase of our collapsing and expanding universe. We now know that it wont expand again after this last coming collapse as Einstein guessed. This is because it will be used to burn the wicked, Satan and his followers. The wicked were created after the Big Bang which was about 14 Billion +/- years ago. Now how did I come up with such material? You have to have read my books and I know your up to speed. This Appendix "B" should be your last reading or lecture.

Now there was once a sheep called Janice. Janice was created by Jesus Christ a 100 billion years ago +/-. Janice woke up with the others. The first person Janice saw when she woke up was Jesus Christ. Just like there is an imprinting among ducklings and chicks, Janice soul was imprinted with Jesus her Shepherd the moment she woke up, and she followed Him. Jesus was the first face that Janice saw and He called her " Janice". That was her secret name between the Lord and her- her "white stone".

Janice the little girl skipped and hopped after Jesus as she tried out her new feet and her new life. She was like a brand new white piece of paper with nothing written on it except " Jesus loves Janice, and Janice loves Jesus". So together they went over to where the others were crowded together and when they saw Jesus return with a brand new family member, the crowd cheered, wept and wailed for Jesus. Jesus radiated love all around Him. It was just a lovely force, that made everyone weep before Him. He loved His sheep and they loved Him.

Janice was a newcomer to this flock and every sheep it seemed wanted to know her and play with her. They showered her with love and attention. They wanted to know what her favorite color was and since Janice did not know they had to show her a rainbow that was over Christ's throne for her to pick. Then they taught her Christian songs to love and cherish the Lord with. So at the end of the day she could sing the little song " Jesus loves me, yes I know, for the Bible tells me so". She was having a hard time remembering the rest, but by the next day she knew the whole song by memory. She also read the Psalms and her favorite Psalms was 23 and 86,

So for many days, in the first universe Janice played with her friends, and on Sunday's, the Sabbath, she went to Church and worshipped the God of Israel. Janice was put in the Hispanic nations by Jesus but she went out and played with the Vietnamese sheep. They were her favorite other sheep. Also Janice would play with the Angels of Jesus Christ- Michael and his nation. The Jewish nation had the task of being the priests of the Lord. Janice because she was a woman could only play Evangelist and prophet for Jesus like Deborah the prophet. She also played as an actor in the Church theaters and plays. So for billions of years Janice was a very happy sheep and was glad Jesus created her and gave life to her unlike the rocks which had no life.

After billions of years of playing and having fun- Janice's point of view lacked something. She couldn't point it out but Jesus knew that all of His sheep were immature. So Jesus who had written the Bible trillions of years ago decided to introduce conflict into the lives of His sheep. Jesus then called a conference for all the sheep to attend.

Janice walked into the palace with the other sheep. The palace was made out of crystal gems and there was a hue of myraid colors radiating from the walls. Jesus spoke for a moment. The King of kings and Lord of lords spoke about the fact that the sheep only knew light and no darkness. Darkness was the opposite of light. As a matter of fact when the sheep were deployed on battlefield Earth they would all be blind. Blind to the spirit world but able to see the world of flesh. It was going to be a struggle between Love and hate, Spirit and flesh, Truth vs lies, Right vs wrong, Jesus vs Satan, Christians vs nonChristians, Sheep vs goats. It was going to be called - The Invisible War-.

Janice was very interested in the war. She had read the Bible and she knew that it was supposed to happen in the future, but her role in the battle was still undecided. Jesus was looking for volunteers for the Invisible War. At first Janice was just curious, then she decided to go to war to show Jesus how much she was willing to suffer for Him. Jesus had told the sheep that He was going to die a horrible, slow painful death for the sheep, because He loved them so much. The volunteering was 40+/- billion years ago, right after the conference was held.

Jesus sat on His throne as the sheep came before Him and pledged their loyalty and volunteered for the war. (Psalm 24:3 Who shall ascend into the hill of the Lord? or who shall stand in His holy place? 4 He that hath clean hands, and a pure heart; who hath not lifted up his soul unto vanity, nor sworn deceitfully).

The Angels wrote everyones name in a Book called "The Book of Life". That way no sheep would be lost and no goat would be saved. Janice came before the great white throne and told Jesus that she was willing to suffer for Him on a faraway planet and different universe. She did not know it, but she would be teleported far into the futre, be slaughtered like sheep in WWIII- 40 billion Ad+/- by

144

the Beast, then she would be teleported to around 2000Ad+/- where she would be beat and spit upon by the Texan K.K.K and raped by the Hells angels in Los Angelos. After that ordeal she would be born again and join the Salvation Army and become a soldier for Christ in Chicago. Janice did not know that she would meet the Lord again at His return while she ran a Kettle for Christmas. But she volunteered anyway like all Christians did 40 billion BC +/-. God was also going to make her a Latino Queen one day in the billions of Hispanic universes that Jesus had for her nation after the collapse of The Invisible War Universe.

After voluntteering for the war, her present universe went into Blue shift and became a singularity. Janice was teleported to heaven where she and her friends stayed with Jesus. This was a wonderful time, being in heaven. Some say it was al surreal with beautiful music with every thought and movement. Love was everywhere, its like being in a womb of love, the best of everything. Janice was very happy in heaven, but one day Jesus came to her and asked her again if she wanted to volunteer for the Invisible War . Janice was determined to go and not dissapoint her Shepherd.

So Janice left heaven and was born to a Latino family in 40 billion AD+/- in a Hispanic nation. The Hispanic or Latino nation was part of Shem. Shem's teritory, even though was beginning to become less and less as the universe imploded, was the top or Northern hemisphere of the universe, about 10-20 billion galaxies. I think the nation of Janice had about 4 million galaxies as its territory. Fortunately and unfortunately for Janice she was born in the Royal family. Her uncle was the king of Argentina the Great. Now it would seem that it was a good thing to be born in this Royal family, but these were times of trouble.

Janice was born on a planet called Aphix. It was earthlike in everything except it did not have animals that looked like primates. The butterflys were dazzling in colors and the bird species were into the millions. The vegetation was red and not green. For some reason God had made the chlorophyll on this planet red, so for human eyes it took some getting used to. The water was the same with myraid of fish forms filling the oceans.

Janice opened her eyes at birth and she started to cry. Her midwife and Doctor were robots and they handed the precious little Janice to her mother Elizabeth. Elizabeth or Liz felt no pain in her chilbearing, for Jesus had eliminated that problem billions of years ago around 2000AD+/-. He had given a medical cure for it and all the hospitals followed His recommendations. Today was 40 billion AD+/- and she felt no pain. She held her bundle of joy in her strong hands and she decided to call the baby girl Mykala.

Mykala grew up on Aphix and felt the joy of being in the Royal family. Unknowing to her, Satan, his demons and his goats were also released into the universe, the kingdom of Jesus Christ. So some of Mykala's birthmates were goats and lied as soon as they were born, crying to their mothers needlessly as babies, as they learned to lie. Mykala did not go to school but her memory was first ingrained by the Educator with rudimentery childish education. She knew how ro read and write at four years old and could handle all the buttons her ergonomic environment provided her at age seven. She also learned about the Bible and to love Jesus whom she came to love as she went to Church.

Satan was released from the Bottomless Pit in 40 billion AD+/- and he was happy. Actually he kept screaming and he couldn't distinguish between plain touching and pain for a few months after he was released. All he could remember was pain and the group of flies, caterpillars, locusts and lice demons surrounding him were also crying. Also Satan had a frog demon in his mouth who couldnt and wouldnt stop screaming as he thought he was still being burned in the Bottomless Pit. It took awhile for the troop to realize that they were not in the fire any longer, that the punishment had stopped. After a few months of this weeping and screaming session they stopped. The Beast angel who was with Satan looked around and since he had forgotten how to speak grunted loudly at the other demons. Satan the wisest tried to remember, then Jesus appeared in front of them and told them who they were. That Satan was the leader of the pack and that they had been burned for 40 billion 800 million years+/- for fighting God a long time ago. That they were being released out of the fire to see if they could fight God like they boasted they could if only they were given an army big enough. Jesus told them that He was going to give them the whole universe of nations and they were welcome to try again. Satan could not recognize Jesus, but he was afraid of Him, all Satan could remember about the past was pain. Then they read the Bible. Satan and his troop learned about Christianity that encompassed the universe, they learned how to talk and they learned how to sin again. Before long the fires of the Bottomless pit was a distant memory. Satan seeing that he was relegated to the toilets of the earth became angry and he organized his demons around himself. This all took a few years, but before long Satan had become a force against the Christian kingdom of Jesus Christ.

Mykala grew up only knowing that WWIII was about to happen. Jesus Christ who was on the Jerusalem planet and Ariel galaxy told the Christians that there was going to be a "falling away first", where the kingdom was going to be decayed by the influx of goats who were coming out of hell as babies. A goat called Melissa became Mykala's friend. Mykala did not know that Melissa was a goat until Melissa lost her virginity before she was married. This was happening throughout the kingdom of Jesus Christ. There was violence and lieing everywhere and it appeared that Jesus was losing control of His kingdom.

Mykala kept going to Church but times were changing. Revolution was in the air. The nations did not like the status quo that had been in place for 40 billion years. The nations including Argentina the Great did not like Jesus, the Jews or Israel. There was wickedness and whoredom in the air and an atmosphere of rebellion. No one knew where it came from, but it became rather nice to hate Jesus. Satan fanned the flames he started.

Mykala talked to Melissa about this new trend in politics. Melissa was an outgoing type of girl, a real goat. She could never rest- she was progressive, and she told her friend Mykala that Jesus was old fashioned, that she was going to leave Aphix and join a political group in the outskirts of the universe in Shem's space, people who were against Jesus. Also she wanted Mykala to go with her. It would be a lot of fun and she really did not need her parents permission, for they were old fashioned and weren't hip.

Now God had written about this day in Isaiah. The Beasts of the forest or those who were in hell and the Bottomless Pit were told to come out and devour the sheep. But the Church slept.

Isaiah.56:9. All ye beasts of the field, come to devour, yea, all ye beasts in the forest.

10. His watchmen are blind: they are all ignorant, they are all dumb dogs, they cannot bark; sleeping, lying down, loving to slumber.

11. Yea, they are greedy dogs which can never have enough, and they are shepherds that cannot understand: they all look to their own way, every one for his gain, from his quarter.

Come ye, say they, I will fetch wine, and we will fill ourselves with strong drink; and to morrow shall be as this day, and much more abundant.

Isaiah 57

1. The righteous perisheth, and no man layeth it to heart: and merciful men are taken away, none considering that the righteous is taken away from the evil to come.
2. He shall enter into peace: they shall rest in their beds, each one walking in his uprightness.
3. But draw near hither, ye sons of the sorceress, the seed of the adulterer and the whore.

4. Against whom do ye sport yourselves? against whom make ye a wide mouth, and draw out the tongue? are ye not children of transgression, a seed of falsehood.

5. Enflaming yourselves with idols under every green tree, slaying the children in the valleys under the clifts of rocks?

6. Among the smooth stones of the stream is thy portion; they, they are thy lot: even to them hast thou poured a drink offering, thou hast offered a meat offering. Should I receive comfort in these?

7. Upon a lofty and high mountain hast thou set thy bed: even thither wentest thou up to offer sacrifice.

8. Behind the doors also and the posts hast thou set up thy remembrance: for thou hast discovered thyself to another than me, and art gone up; thou hast enlarged thy bed, and made thee a covenant with them; thou lovedst their bed where thou sawest it.

9. And thou wentest to the king with ointment, and didst increase thy perfumes, and didst send thy messengers far off, and didst debase thyself even unto hell.

10. Thou art wearied in the greatness of thy way; yet saidst thou not, There is no hope: thou hast found the life of thine hand; therefore thou wast not grieved.

11. And of whom hast thou been afraid or feared, that thou hast lied, and hast not remembered me, nor laid it to thy heart? have not I held my peace even of old, and thou fearest me not?

12. I will declare thy righteousness, and thy works; for they shall not profit thee.

13. When thou criest, let thy companies deliver thee; but the wind shall carry them all away; vanity shall take them: but he that putteth his trust in me shall possess the land, and shall inherit my holy mountain;

14. And shall say, Cast ye up, cast ye up, prepare the way, take up the stumblingblock out of the way of my people.

15. For thus saith the high and lofty One that inhabiteth eternity, whose name is Holy; I dwell in the high and holy place, with him also that is of a contrite and humble spirit, to revive the spirit of the humble, and to revive the heart of the contrite ones.

16. For I will not contend for ever, neither will I be always wroth: for the spirit should fail before me, and the souls which I have made.

17. For the iniquity of his covetousness was I wroth, and smote him: I hid me, and was wroth, and he went on frowardly in the way of his heart.

18. I have seen his ways, and will heal him: I will lead him also, and restore comforts unto him and to his mourners.

19. I create the fruit of the lips; Peace, peace to him that is far off, and to him that is near, saith the Lord; and I will heal him.

20. But the wicked are like the troubled sea, when it cannot rest, whose waters cast up mire and dirt.

21. There is no peace, saith my God, to the wicked.

After talking to Melissa and her strange views, Mykala was confused. But the Holy Spirit inside her tugged at her spirit. The Holy Spirit reminded her to read the Bible. She heard about the Beast 666, but was this the time? She piloted her antigravity vehicle to her parents city that hung in the clouds of Aphix, about half a mile above the red forest floor. She never knew that she would one day have to die for Jesus, nor did Mykala remember her volunteering for the Invisible War in WWIII.

She parked her antigravity vehicle in the parking lot and she walked over to her parents house.

Everything in the Royal family was abuzz about the politics of the day. Argentina the Great had seceded from the Commonwealth of Israel. There was a new king whom God had chosen to replace Jesus, because of all the sinning in the universe. This new king was Asian. It was king Leopid the III. Leopid had just been assasinated a week ago, but he came back to life like Jesus did, so long time ago as the gospels preached.

Now no one knew that Leopid the III was actually dead, and that his spirit had gone someplace else. His empty shell or body was replaced by the Beast angel who happened to be Satan's homosexual husband.

Mykala sensed that something big was happening in the universe. All the planets were in Revolutionary turmoil as the goats tried to break the chains of Jesus Christ.

Psalms 2

1. Why do the heathen rage, and the people imagine a vain thing?
2. The kings of the earth set themselves, and the rulers take counsel together, against the Lord, and against his anointed, saying,
3. Let us break their bands asunder, and cast away their cords from us.
4. He that sitteth in the heavens shall laugh: the Lord shall have them in derision.
5. Then shall he speak unto them in his wrath, and vex them in his sore displeasure.
6. Yet have I set my king upon my holy hill of Zion.
7. I will declare the decree: the Lord hath said unto me, Thou art my son; this day have I begotten thee.
8. Ask of me, and I shall give thee the heathen for thine inheritance, and the uttermost parts of the earth for thy possession.
9. Thou shalt break them with a rod of iron; thou shalt dash them in pieces like a potter's vessel.
10. Be wise now therefore, O ye kings: be instructed, ye judges of the earth.
11. Serve the Lord with fear, and rejoice with trembling.
12. Kiss the son, lest he be angry, and ye perish from the way, when his wrath is kindled but a little. Blessed are all they that put their trust in him.

Mykala went to her room in her parents palace and she opened the Bible. And there it was- chpt 13 Revelations. She had to warn Melissa her friend before she went to serve that new political party. Now the Bible said a false prophet would come around to serve the AntiChrist and she looked to see whom in the news would fit the discription. To her surprise it wasnt hard to find- for the next day the notable Reverend Dorchester told the universe wide church to worship king Leopid and that he was the new Christ. This was too much to take. Mykala put everything together and realized that this was the end time battle- WWIII was next. She had to choose sides. She ran to tell her mother Liz what she discovered in the Bible. Elizabeth was sitting in the kitchen programming the robots to cook tonights meal. She heard her daughter enter the kitchen. " Whats going on, little girl" she cooed. she knew that Mykala was sixteen now, but she couldnt give up on her little sweet girl yet. She loved her too much. " Mammy," Mykala shouted " I found what the Bible is saying about the Beast and WWIII"!. Elizabeth knew what her daughter was talking about- first there was no proof that king Leopid was the Beast 666- he did not even have six letters in his names, besides things change- the old ways had to go. Elizabeth was with Argentina the Great. She was tired of Jesus. So she tried to get her daughter to get with the program. She said-" Jesus is old fashioned, times have changed little girl". Mykala was shocked, how could her mother say such things? Then the argument continued for three more days. The two would par and try to get one another to agree. But it was to no avail. The Holy Spirit had Mykala and a demon had her mother.

Then things started to change for Mykala. The Church she attended switched to worshipping the new king Leopid. That was the last straw, just like the Church's before the Second Coming started to accept homosexuals, the Church fell again and rationalized worshipping king Leopid. Did he not come back from the dead? The Christians of Aphix and the Leopidvites of Aphix separated. And just like the Jews in WWII had to wear the Star of David, Christians began to wear the cross to distinguish themselves from the Leopidvites. Mykala was joyful to wear her cross and she tried to get Melissa to wear one too. Melissa after giving Mykala a lecture, stopped being her friend, but the Lord showed Mykala new friends who were Christians. Thats when Mykala ran away from home.

Christians had holed up from all the pressure on a mountain on the planet. It was like Woodstock in the olden days before the Second coming. Mykala took a job among the Christians as a toddler instructor within the camp. But the Argentinian government sent robot soldiers to their camp and arrested most of everyone. Some escaped. But Mykala did not escape.The robots were almost human in intelligence, they were well programmed. Someone had once told Mykala- "that a robot was only just as good as the human who programmed it". The robots were the color red for camoflouge, looked human but could fly since they had built in antigravity. There was no place to teleport to or time, for they were all caught by surprise and it was a swift operation.

Mykala was put in a cage. All her electronic gear was taken from her and she felt naked. She prayed to the Lord for strength. For some reason she could hum the song -" Jesus loves me, this I know, for the Bible tells me so..." She could not figure out where she got the song, but it was in her subconcious from billions of years ago.

The cage had a toilet and a sink for running water. After a month of this, a small robot came to her cage. It put a forcefield around her and paralyzed her. Then it carried her to the Court room where the goverment was putting Christians on trial. She was put in front of a judge who was a robot who asked her whether she would reject Jesus and worship Leopid. And if she did reject Christ she would recieve a mark on her hand as a Leopidvite or she could have her mind ingrained with the Leopide Bible- a mark on her forehead. Argentina the Great was now serving king Leopid and not the God of Israel.

Satan who had stopped screaming a few years back, maybe a 100 years ago had brought this tragedy to Christians. He had destroyed the fabric of society and everyone was blaming Jesus for the mess. So he told the sheep that God had fired Jesus using the false prophet Dorchester. King Leopid was the new son of God. Not only that king Leopid was going to stop everyone from dying when the universe imploded, for the human race had its back against the wall and Jesus had not yet offered a solution. Chpt 13 Revelation came to come true.

Revelation 13

1. And I stood upon the sand of the sea, and saw a beast rise up out of the sea, having seven heads and ten horns, and upon his horns ten crowns, and upon his heads the name of blasphemy.
2. And the beast which I saw was like unto a leopard, and his feet were as the feet of a bear, and his mouth as the mouth of a lion: and the dragon gave him his power, and his seat, and great authority.
3. And I saw one of his heads as it were wounded to death; and his deadly wound was healed: and all the world wondered after the beast.

4. And they worshipped the dragon which gave power unto the beast: and they worshipped the beast, saying, Who is like unto the beast? who is able to make war with him?

5. And there was given unto him a mouth speaking great things and blasphemies; and power was given unto him to continue forty and two months.

6. And he opened his mouth in blasphemy against God, to blaspheme his name, and his tabernacle, and them that dwell in heaven.

7. And it was given unto him to make war with the saints, and to overcome them: and power was given him over all kindreds, and tongues, and nations.

8. And all that dwell upon the earth shall worship him, whose names are not written in the book of life of the Lamb slain from the foundation of the world.

9. If any man have an ear, let him hear.

10. He that leadeth into captivity shall go into captivity: he that killeth with the sword must be killed with the sword. Here is the patience and the faith of the saints.

11. And I beheld another beast coming up out of the earth; and he had two horns like a lamb, and he spake as a dragon.

12. And he exerciseth all the power of the first beast before him, and causeth the earth and them which dwell therein to worship the first beast, whose deadly wound was healed.

13. And he doeth great wonders, so that he maketh fire come down from heaven on the earth in the sight of men,

14. And deceiveth them that dwell on the earth by the means of those miracles which he had power to do in the sight of the beast; saying to them that dwell on the earth, that they should make an image to the beast, which had the wound by a sword, and did live.

15. And he had power to give life unto the image of the beast, that the image of the beast should both speak, and cause that as many as would not worship the image of the beast should be killed.

16. And he causeth all, both small and great, rich and poor, free and bond, to receive a mark in their right hand, or in their foreheads:

17. And that no man might buy or sell, save he that had the mark, or the name of the beast, or the number of his name.

18. Here is wisdom. Let him that hath understanding count the number of the beast: for it is the number of a man; and his number is Six hundred threescore and six.

Mykala knew that she was going to die. It had come to this. But the Holy Spirit gave her peace. It was like being in a den or arena full of lions. It was not new to Christians. She told the robot Judge she would remain a Christian. So she who was immobolized was carted away to the " To be Terminated Compound". It had come to this. She would die like this, but those Christians who had escaped would form a defense and would fight a universe wide civil war and win. Mykala was terminated on St. Peter's day.

Janice woke up in heaven. Jesus came to meet her. She was happy to be with the Lord again. Jesus congratulated her on her bravery. She would get a "Whitestone" and a "White garment". She was a dyed in the wool Christian. After talking to Jesus, who told her what happened after she died in the universe wide civil war, she relaxed. Jesus told her that Satan had been given all the nations to use in his battle against God except for Israel and the Church. He even was given Jerusalem and the Ariel galaxy. They put king Leopid in the Temple and Satan made the people worship the Beast angel inside Leopids body. They put the Beast angel- the abomination that maketh desolate- in the Temple and the false prophet Dochester made everyone worship him. He did miracles in front of the people and convinced them for they thought God was with him. But the Christians fought. They reprogrammed the robots, the computers and spaceships fought spaceships, whole planets were contested. The God of Israel fought and Jesus returned as Chpt 19 Revelations dictated with all of His Angels to destroy Satan and his angels who possessed the goats.

Revelation chpt 19,

THE BEAST IS CAPTURED.

Revelation 19:11-21

11. And I saw heaven opened, and behold a white horse; and he that sat upon him was called Faithful and True, and in righteousness he doth judge and make war.
12. His eyes were as a flame of fire, and on his head were many crowns; and he had a name written, that no man knew, but he himself.
13. And he was clothed with a vesture dipped in blood: and his name is called The Word of God.
14. And the armies which were in heaven followed him upon white horses, clothed in fine linen, white and clean.
15. And out of his mouth goeth a sharp sword, that with it he should smite the nations: and he shall rule them with a rod of iron: and he treadeth the winepress of the fierceness and wrath of Almighty God.
16. And he hath on his vesture and on his thigh a name written, KING OF KINGS, AND LORD OF LORDS.
17. And I saw an angel standing in the sun; and he cried with a loud voice, saying to all the fowls that fly in the midst of heaven, Come and gather yourselves together unto the supper of the great God;
18. That ye may eat the flesh of kings, and the flesh of captains, and the flesh of mighty men, and the flesh of horses, and of them that sit on them, and the flesh of all men, both free and bond, both small and great.
19. And I saw the beast, and the kings of the earth, and their armies, gathered together to make war against him that sat on the horse, and against his army.
20. And the beast was taken, and with him the false prophet that wrought miracles before him, with which he deceived them that had received the mark of the beast, and them that worshipped his image. These both were cast alive into a lake of fire burning with brimstone.
21. And the remnant were slain with the sword of him that sat upon the horse, which sword proceeded out of his mouth: and all the fowls were filled with their flesh.

THE BEAST AND SATAN TEMPT THE NATIONS

Revelation 20:8-9 says the Beast and Satan went out and created a marvelous nation in the fringes of the universe with the pomp of Germany as they did in WWII. The human race had expanded far into the universe. Ezekiel chpt 38 tells the story of what happened.

Ezekiel 38

1. And the word of the Lord came unto me, saying,
2. Son of man, set thy face against Gog, the land of Magog, the chief prince of Meshech and Tubal, and prophesy against him,
3. And say, Thus saith the Lord God; Behold, I am against thee, O Gog, the chief prince of Meshech and Tubal:
4. And I will turn thee back, and put hooks into thy jaws, and I will bring thee forth, and all thine army, horses and horsemen, all of them clothed with all sorts of armour, even a great company with bucklers and shields, all of them handling swords:
5. Persia, Ethiopia, and Libya with them; all of them with shield and helmet:
6. Gomer, and all his bands; the house of Togarmah of the north quarters, and all his bands: and many people with thee.
7. Be thou prepared, and prepare for thyself, thou, and all thy company that are assembled unto thee, and be thou a guard unto them.
8. After many days thou shalt be visited: in the latter years thou shalt come into the land that is brought back from the sword, and is gathered out of many people, against the mountains of Israel, which have been always waste: but it is brought forth out of the nations, and they shall dwell safely all of them.
9. Thou shalt ascend and come like a storm, thou shalt be like a cloud to cover the land, thou, and all thy bands, and many people with thee.
10. Thus saith the Lord God; It shall also come to pass, that at the same time shall things come into thy mind, and thou shalt think an evil thought:
11. And thou shalt say, I will go up to the land of unwalled villages; I will go to them that are at rest, that dwell safely, all of them dwelling without walls, and having neither bars nor gates,
12. To take a spoil, and to take a prey; to turn thine hand upon the desolate places that are now inhabited, and upon the people that are gathered out of the nations, which have gotten cattle and goods, that dwell in the midst of the land.
13. Sheba, and Dedan, and the merchants of Tarshish, with all the young lions thereof, shall say unto thee, Art thou come to take a spoil? hast thou gathered thy company to take a prey? to carry away silver and gold, to take away cattle and goods, to take a great spoil?
14. Therefore, son of man, prophesy and say unto Gog, Thus saith the Lord God; In that day when My people of Israel dwelleth safely, shalt thou not know it?
15. And thou shalt come from thy place out of the north parts, thou, and many people with thee, all of them riding upon horses, a great company, and a mighty army:

"North" parts means religous revolution
16. And thou shalt come up against My people of Israel, as a cloud to cover the land; it shall be in the latter days, and I will bring thee against my land, that the heathen may know me, when I shall be sanctified in thee, O Gog, before their eyes.

Satan sanctified the name of the Lord before he died

17. Thus saith the Lord God; Art thou he of whom I have spoken in old time by my servants

the prophets of Israel, which prophesied in those days many years that I would bring thee against them?

18. And it shall come to pass at the same time when Gog shall come against the land of Israel, saith the Lord God, that my fury shall come up in my face.

19. For in my jealousy and in the fire of my wrath have I spoken, surely in that day there shall be a great shaking in the land of Israel;

20. So that the fishes of the sea, and the fowls of the heaven, and the beasts of the field, and all creeping things that creep upon the earth, and all the men that are upon the face of the earth, shall shake at my presence, and the mountains shall be thrown down, and the steep places shall fall, and every wall shall fall to the ground.

21. And I will call for a sword against him throughout all my mountains, saith the Lord God: every man's sword shall be against his brother.

That meant a universe wide civil war.

22. And I will plead against him with pestilence and with blood; and I will rain upon him, and upon his bands, and upon the many people that are with him, an overflowing rain, and great hailstones, fire, and brimstone.

23. Thus will I magnify myself, and sanctify myself; and I will be known in the eyes of many nations, and they shall know that I am the Lord.

Think of the outer fringes of the universe being contaminated with Babylon. Meditation. Mine eyes shall be upon the faithful of the land, that they may dwell with Me: he that walketh in a perfect way, he shall serve Me.

MAP OF TIME   40 BILLION AD+/-

THE BEAST GATHERS THE NATIONS AGAINST CHRIST.

The nations commit fornication with the new nation. Jesus who is in the universe in Jerusalem planet is perturbed that people have turned to Satan's physical and spiritual nation again. After about 2000 years or a season, Christian children fret against Jesus and turn to Satan. Then there are wars in Christ's peaceful kingdom again after 40 billion years of peace.

Think of Satan causing wars again. Meditation. In thee, O Lord, do I put my trust; let me never be ashamed: deliver me in thy righteousness.

MAP OF TIME   40 BILLION AD+/-

KINGS ARE CHANGED.

Satan sets up his kings instead of Christ's appointed kings and the Bible says they have power for one hour with the Beast.

Revelation 17:9-12

9. And here is the mind which hath wisdom. The seven heads are seven mountains, on which the woman sitteth.

10. And there are seven kings: five are fallen, and one is, and the other is not yet come; and when he cometh, he must continue a short space.

11. And the beast that was, and is not, even he is the eighth, and is of the seven, and goeth into perdition.

12. And the ten horns which thou sawest are ten kings, which have received no kingdom as yet; but receive power as kings one hour with the beast.

Think of the kings serving the Beast. Meditation. Bow down thine ear to me; deliver me speedily: be thou my strong rock, for an house of defence to save me.

<u>MAP OF TIME</u>   40 BILLION AD+/-

DANIELS PROPHECY

This is where Daniel's prophecy Chpt 11:29 fits in. The appointed time is 40 billion years away. So between 11:28 and 11:29 is 40 billion years just like there is a long time between Genesis 1:1 and Genesis 1:2. One of the kings is killed by Satan and his body is resurrected by the Beast. Wounded by a sword unto death. Satan tried to set up Ronald Wilson Reagan that way when he got shot. It was all a set up to smear him. But anyway the body they put to death is possessed by the abomination of desolation and people worship him just like Jesus. Christians are killed and hunted down with the help of demons, just like the Jews were hunted down by the Nazi's with a little help.

Daniel 11:29-45

29. At the time appointed he shall return, and come toward the south; but it shall not be as the former, or as the latter.

30. For the ships of Chittim shall come against him: therefore he shall be grieved, and return, and have indignation against the holy covenant: so shall he do; he shall even return, and have intelligence with them that forsake the holy covenant.

31. And arms shall stand on his part, and they shall pollute the sanctuary of strength, and shall take away the daily sacrifice, and they shall place the abomination that maketh desolate.

32. And such as do wickedly against the covenant shall he corrupt by flatteries: but the people that do know their God shall be strong, and do exploits.

33. And they that understand among the people shall instruct many: yet they shall fall by the sword, and by flame, by captivity, and by spoil, many days.

34. Now when they shall fall, they shall be holpen with a little help: but many shall cleave to them with flatteries.

35. And some of them of understanding shall fall, to try them, and to purge, and to make them white, even to the time of the end: because it is yet for a time appointed.

36. And the king shall do according to his will; and he shall exalt himself, and magnify himself above every god, and shall speak marvellous things against the God of gods, and shall prosper till the indignation be accomplished: for that that is determined shall be done.

37. Neither shall he regard the God of his fathers, nor the desire of women, nor regard any god: for he shall magnify himself above all.

38. But in his estate shall he honour the God of forces: and a god whom his fathers knew not shall he honour with gold, and silver, and with precious stones, and pleasant things.

39. Thus shall he do in the most strong holds with a strange god, whom he shall acknowledge and increase with glory: and he shall cause them to rule over many, and shall divide the land for gain.

40. And at the time of the end shall the king of the south push at him: and the king of the north shall come against him like a whirlwind, with chariots, and with horsemen, and with many ships; and he shall enter into the countries, and shall overflow and pass over.

41. He shall enter also into the glorious land, and many countries shall be overthrown: but these shall escape out of his hand, even Edom, and Moab, and the chief of the children of Ammon.

42. He shall stretch forth his hand also upon the countries: and the land of Egypt shall not escape.

43. But he shall have power over the treasures of gold and of silver, and over all the precious things of Egypt: and the Libyans and the Ethiopians shall be at his steps.

44. But tidings out of the east and out of the north shall trouble him: therefore he shall go forth with great fury to destroy, and utterly to make away many.

45. And he shall plant the tabernacles of his palace between the seas in the glorious holy mountain; yet he shall come to his end, and none shall help him.

Think of the abomination of desolation in the sanctuary of strength the Church. Meditation. Pull me out of the net that they have laid privily for me: for thou art my strength. Into thine hand I commit my spirit: thou hast redeemed me, O Lord God of truth.

MAP OF TIME   40 BILLION A.D +/-

PLAGUES FROM GOD .

God plagued Satan's nation marvelously. Read Revelation. But also Ezekiel.

Ezekiel Chpt 39.

1. Therefore, thou son of man, prophesy against Gog, and say, Thus saith the Lord God; Behold, I am against thee, O Gog, the chief prince of Meshech and Tubal:

2. And I will turn thee back, and leave but the sixth part of thee, and will cause thee to come up from the north parts, and will bring thee upon the mountains of Israel:

The sixth part has many Theologians confused. The sixth part here is the same as 666 in Revelation chpt 13. It means that Satans full capibilities when he was a priest was seven. But God took his priesthood away from him so he became a lower sixth, but fully capable- all of his might was given to him to contest God.

3. And I will smite thy bow out of thy left hand, and will cause thine arrows to fall out of thy right hand.

4. Thou shalt fall upon the mountains of Israel, thou, and all thy bands, and the people that

is with thee: I will give thee unto the ravenous birds of every sort, and to the beasts of the field to be devoured.

5. Thou shalt fall upon the open field: for I have spoken it, saith the Lord God.

6. And I will send a fire on Magog, and among them that dwell carelessly in the isles: and they shall know that I am the Lord.

7. So will I make my holy name known in the midst of my people Israel; and I will not let them pollute my holy name any more: and the heathen shall know that I am the Lord, the Holy One in Israel.

8. Behold, it is come, and it is done, saith the Lord God; this is the day whereof I have spoken.

9. And they that dwell in the cities of Israel shall go forth, and shall set on fire and burn the weapons, both the shields and the bucklers, the bows and the arrows, and the handstaves, and the spears, and they shall burn them with fire seven years:

10. So that they shall take no wood out of the field, neither cut down any out of the forests; for they shall burn the weapons with fire: and they shall spoil those that spoiled them, and rob those that robbed them, saith the Lord God.

11. And it shall come to pass in that day, that I will give unto Gog a place there of graves in Israel, the valley of the passengers on the east of the sea: and it shall stop the noses of the passengers: and there shall they bury Gog and all his multitude: and they shall call it the valley of Hamongog.

12. And seven months shall the house of Israel be burying of them, that they may cleanse the land.

13. Yea, all the people of the land shall bury them; and it shall be to them a renown the day that I shall be glorified, saith the Lord God.

14. And they shall sever out men of continual employment, passing through the land to bury with the passengers those that remain upon the face of the earth, to cleanse it: after the end of seven months shall they search.

15. And the passengers that pass through the land, when any seeth a man's bone, then shall he set up a sign by it, till the buriers have buried it in the valley of Hamongog.

16. And also the name of the city shall be Hamonah. Thus shall they cleanse the land.

17. And, thou son of man, thus saith the Lord God; Speak unto every feathered fowl, and to every beast of the field, assemble yourselves, and come; gather yourselves on every side to my sacrifice that I do sacrifice for you, even a great sacrifice upon the mountains of Israel, that ye may eat flesh, and drink blood.

18. Ye shall eat the flesh of the mighty, and drink the blood of the princes of the earth, of rams, of lambs, and of goats, of bullocks, all of them fatlings of Bashan.

19. And ye shall eat fat till ye be full, and drink blood till ye be drunken, of my sacrifice which I have sacrificed for you.

20. Thus ye shall be filled at my table with horses and chariots, with mighty men, and with all men of war, saith the Lord God.

21. And I will set my glory among the heathen, and all the heathen shall see my judgment that I have executed, and my hand that I have laid upon them.

22. So the house of Israel shall know that I am the Lord their God from that day and forward.

23. And the heathen shall know that the house of Israel went into captivity for their iniquity: because they trespassed against me, therefore hid I my face from them, and gave them into the hand of their enemies: so fell they all by the sword.

24. According to their uncleanness and according to their transgressions have I done unto them, and hid my face from them.

25. Therefore thus saith the Lord God; Now will I bring again the captivity of Jacob, and have mercy upon the whole house of Israel, and will be jealous for my holy name;

26. After that they have borne their shame, and all their trespasses whereby they have trespassed against me, when they dwelt safely in their land, and none made them afraid.

27. When I have brought them again from the people, and gathered them out of their enemies' lands, and am sanctified in them in the sight of many nations;

28. Then shall they know that I am the Lord their God, which caused them to be led into captivity among the heathen: but I have gathered them unto their own land, and have left none of them any more there.

29. Neither will I hide my face any more from them: for I have poured out my spirit upon the house of Israel, saith the Lord God.

Think of all the Plagues of Revelation from God's altar. Meditation. He that sitteth in the heavens shall laugh: the Lord shall have them in derision. Then shall He speak unto them in His wrath, and vex them in His sore displeasure

After the war those who were alive, the Christians took and looted all of Satan's army throughout the universe and it was indescribable the amount of loot that they captured. It took a long time to cleanse the universe.

Satan went before the Lord, the Beast and the false prophet were already in the middle of the imploding universe, but Satan went before the Lord for the last time. He remembered the Bottomless pit and the pain and he knew that this was the last time. He sanctified the name of the God of Israel in his heart (Ezekiel 38:16   ). He begged the Lord not to throw him away forever as the Bible said He would. The fact that he had boasted that with enough men he could defeat God was forgotten. I dont know what Jesus said to him, but the Bible said- we the Church shall judge angels. And the Church did. Satan and his whole crew was thrown into the Lake of fire, the collapsed universe forever. The Church had receieved its vengeance and that was the end of Satan and his whole house. There was a long scream, then there was silence.

The people lived on until the universe collapsed and judgment day came and went. You will have to ask Jesus how He is going to evacuate the universe as it implodes. Those who were not in the Book of Life were thrown into hell and hell was thrown into the lake of fire.

Janice listened to the Lord, then she asked Him, what was next? Jesus told her that since she died in WWIII she could go to around the year 2000+/- AD and welcome Him at the Second Coming on the planet where the human race was begun in this universe. The Lord told her that she would be in trouble, but He would come and save her. So Janice skipped away happy- all in white- a garment she earned by dying for the Lord in WWIII.- 40 billion AD+/-.

Then after a while, probably a million years- Jesus called Janice again, and she said " here I am" The Lord told her it was time to send her again into the Invisible War., back in time to the year 2000+/- AD. She would welcome the Lord.

Janice woke up in Mexico city in 1963 AD. She started to cry. Her mother stopped screaming when she was born. She was born in the Shanty town suburbs of Mexico city. Soon there would be 30 million people in Mexico city. But Janice did not know that, she was only a child. Her mother called her Kizzy, but her father called her Paula. So Paula was her name. Paula grew up in the worst place possible. She never went to school until the Christians Children Fund people found her, fed her and took her to school. She learned spanish and grew up to be a sexy latino girl. Paula survived all the childhood diseases of her enviroment and one day her parents decided to go to the U.S.A. to escape the poverty of Mexico city.

Paula wasn't a Christian- not yet anyway- and she started to smoke cigarettes at an early age. Before long she was embroiled in prostitution and drugs. That was her life until she turned sixteen and her parents decided to go north to take them to Los Angelos. So in 1979 the family crossed over into the U.S.A. It could have been a tragic story but for some reason God was with the family. The coyote was a friendly man but all he really cared was about the money. Paula settled into L.A.nicely. She wanted to be an actor in HollyWood but her English language skills were terrible. Latino's were not welcomed in the U.S.A. and were treated like second class citizens, but much better then her black neighbours.

Paula became a Prostitute on the streets of L.A. and drifted into the drug world. There were Mexican gangs in L.A. and the whole city seemed segregated. Paula one day told her parents that she did not like L.A and that she was moving to San Antonia Texas. She traveled there by bus and ended up street walking on the same street that the Alamo Fort was on. She would captivate young Army medical soldiers who had come back from deployment in Vietnam. They lived through it, so they cared less if they spent their time with a prostitute.

One day Paula was street walking on the night shift when she accidently walked down a dark allyway. As she was walking on the sidewalk a Dodge van pulled up to her and three young men jumped out. Paula was calloused by the streets and she carried a blade in her purse, but these young boys looked mean. " Hey Mexican" said one- a young man wearing a red shirt. " Must be a Mexican" another one said wearing a cowboy hat. They ran up to her and tried to pull her into the van. Paula knew the men were going to rape her and kill her. They were white Aryan supremicists and they did not like Latinos in Texas. Her form of dress, tight miniskirt and lace told them she was a hooker. Where were the police when you needed them. Paula pulled out her knife, but before she could unfold it one of the bruisers hit her on the cheek. She screamed for help. The men were only having fun. The Texas way. They were cattleherding cowboys who loved the U.S.A. They beat Paula up and left her for dead. But the Lord was with her and she did not die. A passerby saw her after the van left and called the Police. The Police and an ambulance arrived.

She was taken to the hospital- St. John's Memorial Hospital. The police didn't care about her and the paramedics thought " Just some more meat to clean off the streets". No one cared for Paula, except for the Lord.

When she got well three days later, Paula snuck out of the hospital. She knew if the police knew about her true identity they would deport her to Mexico. So she took the little amount of money she had saved and took a bus back to L.A. Texas was a hateful Right wing State, maybe it will be better in California.

She arrived in L.A. and she found out from her fellow Street Walkers that her parents had been captured and deported back to Mexico. Someone had informed the police about them and the Immigration Dept was swift. Paula felt despair for once in her life. There had to be a better way. But it had to take one more gruesome incident to convince Paula that Christ was the only way out.

Paula survived the winter as a streetwalker. She did not have a pimp who could protect her, so life was very dangerous for her. The average lifespan for a hooker was about 35 +/-. One day she walked into a Biker Bar. A young biker- hells angels- possessed by demons of Satan who had not yet tasted the Bottomless Pit, asked Paula for a trick. They went upstairs to a room and he told her to wait while he went and got some more drinks. She undressed. When he came back, he came back with three of his friends.

It took three hours, but the four of them abused Paula terribly. They left her a bleeding mess and there was despair deep down in her soul. no one cared for her, she let out a scream , then she collapsed into a whimpering little girl.

She looked around the room for a cigarrette and she opened and slammed the drawers of furniture in the room. She opened one drawer and saw a Gideons Bible in Spanish. She opened it and she read psalm 138 and she cried to the Lord.

Psalms 138

1. I Will praise thee with my whole heart: before the gods will I sing praise unto thee.
2. I will worship toward thy holy temple, and praise thy name for thy lovingkindness and for thy truth: for thou hast magnified thy word above all thy name.
3. In the day when I cried thou answeredst me, and strengthenedst me with strength in my soul.
4. All the kings of the earth shall praise thee, O Lord, when they hear the words of thy mouth.
5. Yea, they shall sing in the ways of the Lord: for great is the glory of the Lord.
6. Though the Lord be high, yet hath he respect unto the lowly: but the proud he knoweth afar off.
7. Though I walk in the midst of trouble, thou wilt revive me: thou shalt stretch forth thine hand against the wrath of mine enemies, and thy right hand shall save me.
8. The Lord will perfect that which concerneth me: thy mercy, O Lord, endureth for ever: forsake not the works of thine own hands.

"Where are you Lord?" she whimpered. "If you are real, please show yourself." she cried. She couldn't take it anymore She opened the Bible and read Psalm 86.

Psalm 86.

Psalm 86 describes the nature of God.

Psalms 86

1. Bow down thine ear, O Lord, hear me: for I am poor and needy.
2. Preserve my soul; for I am holy: O thou my God, save thy servant that trusteth in thee.
3. Be merciful unto me, O Lord: for I cry unto thee daily.
4. Rejoice the soul of thy servant: for unto thee, O Lord, do I lift up my soul.
5. For thou, Lord, art good, and ready to forgive; and plenteous in mercy unto all them that call upon thee.
6. Give ear, O Lord, unto my prayer; and attend to the voice of my supplications.
7. In the day of my trouble I will call upon thee: for thou wilt answer me.
8. Among the gods there is none like unto thee, O Lord; neither are there any works like unto thy works.
9. All nations whom thou hast made shall come and worship before thee, O Lord; and shall glorify thy name.
10. For thou art great, and doest wondrous things: thou art God alone.
11. Teach me thy way, O Lord; I will walk in thy truth: unite my heart to fear thy name.

12. I will praise thee, O Lord my God, with all my heart: and I will glorify thy name for evermore.

13. For great is thy mercy toward me: and thou hast delivered my soul from the lowest hell.

14. O God, the proud are risen against me, and the assemblies of violent men have sought after my soul; and have not set thee before them.

15. But thou, O Lord, art a God full of compassion, and gracious, longsuffering, and plenteous in mercy and truth.

16. O turn unto me, and have mercy upon me; give thy strength unto thy servant, and save the son of thine handmaid.

17. Shew me a token for good; that they which hate me may see it, and be ashamed: because thou, Lord, hast holpen me, and comforted me.

She knew that the Lord existed, she felt an inner peace. So she walked out with the Bible clutched in her hand and she knew that she must find God. It was a Saturday and it was raining in this "city of demons" of "fallen angels"- Los Angelos. Paula found an abandoned building to sleep in. She knew that she had to go to Church the next day and thats what she did. Now what Church should she go to? That question really did not bother her as long as God was there. She walked into a magnificent Catholic Church and she worshipped the Lord in her own special way. She couldn't understand why everyone would stare at her then look quickly away. But she soon realized that she was dressed like a hooker with smudged paint on her face from all of her recent tears. She did not care, her soul was hungry for the Bread of Life- the Words of Christ. That days sermon was about the prodigal son. She called out to Jesus.

After the ceremony, still clutching her Gideons spanish Bible, she decided to leave her profession as a prostitute and become a christian. All she had was ten dollars and nowhere to live. Paula knew that the Salvation Army stores had cheap clothing- so she found one near the Catholic Church and bought a backpack, jeans and a blouse to wear like a young lady.

Once she bought the clothes she asked the Salvation Army worker where she might find a place to eat and a shelter for the night. The Salvation Army had places to eat- soup kitchens. The soldier also gave her a list of all the Churchs that fed the poor in the city. The Christians were following Christs commandment to feed the poor- Mother Church- from the Catholics, to the Baptists, to the Lutherans and Salvation Army was feeding the poor in the city of Angels. The Christians were the Angels of Jesus and the hells angels were the demon possessed angels of . Satan.So a struggle- an Invisible War- was going on.

So Paula roamed the streets that summer going from one Church to another. One day she walked again into the Salvation Army thrift store and asked for a job. She got some work folding clothes and after a while, about three years later, she joined the Salvation Army Church in L.A.

She did not like the city, so Paula decided after praying for a week to go to Chicago. The Lord answered her prayers when she had a dream that she was standing in front of a Lake in the windy city holding and cuddling three of her own children.

Thats all the prompting she needed and after receiving a transfer welcome to Chicago's Salvation Army thrift store she left L.A. with bittersweet feelings, for she missed her family.

Chicago was a more forgiving city then L.A., but the winters were cold. The Salvation Army provided for her needs and she became a soldier with a uniform. She met a young man from Texas and they got married. He was a kind man who had the love of Jesus in his heart. Not all Texans are bad. His name was Brad and he loved his Latino wife. They were a cute couple and even after she told him her life story he still loved her. She was beautiful. That was in 1985 and the question of Amnesty for Hispanic and Latino population was about to hit the nation.

Satan in 1985 was also having his problems. He was in a life and death struggle with Jesus Christ and a sheep called the Carcase or the Earth who had just swallowed up his whole war. First in WWI Satan had tried to jump the gun for he knew his time was short and that God was going to give him Germany to make his last stand, so he caused WWI in anticipation. When that failed 25 years later he tried again, hoping he could destroy all the Jews with WWII. That way they could not become a nation. When that failed he tried to nuke the earth by escalating the cold war. When that failed- the Carcase who was to prepare the way for Jesus came on station. He contested for the Carcase against Jesus but that failed. Read Melek Lotegeluaki's books on how that happened. The carcase had gotten out of the U.S Army and he wanted to get married instead of going to Cambodia. An Invisible war was fought with Jesus and the U.S.S.R fell. The Carcase prepared the way for Jesus Christ by taking information that he got from Jesus through the Holy Spirit and wrote seven Books, and Appendix A and this Appendix B.

Satan fought hard, he sent three frogs to kill or divert the Carcase, also due to the fact that the Carcase planned on stealing the Trident Submarine and rally all the Christians behind him to attack the U.S.S.R., he tried to outsmart him by destroying the U.S.S.R.. The Christians couldnt rally and God's prophecy of WWIII would be a lie in the Bible. That failed, but with Vietnam, Cambodia, Kosovo, Bosnia, Rwanda, Burundi, Congo, Sudan, Somalia, South Africa, Arab spring (Isaiah 19:22-25) Iraq and Afganistan, and the recent economic upheavel- SATAN TRIED HIS BEST TO RUN AWAY FROM JESUS! before the Second Coming- THE RETURN OF THE KING.

Also Satan read some of the material the Carcase wrote, his seven books and two Appendix's and there was a long, wailing, piercing scream come out of Pandamonia as Satan and his demons realized that they had been created after the Big Bang and that everyone else including the good Angels were created before in 100 billion B.C +/-. They have been fated from the very beginning. So that means God is truly Holy and there was no unrighteousness in Him, for Satan always thought his rebellion proved God made mistakes. Now he knew it was all planned. So he has to get rid of those books and kill this Carcase who also wrote that they Satan and his house of demons would spend 40 billion years plus in the Bottomless Pit instead of the 1000 years they thought Revelation mentioned. What is even worse there was going to be no war and he had destroyed the U.S.S.R. How terrible can things be? To be roasted alive for 40 billion 800 million Years?.

The Lord arrived " In that day". It was a surprise to everyone. To the Church it was a welcome surprise. The sky's were clear "in that day". and 2.3 billion people lost their lives.

Janice cuddled her children around her. The ambulance sirens did not stop. But the Angels were here. " Paula" was what her husband called her and their whole family had been spared unlike many other families on earth that did not claim Jesus as King and Saviour. They had been burying and burning the bodies of the billions who died all over the earth. God had done His "strange act" and had come down to punish the earth for their iniquity. They were not expecting this "Thunderclap" this sudden death of billions as psalm 110 said it would happen.

psalm 110--------------

Psalm 110 is a Second Coming Psalm.

Psalms 110

1. The Lord said unto my Lord, Sit thou at my right hand, until I make thine enemies thy footstool.

2. The Lord shall send the rod of thy strength out of Zion: rule thou in the midst of thine enemies.
3. Thy people shall be willing in the day of thy power, in the beauties of holiness from the womb of the morning: thou hast the dew of thy youth.
4. The Lord hath sworn, and will not repent, Thou art a priest for ever after the order of Melchizedek.
5. The Lord at thy right hand shall strike through kings in the day of his wrath.
6. He shall judge among the heathen, he shall fill the places with the dead bodies; he shall wound the heads over many countries.
7. He shall drink of the brook in the way: therefore shall he lift up the head.

Lets look at Psalm 110 more closely- for it summarizes the Second coming and the tribulation war nicely.

The Lord's are Abba and Jesus and they sit side by side in the throne room of heaven.

Psalm 110:1

1. The Lord said unto my Lord, Sit thou at my right hand, until I make thine enemies thy footstool.

The Lord shall send His Holy Spirit- "the rod out of Zion" and rule His Christians on the earth in the midst of their enemies- demons, goats and Satan. (Also note- the Holy Spirit is the rod of Iron in Revelation Chpt 12).

Psalm 110:2.

2. The Lord shall send the rod of thy strength out of Zion: rule thou in the midst of thine enemies.

Jesus came in the "morning" of history and He has the "dew of His Youth" - or He will be frozen at the age of 33 forever. He still has that childishness in Him at 33. Christians volunteered to work in His kingdom for free at the Second Coming.

Psalm 110:3.

3. Thy people shall be willing in the day of thy power, in the beauties of holiness from the womb of the morning: thou hast the dew of thy youth.

Melchizedek was Jesus Christ for Jesus is so great He does not take after the titles of men. Where have Theologians been? Hebrews chpt 7 says Jesus is Melchizedek.

Psalm 110:4.

4. The Lord hath sworn, and will not repent, Thou art a priest for ever after the order of Melchizedek.

At the Second Coming there will be a Planetary Coupe de tat where God is going to kill all the leaders of the earth.

Psalm 110:5.

5. The Lord at thy right hand shall strike through kings in the day of his wrath.
The "taken" in Mt. 24 etc are the dead people of Psalm 110:6.
6. He shall judge among the heathen, he shall fill the places with the dead bodies; he shall wound the heads over many countries.

Then God will eliminate the political barriers that Satan set up against Jesus (the brook) and He will crown Jesus as King.

Psalm 110:7.

7. He shall drink of the brook in the way: therefore shall he lift up the head.

Isaiah 26

1. In that day shall this song be sung in the land of Judah; We have a strong city; salvation will God appoint for walls and bulwarks.
2. Open ye the gates, that the righteous nation which keepeth the truth may enter in.
3. Thou wilt keep him in perfect peace, whose mind is stayed on thee: because he trusteth in thee.
4. Trust ye in the Lord for ever: for in the Lord Jehovah is everlasting strength:
5. For he bringeth down them that dwell on high; the lofty city, he layeth it low; he layeth it low, even to the ground; he bringeth it even to the dust.
6. The foot shall tread it down, even the feet of the poor, and the steps of the needy.
7. The way of the just is uprightness: thou, most upright, dost weigh the path of the just.
8. Yea, in the way of thy judgments, O Lord, have we waited for thee; the desire of our soul Is to thy name, and to the remembrance of thee.
9. With my soul have I desired thee in the night; yea, with my spirit within me will I seek thee early: for when thy judgments are in the earth, the inhabitants of the world will learn righteousness.
10. Let favour be shewed to the wicked, yet will he not learn righteousness: in the land of uprightness will he deal unjustly, and will not behold the majesty of the Lord.
11. Lord, when thy hand is lifted up, they will not see: but they shall see, and be ashamed for their envy at the people; yea, the fire of thine enemies shall devour them.
12. Lord, thou wilt ordain peace for us: for thou also hast wrought all our works in us.
13. O Lord our God, other lords beside thee have had dominion over us: but by thee only will we make mention of thy name.
14. They are dead, they shall not live; they are deceased, they shall not rise: therefore hast thou visited and destroyed them, and made all their memory to perish.
15. Thou hast increased the nation, O Lord, thou hast increased the nation: thou art glorified: thou hadst removed it far unto all the ends of the earth.
16. Lord, in trouble have they visited thee, they poured out a prayer when thy chastening was upon them.
17. Like as a woman with child, that draweth near the time of her delivery, is in pain, and crieth out in her pangs; so have we been in thy sight, O Lord.

18. We have been with child, we have been in pain, we have as it were brought forth wind; we have not wrought any deliverance in the earth; neither have the inhabitants of the world fallen.

19. Thy dead men shall live, together with my dead body shall they arise. Awake and sing, ye that dwell in dust: for thy dew is as the dew of herbs, and the earth shall cast out the dead.

20. Come, my people, enter thou into thy chambers, and shut thy doors about thee: hide thyself as it were for a little moment, until the indignation be overpast.

For, behold, the Lord cometh out of his place to punish the inhabitants of the earth for their iniquity: the earth also shall disclose her blood, and shall no more cover her slain.

Isaiah 27

1. In that day the Lord with his sore and great and strong sword shall punish leviathan the piercing serpent, even leviathan that crooked serpent; and he shall slay the dragon that is in the sea.

2. In that day sing ye unto her, A vineyard of red wine.

Satan is Leviathan the dragon, and the Lord's vineyard is His Christian Church. He will feed it becuase she is starving. Satan tried to set up briers and thorns to stop the Lord like writing those " left behind" series books and the whole scenario of confusion in Second Coming doctrine. He tried to stop the Carcase work by providing utter confusion in Christianity. But the Lord burned all the Briers and thorns. Read the seven books of the Carcase and his two Appendix, A and B. The "Red wine" is the gospel of love from the Church.

3. I the Lord do keep it; I will water it every moment: lest any hurt it, I will keep it night and day.

4. Fury is not in me: who would set the briers and thorns against me in battle? I would go through them, I would burn them together.

5. Or let him take hold of my strength, that he may make peace with me; and he shall make peace with me.

6. He shall cause them that come of Jacob to take root: Israel shall blossom and bud, and fill the face of the world with fruit.

7. Hath he smitten him, as he smote those that smote him? or is he slain according to the slaughter of them that are slain by him?

8. In measure, when it shooteth forth, thou wilt debate with it: he stayeth his rough wind in the day of the east wind.

9. By this therefore shall the iniquity of Jacob be purged; and this is all the fruit to take away his sin; when he maketh all the stones of the altar as chalkstones that are beaten in sunder, the groves and images shall not stand up.

10. Yet the defenced city shall be desolate, and the habitation forsaken, and left like a wilderness: there shall the calf feed, and there shall he lie down, and consume the branches thereof.

11. When the boughs thereof are withered, they shall be broken off: the women come, and set them on fire: for it is a people of no understanding: therefore he that made them will not have mercy on them, and he that formed them will shew them no favour.

12. And it shall come to pass in that day, that the Lord shall beat off from the channel of

the river unto the stream of Egypt, and ye shall be gathered one by one, O ye children of Israel.

And it shall come to pass in that day, that the great trumpet shall be blown, and they shall come which were ready to perish in the land of Assyria, and the outcasts in the land of Egypt, and shall worship the Lord in the holy mount at Jerusalem.

In the day that the great towers fell, the great slaughter.is today. The Second Coming.

Isaiah. 30:25

25. And there shall be upon every high mountain, and upon every high hill, rivers and streams of waters in the day of the great slaughter, when the towers fall.

Today Janice was happy. It was the day that Jesus will come down. She watched on T.V as the skies in Jerusalem were scanned by the T.V crews. There were people who floated into the air around Jerusalem and flew like birds as the Holy Spirit gave them power to meet Jesus in the air as He came down. There was a collective wailing around the world as Jesus appeared in the sky. The Angels, all as white as Lightening, around the whole world began to cheer and clap.
THE KING OF kings HAS RETURNED.!

Psalms 24

1. The earth is the Lord's, and the fulness thereof; the world, and they that dwell therein.
2. For he hath founded it upon the seas, and established it upon the floods.
3. Who shall ascend into the hill of the Lord? or who shall stand in his holy place?
4. He that hath clean hands, and a pure heart; who hath not lifted up his soul unto vanity, nor sworn deceitfully.
5. He shall receive the blessing from the Lord, and righteousness from the God of his salvation.
6. This is the generation of them that seek him, that seek thy face, O Jacob. Selah.
7. Lift up your heads, O ye gates; and be ye lift up, ye everlasting doors; and the King of glory shall come in.
8. Who is this King of glory? The Lord strong and mighty, the Lord mighty in battle.
9. Lift up your heads, O ye gates; even lift them up, ye everlasting doors; and the King of glory shall come in.
10. Who is this King of glory? The Lord of hosts, he is the King of glory. Selah.

Jesus returned to Jerusalem as Psalm 24 dictated. It was written for this day. The Church was happy and the sheep were just so joyful He was back. Here was their Shepherd- the Lord. The Carcase introduced the Lord. It was the Carcase who was supposed to have warned the earth that Jesus was coming back. He failed in every attempt, he never got his chance, but it was all planned that way by the Lord. (unknown to the Carcase).

The Carcase told his fellow sheep that Jesus Christ was Almighty God in the flesh. Those Arabs who were of Islam and were spared from the death understood. Kedar wept for the Lord. Satan had abused them, but God- The God of Israel did not forsake them. They were alive.

The Church had questions for Jesus. What about Dispensationalism?, the Rapture, pretribulation, prewrathtribulation, , posttribulation. It was all nonsense. God had put a curse on the visions of the Second Coming in chpt 22 Isaiah. Also Satan had hoodwinked the Church with those " Left behind" series books. The people will untangle themselves with the seven books written by Melek Lotegeluaki.

Now it will be clear skies forever. True the earth had to be divided up, the spoils from Satan, but Jesus is fair and Righteous. He will not be hoodwinked by special interest, or the rich. The Christian World Order was fair. Everyone got a piece of the pie. The Indians were resurrected and given some land, the crowded Chinese got more land, the oppressed Black nation was united worldwide. The Polynesians got their own nation. Shem got billions of earthlike planets in the universe.

But after it was all divided, the nations blessed the Lord, for the Lord had divided the known universe to the nations- this finite universe with its billions of earthlike planets. The nations were like fat sheep now with billions of earths available to them. There were many celebrations on earth when the Lord returned.

The Lord met Paula, and He called her " Janice". She responded, like that had been her real name. Jesus told her the story of her life, from creation to the Second coming. Jesus brought Antigravity vehicles, spaceships, robots, teleportation , Education machine and the Disintegrate/Intergrator to the earth. Israel was given more land, from the Euphrates river to Cairo. The nations were given billions of galaxies. Janice was happy to have been saved by Jesus.

Psalm 50 is a Second Coming Psalm and what to expect when Jesus lands on the earth with all of His Angels.

Psalm 50.

1. The mighty God, even the Lord, hath spoken, and called the earth from the rising of the sun unto the going down thereof.
2. Out of Zion, the perfection of beauty, God hath shined.
3. Our God shall come, and shall not keep silence: a fire shall devour before him, and it shall be very tempestuous round about him.
4. He shall call to the heavens from above, and to the earth, that he may judge his people.
5. Gather my saints together unto me; those that have made a covenant with me by sacrifice.
6. And the heavens shall declare his righteousness: for God is judge himself. Selah.
7. Hear, O my people, and I will speak; O Israel, and I will testify against thee: I am God, even thy God.
8. I will not reprove thee for thy sacrifices or thy burnt offerings to have been continually before me.
9. I will take no bullock out of thy house, nor he goats out of thy folds.
10. For every beast of the forest is mine, and the cattle upon a thousand hills.
11. I know all the fowls of the mountains: and the wild beasts of the field are mine.
12. If I were hungry, I would not tell thee: for the world is mine, and the fulness thereof.
13. Will I eat the flesh of bulls, or drink the blood of goats?
14. Offer unto God thanksgiving; and pay thy vows unto the most High:
15. And call upon me in the day of trouble: I will deliver thee, and thou shalt glorify me.
16. But unto the wicked God saith, What hast thou to do to declare my statutes, or that thou shouldest take my covenant in thy mouth?
17. Seeing thou hatest instruction, and castest my words behind thee.

18. When thou sawest a thief, then thou consentedst with him, and hast been partaker with adulterers.
19. Thou givest thy mouth to evil, and thy tongue frameth deceit.
20. Thou sittest and speakest against thy brother; thou slanderest thine own mother's son.
21. These things hast thou done, and I kept silence; thou thoughtest that I was altogether such an one as thyself: but I will reprove thee, and set them in order before thine eyes.
22. Now consider this, ye that forget God, lest I tear you in pieces, and there be none to deliver.
23. Whoso offereth praise glorifieth me: and to him that ordereth his conversation aright will I shew the salvation of God.

Janice died a loving death and left her three children in Christs hands in His new world. After Janice died, she was instantly teleported to heaven. She did not have to meet the Beast and WWIII. She already used up that Time slot in the future. It was all clear skies for her. Satan was spending 40 billion years 800 million years+/- in the Bottomless Pit.

Christians are Time travelers and God can do anything, backwards in Time or Forward in Time. Janice woke up in heaven. Jesus was there with her. After this universe collapsed the nations were given billions, trillions or a googolplex universes to live in. If they wanted more Jesus at the snap of a finger could give them a Grahams number of universes to live in. That was the new earth. The universes knew no pain or sorrow. Our Earth today is built on pain and death, someone had to die all the time for others to live, for example, a worm had to die a painful death for the bird to live. Not so in these new universes. Sorrow was no more. It was all built on love and no pain.

Revelation 21:1-4

1. " And I saw a new heaven and a new earth: for the first heaven and the first earth were passed away; and there was no more sea.
2 And I john saw the holy city, new Jerusalem, coming down from God out of heaven, prepared as a bride adorned for her husband.
3 And I heard a great voice out of heaven saying, Behold, the tabernacle of God is with men, and He will dwell with them, and they shall be His people, and God Himself shall be with them, and be their God.
4 And God shall wipe away all tears from their eyes; and there shall be no more death, neither sorrow, nor crying, neither shall there be any more pain: for the former things are passed away."

At least no pain for the human sheep. A universe for pain will be left within our googolplex universes for Satan and his followers. That universe will never rexplode again.

Isaiah 66:22-24..

22. For as the new heavens and the new earth, which I will make, shall remain before me, saith the Lord, so shall your seed and your name remain.
23. And it shall come to pass, that from one new moon to another, and from one sabbath to another, shall all flesh come to worship before me, saith the Lord.
And they shall go forth, and look upon the carcases of the men that have transgressed against

me: for their worm shall not die, neither shall their fire be quenched; and they shall be an abhorring unto all flesh

But today Janice is a Queen, not in Argentina the Great, for there is no more sea or political sea. Every woman was a Queen in Christs kingdom and life today was like it was before the BigBang 100 billion B.C+/-, before the Invisible War and the Collapse of the Universe 100 billion AD+/-. Just like it was when we were innocent. But this time we knew what darkness was. We were not immature. At least Janice was not immature. And she had a "White garment" and a "White stone" forever. Janice and all the other sheep were happy.

Jesus sat next to His Father on the great white throne and He was wondering what was next on the Agenda.Should He introduce His sheep to His other infinite sheep in the infinite third dimension? The Church did not ask, they needed to rest for a little bit, but maybe one day to liven things up like He did with the Invisible War- what was their collective wants ? He was the Shepherd.

Psalms 23

1. The Lord is my shepherd; I shall not want.
2. He maketh me to lie down in green pastures: he leadeth me beside the still waters.
3. He restoreth my soul: he leadeth me in the paths of righteousness for his name's sake.
4. Yea, though I walk through the valley of the shadow of death, I will fear no evil: for thou art with me; thy rod and thy staff they comfort me.
5. Thou preparest a table before me in the presence of mine enemies: thou anointest my head with oil; my cup Runneth over.
6. Surely goodness and mercy shall follow me all the days of my life: and I will dwell in the house of the Lord for ever.

Psalms 37

1. Fret not thyself because of evildoers, neither be thou envious against the workers of iniquity.
2. For they shall soon be cut down like the grass, and wither as the green herb.
3. Trust in the Lord, and do good; so shalt thou dwell in the land, and verily thou shalt be fed.
4. Delight thyself also in the Lord: and he shall give thee the desires of thine heart.
5. Commit thy way unto the Lord; trust also in him; and he shall bring it to pass.
6. And he shall bring forth thy righteousness as the light, and thy judgment as the noonday.
7. Rest in the Lord, and wait patiently for him: fret not thyself because of him who prospereth in his way, because of the man who bringeth wicked devices to pass.
8. Cease from anger, and forsake wrath: fret not thyself in any wise to do evil.
9. For evildoers shall be cut off: but those that wait upon the Lord, they shall inherit the earth.
10. For yet a little while, and the wicked shall not be: yea, thou shalt diligently consider his place, and it shall not be.
11. But the meek shall inherit the earth; and shall delight themselves in the abundance of peace.

12. The wicked plotteth against the just, and gnasheth upon him with his teeth.

13. The Lord shall laugh at him: for he seeth that his day is coming.

14. The wicked have drawn out the sword, and have bent their bow, to cast down the poor and needy, and to slay such as be of upright conversation.

15. Their sword shall enter into their own heart, and their bows shall be broken.

16. A little that a righteous man hath is better than the riches of many wicked.

17. For the arms of the wicked shall be broken: but the Lord upholdeth the righteous.

18. The Lord knoweth the days of the upright: and their inheritance shall be for ever.

19. They shall not be ashamed in the evil time: and in the days of famine they shall be satisfied.

20. But the wicked shall perish, and the enemies of the Lord shall be as the fat of lambs: they shall consume; into smoke shall they consume away.

21. The wicked borroweth, and payeth not again: but the righteous sheweth mercy, and giveth.

22. For such as be blessed of him shall inherit the earth; and they that be cursed of him shall be cut off.

23. The steps of a good man are ordered by the Lord: and he delighteth in his way.

24. Though he fall, he shall not be utterly cast down: for the Lord upholdeth him with his hand.

25. I have been young, and now am old; yet have I not seen the righteous forsaken, nor his seed begging bread.

26. He is ever merciful, and lendeth; and his seed is blessed.

27. Depart from evil, and do good; and dwell for evermore.

28. For the Lord loveth judgment, and forsaketh not his saints; they are preserved for ever: but the seed of the wicked shall be cut off.

29. The righteous shall inherit the land, and dwell therein for ever.

30. The mouth of the righteous speaketh wisdom, and his tongue talketh of judgment.

31. The law of his God is in his heart; none of his steps shall slide.

32. The wicked watcheth the righteous, and seeketh to slay him.

33. The Lord will not leave him in his hand, nor condemn him when he is judged.

34. Wait on the Lord, and keep his way, and he shall exalt thee to inherit the land: when the wicked are cut off, thou shalt see it.

35. I have seen the wicked in great power, and spreading himself like a green bay tree.

36. Yet he passed away, and, lo, he was not: yea, I sought him, but he could not be found.

37. Mark the perfect man, and behold the upright: for the end of that man is peace.

38. But the transgressors shall be destroyed together: the end of the wicked shall be cut off.

39. But the salvation of the righteous is of the Lord: he is their strength in the time of trouble.

40. And the Lord shall help them, and deliver them: he shall deliver them from the wicked, and save them, because they trust in him.

Psalm 145 is a vision for kings, Queens and all peoples.

Psalms 145

1. I will extol thee, my God, O king; and I will bless thy name for ever and ever.

2. Every day will I bless thee; and I will praise thy name for ever and ever.

3. Great is the Lord, and greatly to be praised; and his greatness is unsearchable.

4. One generation shall praise thy works to another, and shall declare thy mighty acts.

5. I will speak of the glorious honour of thy majesty, and of thy wondrous works.

6. And men shall speak of the might of thy terrible acts: and I will declare thy greatness.

7. They shall abundantly utter the memory of thy great goodness, and shall sing of thy righteousness.

8. The Lord is gracious, and full of compassion; slow to anger, and of great mercy.

9. The Lord is good to all: and his tender mercies are over all his works.

10. All thy works shall praise thee, O Lord; and thy saints shall bless thee.

11. They shall speak of the glory of thy kingdom, and talk of thy power;

12. To make known to the sons of men his mighty acts, and the glorious majesty of his kingdom.

13. Thy kingdom is an everlasting kingdom, and thy dominion endureth throughout all generations.

14. The Lord upholdeth all that fall, and raiseth up all those that be bowed down.

15. The eyes of all wait upon thee; and thou givest them their meat in due season.

16. Thou openest thine hand, and satisfiest the desire of every living thing.

17. The Lord is righteous in all his ways, and holy in all his works.

18. The Lord is nigh unto all them that call upon him, to all that call upon him in truth.

19. He will fulfil the desire of them that fear him: he also will hear their cry, and will save them.

20. The Lord preserveth all them that love him: but all the wicked will he destroy.

21. My mouth shall speak the praise of the Lord: and let all flesh bless his holy name for ever and ever.

CREDITS AND EXCELLENT BOOKS TO READ.

THE INVISIBLE WAR, BY DR. DONALD GREY BARNHOUSE.
WAR ON THE SAINTS, BY JESSE PENN-LEWIS AND EVAN ROBERTS-(THE OVERCOMER LITERATURE TRUST

3 MUNSTER ROAD, PARKSTONE, POOLE, DORSET, ENGLAND. AGENTS IN USA-THE CHRISTIAN LITERATURE CRUSADE- FORT WASHINGTON, PENNA:

MADE AND PRINTED IN GREAT BRITAIN BY- STANLEY L HUNT (PRINTERS) LTD., GEORGE STREET, RUSHDEN, NORTHANTS.

BOOKS FROM STANLEY O LOTEGELUAKI

1.) CHRISTIANS EXISTED BEFORE THE BIG BANG AND WILL EXIST AFTER THE COLLAPSE OF THIS UNIVERSE.

2.) WHAT THE BIBLE SAYS ABOUT THE COLLAPSE OF THE UNIVERSE. BOOK II.

3.) JESUS CHRIST IS LORD AND IS WORSHIPPED IN INFINITE MULTIPLE UNIVERSES THROUGHOUT INFINITY.

4.) THE HOLY BIBLE: THE REFRESHING.

5.) THE SECOND COMING OF JESUS CHRIST: THE RETURN OF THE KING.

6.) INTERGALACTIC JESUS CHRIST SUPERSTAR.

7.) AFRICA: INTERGALACTIC FEDERATION OF AFRICAN TRIBES

To be published alone, but inserted in this Book

8.) JESUS CHRIST IS REALLY ALMIGHTY GOD.

To be published alone, but inserted in this Book.

9.) SALVATION FROM THE LAKE OF FIRE AND BEING BURNED ALIVE FOREVER. JESUS IS THE SAVIOR.

10.) THE WRATH OF THE LAMB

WORMWOOD! SATAN AND HIS DEMONS WILL BE BURNED IN THE BOTTOMLESS PIT FOR 40 BILLION +/- YEARS, THEN WWIII.

11.) CHRISTIANS THERE IS NO RAPTURE OR WAR BEFORE THE SECOND COMING, YOU HAVE BEEN FOOLED BY SATAN.

12.) ARMAGEDDON IS 40 BILLION +/- YEARS FROM NOW, WWIII, AND THE LAKE OF FIRE.

go to Church- they are all preaching about Salvation (Mainstream Church's- not Jehovah Witness, Christian Science, Mormons, etc) but go to Mainstream Churchs- Catholics, Baptist, Lutherans, Pentecostal, Salvation Army etc. Go to real churches that say Jesus is Almighty God and the God of Israel and is the sinless Lamb sacrificed for all of our sins.

Psalm 131 is one of my favorite Psalms. Try to memorize this psalm if you couldn't memorize Psalm 119.

Psalms 131

1. Lord, my heart is not haughty, nor mine eyes lofty: neither do I exercise myself in great matters, or in things too high for me.
2. Surely I have behaved and quieted myself, as a child that is weaned of his mother: my soul is even as a weaned child.
3. Let Israel hope in the Lord from henceforth and for ever.

CHAPTER SEVEN
SALVATION FOR HUMANS

SALVATION FROM THE LAKE OF FIRE AND BEING BURNED ALIVE FOREVER. JESUS IS THE SAVIOR.

BOOK XIV THIS BOOK IS UNEDITED
EINSTEIN AND THE BIBLE AGREE ABOUT THE COLLAPSE OF THE UNIVERSE. CHRISTIANS CALL THE COLLAPSED UNIVERSE THE LAKE OF FIRE- SCIENTICISTS CALL IT GRAVITATIONAL EQUILIBRIUM, THE BIG CRUNCH. IN A 100 BILLION A.D. BLUESHIFT, THE WICKED WILL BE BURNED IN THE CORE OF THE COLLAPSED UNIVERSE FOREVER IN THE MIDDLE OF FIERY STARS AND HOT GALAXIES SMASHED TOGETHER. THE LAKE OF FIRE. II PETER 3:7. BLOOD, FIRE AND PILLARS OF SMOKE

The Fourteen books I wrote is the food prophesied in Isaiah to be fed to the people of the Second Coming. Mother Church you are the Woman of Revelation 12 and these TEN books are the nourishment of Rev:12:14. I have prepared the way of the Lord for the Second Coming like John the Baptist did for the first arrival. This is the Second Coming preparation and that is what I was born for. Eat and be merry Mother Church, even Einstein is on our side. He confirms the Bible, The Lake of Fire. But Jesus will come back in my lifetime.

Isaiah 25

6. And in this mountain shall the Lord of hosts make unto all people a feast of fat things, a feast of wines on the lees, of fat things full of marrow, of wines on the lees well refined.
7. And he will destroy in this mountain the face of the covering cast over all people, and the vail that is spread over all nations.
8. He will swallow up death in victory; and the Lord God will wipe away tears from off all faces; and the rebuke of his people shall he take away from off all the earth: for the Lord hath spoken it.

Stanley O Lotegeluaki. Messenger of Isaiah. Herald of Christ.

GIVE THIS BOOK TO YOUR LOVED ONES, CLOSE CIRCLE OF FRIENDS WHO YOU WANT TO SPEND ETERNITY IN PARADISE WITH, IN HEAVEN, SAVE THEM IF YOU CARE. FRIEND I CARE, SPEND ETERNITY WITH ME AND JESUS.
JOEL 2:32 AND IT SHALL COME TO PASS, THAT WHOSOEVER SHALL CALL ON

THE NAME OF THE LORD SHALL BE DELIVERED: FOR IN MOUNT ZION AND IN JERUSALEM SHALL BE DELIVERANCE, AS THE LORD HATH SAID, AND IN THE REMNANT WHOM THE LORD SHALL CALL.

JOHN 3:16 FOR GOD SO LOVED THE WORLD, THAT HE GAVE HIS ONLY BEGOTTEN SON, THAT WHOSOEVER BELIEVETH IN HIM SHOULD NOT PERISH, BUT HAVE EVERLASTING LIFE.

Isaiah 31: 4. For thus hath the Lord spoken unto me, Like as the lion and the young lion roaring on his prey, when a multitude of shepherds is called forth against him, he will not be afraid of their voice, nor abase himself for the noise of them: so shall the Lord of hosts come down to fight for mount Zion, and for the hill thereof.

5. As birds flying, so will the Lord of hosts defend Jerusalem; defending also he will deliver it; and passing over he will preserve it.

THE VIOLENT WEATHER, TORNADOES, EARTHQUAKES, TSUNAMI'S, HURRICANES ON EARTH IS BECAUSE THE LORD IS ON HIS WAY BACK.

ISAIAH 29: 6. Thou shalt be visited of the Lord of hosts with thunder, and with earthquake, and great noise, with storm and tempest, and the flame of devouring fire.

ISAIAH 11: 9. They shall not hurt nor destroy in all my holy mountain: for the earth shall be full of the knowledge of the Lord, as the waters cover the sea.

10. And in that day there shall be a root of Jesse, which shall stand for an ensign of the people; to it shall the Gentiles seek: and His rest shall be glorious.

JESUS CHRIST IS LORD !

INTERGALACTIC JESUS CHRIST SUPERSTAR !

INTRODUCTION

John 1:1.

1. In the beginning was the Word, and the Word was with God, and the Word was God.

Next we learn that Jesus has always been with God- forever past.

John 1:2.

2. The same was in the beginning with God.

Jesus created all things.

John 1:3.

3. All things were made by him; and without him was not any thing made that was made.

Jesus is "Life"- thats where we get our conciousness from and He is our "Light".

John 1:4.

4. In him was life; and the life was the light of men.

The great tribulation is over. Satan's camp has been attacked by Jesus Christ with His army the Church. The Catholic's were the first wave to surround and swarm into Satan's camp. They went over the fence first. They got stopped by the layers of wires over the ages, by mines, "foo" gas (burn't at the stake) and machine gun fire from the enemy. They were stopped by the worship of Mary, the belief of purgatory, the inquisition, the selling of indulgences and wars etc.

Then Jesus sent in the second wave- the Protestants. They attacked and assaulted violently Satans camp further in. They destroyed Satan's supplies and took most of Satan's camp. But they were stopped by enemy fire with conformity- the acceptance of homosexuals, abortion, adultery and fornication etc.

Now Jesus is sending in the Third Wave who will completely wipe out Satans command post. The Third Wave are Christians who ate the "Refreshing" and believe in the Bibles version of the collapse of the universe and life before the big bang. They entered Satan's command post and killed the enemy. Now the war is over. Jesus is coming. The Return of the King.

Thats how the Tribulation was fought. The earth is ours. Jerusalem will be the Capital city of Jesus.

THE BANNER - THE DOCTRINE OF THE SECOND COMING.

THE THIRD WAVE.

THE NEW CHRISTIANITY. THE LEADING EDGE OF CHRISTIAN DEVELOPMENT. WE ARE GOING INTO SPACE- TO CONQUER THE STARS WITH JESUS WHEN HE COMES BACK AT THE SECOND COMING.

Christians existed before the Big Bang. We lived with Jesus in peace in a kingdom called the Kingdom of the King of Glory. (before the Big bang, before the goats and Satan were created). Then we Christians all volunteered for the Invisible War to be fought in this universe on a planet called earth. That is why we are here. That war has been fought and the Bible is the history of it. At the Second Coming which is in my lifetime, Jesus will come back. Then Jesus is going to lead the human race into space, to conquer the stars with Christ Technology and Angel Technology. Satan and his goats, the Beast angel and demons will be thrown into the Bottomless Pit while the goat people will be "taken" to comfortable hell for 40 billion years +/- or the 1000 Christ years. 40 billion years from now, or in 1000 Christ years, WWIII will be fought in spaceships against the Beast 666, Satan, demons and goats when they are rereleased into Christ's perfect 1000 year reign or spacekingdom. That is when Armageddon is fought, not now before the Second Coming. Armageddon is after the 1000 years of Christ's reign, it will be fought when the universe is in Blueshift, when the core of the collapsing universe exists or as Christians call it the "Lake of fire" (II Peter 3:7).

After the war the goats and Satan will be thrown into the Lake of fire and we Christians will live in peace until the universe finishes imploding. We Christians will be given a New Heaven and a New earth or universe to live in. Actually the nations will be given billions of universes to live in. Read all of my books to see the entire scenario of the Life before the Big Bang, the Invisible War and the collapse of the universe and the New Christianity. We are the Third Wave. The Catholics were the first wave Jesus sent in, and they discomfited Satans camp. Then Jesus sent in the Second

Wave, the Protestants and they tormented Satans camp and now Jesus is sending in the Third Wave, StarChildren who believe in Life before the Big Bang, the Invisible War and the Collapse of the universe doctrine and they will wipe out Satan's command post completely. Jesus will soon return to give the First, Second and Third Wave medals at the Second Coming. Thus the end of the Invisible War for a 1000 years.

Isaiah 30: 30. And the Lord shall cause his glorious voice to be heard, and shall shew the lighting down of his arm, with the indignation of his anger, and with the flame of a devouring fire, with scattering, and tempest, and hailstones.

Credits: King James Bible Public Domain
Referenced with KJV BIBLE
@COPYRIGHT 2005
HOLMAN BIBLE PUBLISHERS
ALL RIGHTS RESERVED
FONT NOT USED
OTHER CREDITS TO

- Encyclopedia World Book 1988
- The Invisible War. By Dr. D. Grey Barnhouse, Martyr and hero of the Lord.
- Sit, Walk, Stand. By Watchman Nee, Martyr and hero of Christianity.
- Pastor Gong Shengliang. Martyr and hero of Chrisitanity.

SALVATION- WHAT DOES IT MEAN ?

Christians always talk about Salvation and that Jesus is going to save anyone who believes in Him and obeys Him by loving God with all their strength and loving their neighbour , their fellow humans like they love themselves. Also to believe in the cross of Jesus- You have to believe that Jesus was punished on the cross for your sins, as He died for you. You must believe that He was a subsitite for your punishment.

When you believe in Jesus, everytime God looks at you, He sees you through a lens, where Jesus cleansed your sins with His blood. So your clean. So God does not see your sins- He sees Jesus on the cross in pain for your sins.

Isaiah 53:10,11

10. Yet it pleased the Lord to bruise him; he hath put him to grief: when thou shalt make his soul an offering for sin, he shall see his seed, he shall prolong his days, and the pleasure of the Lord shall prosper in his hand.

GOD BRUISED JESUS TO PAY FOR OUR SINS. HE TOOK OUR PUNISHMENT AND WE ARE SAVED. THE CHURCH'S DOCTRINE IS CORRECT.

11. He shall see of the travail of his soul, and shall be satisfied: by his knowledge shall my righteous servant justify many; for he shall bear their iniquities.

John 3:14-18

IF YOU MISS THESE NEXT VERSES YOU MISSED EVERYTHING.

John 3:14-34.

13. And no man hath ascended up to heaven, but he that came down from heaven, even the Son of man which is in heaven.
14. And as Moses lifted up the serpent in the wilderness, even so must the Son of man be lifted up:
15. That whosoever believeth in him should not perish, but have eternal life.
16. For God so loved the world, that he gave his only begotten Son, that whosoever believeth in him should not perish, but have everlasting life.
17. For God sent not his Son into the world to condemn the world; but that the world through him might be saved.
18. He that believeth on him is not condemned: but he that believeth not is condemned already, because he hath not believed in the name of the only begotten Son of God.

I John 4:9-10

9: In this was manifested the love of God toward us, because that God sent His only begotten Son into the world, that we might live through Him.
10: Herin is love, not that we loved God, but that He loved us, and sent His Son to be the propitiation for our sins.

Romans 5: 11-19

11: And not only so, but we also joy in God through our Lord Jesus Christ, by whom we have now received the atonement.
12: Wherefore, as by one man sin entered into the world, and death by sin; and so death passed upon all men, for that all have sinned:
13: (For until the law sin was in the world: but sin is not imputed when there is no law.
14: Nevertheless death reigned from Adam to Moses, even over them that had not sinned after the similitude of Adam's transgression, who is the figure of him that was to come.
15: But not as the offence, so also is the free gift. For if through the offence of one many be dead, much more the grace of God, and the gift by grace, which is by one man, Jesus Christ, hath abounded unto many.
16: And not as it was by one that sinned, so is the gift: for the judgment was by one to condemnation, but the free gift is of many offences unto justification.
17: For if by one man's offence death reigned by one; much more they which receive abundance of grace and of the gift of righteousness shall reign in life by one, Jesus Christ.)
18: Therefore as by the offence of one judgment came upon all men to condemnation; even so by the righteousness of one the free gift came upon all men unto justification of life.

19: For as by one man's disobedience many were made sinners, so by the obedience of one shall many be made righteous.

THAT MEANT ADAM CAUSED ALL MEN TO SIN AND DIE, BUT JESUS CAME AND THROUGH HIS OBEDIENCE TO GOD SAVED A LOT OF PEOPLE.

Romans 3:22-26

22: Even the righteousness of God which is by faith of Jesus Christ unto all and upon all them that believe: for there is no difference:

23: For all have sinned, and come short of the glory of God;

24: Being justified freely by His grace through the redemption that is in Christ Jesus.

25: Whom God hath set forth to be a propitiation through faith in His blood, to declare His righteousness for the remission of sins that are past, through the forbearance of God;

26: To declare, I say, at this time His righteousness: that He might be just, and the justifier of him which believeth in Jesus.

What are you being saved from? You are being saved from being thrown into hell, then into the Lake of fire at the end of time, into the collapsed universe of hot fiery stars and smashed galaxies and burned alive forever. Where your skin will not fall off but will always be fresh to feel the pain. You will never die. Actually whether you believe in Jesus or not you will live forever- its where you will spend eternity that matters, in pure paradise of heaven or the Lake of fire.

So ask Jesus to save you, you only have so many opportunities to accept Him in your lifetime- He is knocking at the door right now as you read this book, if you dont accept His love, then He will leave you to your fate unsaved. If you believe He will be faithful to save you no matter what you have done. No one is beyond Salvation, except Satan and his demons. Satan and his demons even had a concert, a celebration- " the unforgiven" concert by Metallica. Or is Salvation a big joke to you like AC/DC "Highway to hell"?. One out every three humans on earth will be burned in the Lake of fire, your chances of escape are slim indeed. Turn to Jesus.

We could start the story of Salvation with life before the Big Bang where we all volunteered to come to earth and fight a battle against Satan, demons and goats. Thats when our names were put in the Book of Life so no Sheep will be lost and no goat will be saved. When Jesus before the Big Bang volunteered to come to save us from a dragon by dying a horrible painful death. We could start there, but some are unfamiliar with that version, so I will start with Adam and Eve.

Satan tempted Eve to disobey God and eat from a forbidden fruit. The fruit was not important, it was the act of disobedience that was important. You have heard the story of the garden of Eden before. Read Genesis to see what Iam talking about. As you know Moses is the one who penned Genesis with the help of God. But there is also another writing that notes Adams sin and what happened in the garden of Eden, someone who did not even know Moses. It was St. Job.

Job 31:33

33. If I covered my transgressions as Adam, by hiding mine iniquity in my bosom:

St. Job was a second witness in the Bible to Genesis and the witness of two people is usually true. Now what is important about Adam and Eve ? Adam and Eve did not need to be saved at first because they never sinned- Sin only happens when there are rules to break and they only had one rule from God, dont eat from a particular tree. God said if they did they would die. The reason God gave them only one rule was to trap Satan in the Invisible War.

Satan was successful in tempting the pair of humans in the garden to break God's commandment and the first sin came to earth. Now Satan was laden with sin and he was contagious and he contaminated the earth.

Where did Satan come from? You have to read Ezekiel 28 for the whole story about Satans heavenly kingdom after the Big Bang where he was the highpriest for Jesus or God. But what is important here is that Adam and Eve ate from the fruit and they did not die as God said they would, but actually something died and they became gods, their spirits died and the first thing they realized was the difference between good and evil. That if you obey God- thats good, and if you disobey God- thats bad. So they recieved the knowledge. Their spirits began to disintegrate, to fall and they became gods also for they realized they were naked and were ashamed to be naked. They also became afraid of God and hid from Him. That is the reason you hide from God.

So now Adam and Eve needed to be saved from God's terrible wrath, for the wages of sin is death. Someone had to die, someone had to be punished for if God did not punish Adam, He could not punish Lucifer or Satan for doing the same thing. But God is wise. Someone had to be punished- true- so God decided He would punish Himself for our sins. He died on the cross as a punishment for our sins.

But lets go back to Genesis. After Jesus cursed Adam, Eve and Satan the serpent- Jesus promised that a Child of Eve would one day bruise the serpents head (Satan) and the serpent would bruise or kill the Child of Eve (Jesus on the cross). So everything was set in motion for the Invisible War. Now the sin of Adam was in Adam's seed and every baby born from Adam's seed had the original sin passed down to them from the eating of the fruit. All babies - the entire spectrum of the human race born form Adam deserved to be burned in the fires of the Lake of fire forever, becuase they were contaminated from Adam.

Every baby had original sin- but one day God stopped the onward passing down of the seed of Adam- the seed that had known sin. Jesus was born from a virgin, so the sin of Adam was not in Him. He was born a sinless lamb for a sacrifice for all our sins. He was going to save us from the dragon.

Now God began to choose and hint at what type of sacrifice Jesus was going to be- a sinless lamb. It started when Abel and Cain brought in their fruits and burned it to God, so God in heaven could smell the aroma and bless them, men do strange things when it comes to God, but thats what they did. God rejected Cain's offering of plants- probably the smoke blew downward- while Abel's offering of a lamb pleased God, and probably the smoke went upward. But you know the story- Cain killed Abel for that (also note it was Satan who tempted Cain to kill Abel, so he could wipeout the human race before it even budded- for he knew that a Child of Adam and Eve would one day bruise his head.) Genesis 4:7.

What is important here is that God accepted Abel and his sacrifice of a lamb. When God took Moses and Israel out of Egypt God instituted that Lambs and kids be killed as an atonement for sin. The physics of sin is that someone has to die for them.

People say that Moses took the practice of sacrificing animals from the Egyptians and Canaanites, but it was Abel who started it, then Noah, then Abraham, Isaac, Jacob- all sacrificed lambs to God to please Him.

Now when Israel became a nation- there was a lot of sin and a lot of sacrificing was going on, sure there were times when the Israelites turned away from the Lord, but sacrificing animals became an institution, an organization and a religious national event. Millions of lambs were sacrificed until God could not take it anymore. It just did not deter people from sinning- the idea was to stop sinning and not instituting it.

So God decided that one day there will be only one sacrifice- a single sacrifice to atone for all sin. He would sacrifice Himself or His Son Jesus for the remission of all sins. He outlines His plan in Isaiah where He tells the Israelites about Jesus.

JOEL 2:32 AND IT SHALL COME TO PASS, THAT WHOSOEVER SHALL CALL ON THE NAME OF THE LORD SHALL BE DELIVERED: FOR IN MOUNT ZION AND IN JERUSALEM SHALL BE DELIVERANCE, AS THE LORD HATH SAID, AND IN THE REMNANT WHOM THE LORD SHALL CALL.

JOHN 3:16 FOR GOD SO LOVED THE WORLD, THAT HE GAVE HIS ONLY BEGOTTEN SON, THAT WHOSOEVER BELIEVETH IN HIM SHOULD NOT PERISH, BUT HAVE EVERLASTING LIFE.

JOHN CHAPTER THREE.

John chpt 3:1-5.

"water" means "gospel". "Spirit" means the "Holy Spirit".

John 3

1. There was a man of the Pharisees, named Nicodemus, a ruler of the Jews:
2. The same came to Jesus by night, and said unto him, Rabbi, we know that thou art a teacher come from God: for no man can do these miracles that thou doest, except God be with him.
3. Jesus answered and said unto him, Verily, verily, I say unto thee, Except a man be born again, he cannot see the kingdom of God.
4. Nicodemus saith unto him, How can a man be born when he is old? can he enter the second time into his mother's womb, and be born?
5. Jesus answered, Verily, verily, I say unto thee, Except a man be born of water and of the Spirit, he cannot enter into the kingdom of God.

"water" means "gospel". "Spirit" means the "Holy Spirit".

John 3:6-8.

6. That which is born of the flesh is flesh; and that which is born of the Spirit is spirit.
7. Marvel not that I said unto thee, Ye must be born again.
8. The wind bloweth where it listeth, and thou hearest the sound thereof, but canst not tell whence it cometh, and whither it goeth: so is every one that is born of the Spirit.

Christians are a "free" lot. The Spirit takes them in different directions politically and Spiritually but they all follow Jesus.

John 3:9-13.

9. Nicodemus answered and said unto him, How can these things be?
10. Jesus answered and said unto him, Art thou a master of Israel, and knowest not these things?
11. Verily, verily, I say unto thee, We speak that we do know, and testify that we have seen; and ye receive not our witness.
12. If I have told you earthly things, and ye believe not, how shall ye believe, if I tell you of heavenly things?
13. And no man hath ascended up to heaven, but he that came down from heaven, even the Son of man which is in heaven.

IF YOU MISS THESE NEXT VERSES YOU MISSED EVERYTHING.

John 3:14-34.

13. And no man hath ascended up to heaven, but he that came down from heaven, even the Son of man which is in heaven.
14. And as Moses lifted up the serpent in the wilderness, even so must the Son of man be lifted up:
15. That whosoever believeth in him should not perish, but have eternal life.
16. For God so loved the world, that he gave his only begotten Son, that whosoever believeth in him should not perish, but have everlasting life.
17. For God sent not his Son into the world to condemn the world; but that the world through him might be saved.
18. He that believeth on him is not condemned: but he that believeth not is condemned already, because he hath not believed in the name of the only begotten Son of God.
19. And this is the condemnation, that light is come into the world, and men loved darkness rather than light, because their deeds were evil.
20. For every one that doeth evil hateth the light, neither cometh to the light, lest his deeds should be reproved.
21. But he that doeth truth cometh to the light, that his deeds may be made manifest, that they are wrought in God.
22. After these things came Jesus and his disciples into the land of Judaea; and there he tarried with them, and baptized.
23. And John also was baptizing in Aenon near to Salim, because there was much water there: and they came, and were baptized.
24. For John was not yet cast into prison.
25. Then there arose a question between some of John's disciples and the Jews about purifying.
26. And they came unto John, and said unto him, Rabbi, he that was with thee beyond Jordan, to whom thou barest witness, behold, the same baptizeth, and all men come to him.

27. John answered and said, A man can receive nothing, except it be given him from heaven.

28. Ye yourselves bear me witness, that I said, I am not the Christ, but that I am sent before him.

29. He that hath the bride is the bridegroom: but the friend of the bridegroom, which standeth and heareth him, rejoiceth greatly because of the bridegroom's voice: this my joy therefore is fulfilled.

30. He must increase, but I must decrease.

31. He that cometh from above is above all: he that is of the earth is earthly, and speaketh of the earth: he that cometh from heaven is above all.

32. And what he hath seen and heard, that he testifieth; and no man receiveth his testimony.

33. He that hath received his testimony hath set to his seal that God is true.

34. For he whom God hath sent speaketh the words of God: for God giveth not the Spirit by measure unto him.

The reason why Christians can only do a limited amount of miracles is because God has measured out His power to us. But with Jesus He has been given all power. Jesus can do anything. Universes obey Him.

John 3:35-36.

35. The Father loveth the Son, and hath given all things into his hand.
36. He that believeth on the Son hath everlasting life: and he that believeth not the Son shall not see life; but the wrath of God abideth on him.

JOHN CHPT ONE

Jesus Christ is called the Word of God in Revelation.

Revelation chpt 19:13-14.

13. And he was clothed with a vesture dipped in blood: and his name is called The Word of God.

14. And the armies which were in heaven followed him upon white horses, clothed in fine linen, white and clean.

Now why did God choose the word - "Word" as His name? What is so special about the "Word" or "Words of God"? When God creates- He just says it and it appears and also the Bible is the Word of God. So if the Bible as a book could live it would be Jesus. Jesus is the Bible come to life. Also Jesus is the "Word of God". Note* God's Word's are not just words- they are His actions. Whenever He speaks it comes true- so He has to watch out what He says.

John 1:1.

1. In the beginning was the Word, and the Word was with God, and the Word was God.

Next we learn that Jesus has always been with God- forever past.

John 1:2.

2. The same was in the beginning with God.

Jesus created all things.

John 1:3.

3. All things were made by him; and without him was not any thing made that was made.

Jesus is "Life"- thats where we get our conciousness from and He is our "Light".

John 1:4.

4. In him was life; and the life was the light of men.

Satan cannot comprehend Jesus, nor understand Him and Jesus shines into Satan's territory- thus the Invisible War.

John 1:5.

5. And the light shineth in darkness; and the darkness comprehended it not.

Jesus is the "Light" of Genesis 1:3.

Genesis 1:3-5.

3. And God said, Let there be light: and there was light.
4. And God saw the light, that it was good: and God divided the light from the darkness.
5. And God called the light Day, and the darkness he called Night. And the evening and the morning were the first day.

John 1:6-13.
6. There was a man sent from God, whose name was John.
7. The same came for a witness, to bear witness of the Light, that all men through him might believe.
8. He was not that Light, but was sent to bear witness of that Light.
9. That was the true Light, which lighteth every man that cometh into the world.
10. He was in the world, and the world was made by him, and the world knew him not.
11. He came unto his own, and his own received him not.
12. But as many as received him, to them gave he power to become the sons of God, even to them that believe on his name:
13. Which were born, not of blood, nor of the will of the flesh, nor of the will of man, but of God.

As i said before - Jesus is the Bible come to life or the Words of God come to Life.
John 1:14-18.

14. And the Word was made flesh, and dwelt among us, (and we beheld his glory, the glory as of the only begotten of the Father,) full of grace and truth.
15. John bare witness of him, and cried, saying, This was he of whom I spake, He that cometh after me is preferred before me: for he was before me.
16. And of his fulness have all we received, and grace for grace.
17. For the law was given by Moses, but grace and truth came by Jesus Christ.
18. No man hath seen God at any time; the only begotten Son, which is in the bosom of the Father, he hath declared him.

Jesus says He has not seen God - for God fills all infinity- but to "declare" God is to see Him or God "declared" to you.

John 1:19-25.

19. And this is the record of John, when the Jews sent priests and Levites from Jerusalem to ask him, Who art thou?
20. And he confessed, and denied not; but confessed, I am not the Christ.
21. And they asked him, What then? Art thou Elias? And he saith, I am not. Art thou that prophet? And he answered, No.
22. Then said they unto him, Who art thou? that we may give an answer to them that sent us. What sayest thou of thyself?
23. He said, I am the voice of one crying in the wilderness, Make straight the way of the Lord, as said the prophet Esaias.
24. And they which were sent were of the Pharisees.
25. And they asked him, and said unto him, Why baptizest thou then, if thou be not that Christ, nor Elias, neither that prophet?

St. John did not know that he was Elijah.

John 1:26-27.

26. John answered them, saying, I baptize with water: but there standeth one among you, whom ye know not;
27. He it is, who coming after me is preferred before me, whose shoe's latchet I am not worthy to unloose.

I myself am not even worthy to lick the dust off of Christ's sandals let alone behold Him.

John 1:28-29.

28. These things were done in Bethabara beyond Jordan, where John was baptizing.
29. The next day John seeth Jesus coming unto him, and saith, Behold the Lamb of God, which taketh away the sin of the world.

St John declares Christ's mission on earth as the sacrificial lamb that would be sacrificed at the cross to take away the sins of the world- our sins.

John 1:29-48.

29. The next day John seeth Jesus coming unto him, and saith, Behold the Lamb of God, which taketh away the sin of the world.
30. This is he of whom I said, After me cometh a man which is preferred before me: for he was before me.
31. And I knew him not: but that he should be made manifest to Israel, therefore am I come baptizing with water.
32. And John bare record, saying, I saw the Spirit descending from heaven like a dove, and it abode upon him.
33. And I knew him not: but he that sent me to baptize with water, the same said unto me, Upon whom thou shalt see the Spirit descending, and remaining on him, the same is he which baptizeth with the Holy Ghost.
34. And I saw, and bare record that this is the Son of God.
35. Again the next day after John stood, and two of his disciples;
36. And looking upon Jesus as he walked, he saith, Behold the Lamb of God!
37. And the two disciples heard him speak, and they followed Jesus.
38. Then Jesus turned, and saw them following, and saith unto them, What seek ye? They said unto him, Rabbi, (which is to say, being interpreted, Master,) where dwellest thou?
39. He saith unto them, Come and see. They came and saw where he dwelt, and abode with him that day: for it was about the tenth hour.
40. One of the two which heard John speak, and followed him, was Andrew, Simon Peter's brother.
41. He first findeth his own brother Simon, and saith unto him, We have found the Messias, which is, being interpreted, the Christ.
42. And he brought him to Jesus. And when Jesus beheld him, he said, Thou art Simon the son of Jona: thou shalt be called Cephas, which is by interpretation, A stone.
43. The day following Jesus would go forth into Galilee, and findeth Philip, and saith unto him, Follow me.
44. Now Philip was of Bethsaida, the city of Andrew and Peter.
45. Philip findeth Nathanael, and saith unto him, We have found him, of whom Moses in the law, and the prophets, did write, Jesus of Nazareth, the son of Joseph.
46. And Nathanael said unto him, Can there any good thing come out of Nazareth? Philip saith unto him, Come and see.
47. Jesus saw Nathanael coming to him, and saith of him, Behold an Israelite indeed, in whom is no guile!
48. Nathanael saith unto him, Whence knowest thou me? Jesus answered and said unto him, Before that Philip called thee, when thou wast under the fig tree, I saw thee.

Jesus is God and He sees all things- everywhere and knows all thoughts.

John 1:48-51.

48. Nathanael saith unto him, Whence knowest thou me? Jesus answered and said unto him, Before that Philip called thee, when thou wast under the fig tree, I saw thee.

49. Nathanael answered and saith unto him, Rabbi, thou art the Son of God; thou art the King of Israel.

50. Jesus answered and said unto him, Because I said unto thee, I saw thee under the fig tree, believest thou? thou shalt see greater things than these.

51. And he saith unto him, Verily, verily, I say unto you, Hereafter ye shall see heaven open, and the angels of God ascending and descending upon the Son of man.

HUMANBEINGS CAN BE SAVED BUT SATAN AND HIS DEMONS CANNOT BE SAVED FOR THEY COMMITTED THE UNPARDONABLE BLASPHEMY. AND THE UNPARDONABLE BLASPHEMY IS TO TELL PEOPLE YOU ARE GOD AND HAVE THEM WORSHIP YOU AS GOD AND YOU KNOWING THAT YOU ARE NOT GOD. SATAN AND HIS DEMONS HAVE DONE THIS WHEN THEY CREATED OTHER RELIGIONS ON EARTH AND HAD PEOPLE WORSHIP THEM AS GODS- FROM BAAL, ALLAH, ZEUS, HINDU, WICCA, THOR, BUDDHA, TAOISM, ATHIESM, PAGANISM, NEW AGE, ATHIESTIC COMMUNISM, NAZISM, ETC. ALSO WHEN THEY WERE RELEASED OUT OF THE BOTTOMLESS PIT IN 40 BILLION AD+/- THEY COMMITTED THE SAME SIN WHEN THEY HAD PEOPLE WORSHIP THE ANTICHRIST ANGEL THAT POSSESSED A DEAD KING AND CAME BACK TO LIFE. AND THEY WORSHIPPED THE DRAGON WHO IS SATAN. EVEN THOUGH THEY WERE BURNED FOR 40 BILLION YEARS IN THE BOTTOMLESS PIT- THE BIBLE SAYS.

PROVERBS 27:22

22. THOUGH THOU SHOULDEST BRAY A FOOL IN A MORTAR AMONG WHEAT WITH A PESTLE, YET WILL NOT HIS FOOLISHNESS DEPART FROM HIM.

IT WAS MOTHER CHURCH WHO EVENTUALLY DECIDED TO BURN SATAN FOREVER. JESUS ONLY BURNED THEM FOR 40 BILLION 800 MILLION +/- YEARS. WE SHALL JUDGE ANGELS AS ST. PAUL SAID. BUT I STANLEY O LOTEGELUAKI IS CLEAN FROM YOUR BLOOD, FOR NOT ONLY DID I LEAD YOU TO SALVATION BY EXPOSING TO YOU CHPT 1 AND 3 JOHN, BUT I HAVE SHOWN YOU THE ENTIRE HISTORY OF CHRISTIANITY WITH THESE BOOKS. MY HANDS ARE CLEAN- THE SECOND COMING IS IN MY LIFETIME. THESE ARE THE 10 TALENTS JESUS GAVE TO ME, AND I HAVE GIVEN THEM TO YOU. IF YOU BURY THEM, ITS YOUR FAULT, IF YOU TELL OTHER PEOPLE AND SPREAD THE WORD- DO BUSINESS WITH THEM, THEN YOU HAVE DONE WELL. BUT THESE NEXT IS THE WORD OF GOD, FOOD MENTIONED IN ISAIAH 25:6-9.

6. And in this mountain shall the Lord of hosts make unto all people a feast of fat things, a feast of wines on the lees, of fat things full of marrow, of wines on the lees well refined.

7. And he will destroy in this mountain the face of the covering cast over all people, and the vail that is spread over all nations.

8. He will swallow up death in victory; and the Lord God will wipe away tears from off all faces; and the rebuke of his people shall he take away from off all the earth: for the Lord hath spoken it.

9. And it shall be said in that day, Lo, this is our God; we have waited for him, and he will save us: this is the Lord; we have waited for him, we will be glad and rejoice in his salvation.

THESE BOOKS OF MINE ARE THE NOURISHMENT FOR THE WOMAN -MOTHER CHURCH WHO IS IN THE WILDERNESS RIGHT NOW.

REVELATION CHPT 12.

12. Therefore rejoice, ye heavens, and ye that dwell in them. Woe to the inhabiters of the earth and of the sea! for the devil is come down unto you, having great wrath, because he knoweth that he hath but a short time.

13. And when the dragon saw that he was cast unto the earth, he persecuted the woman which brought forth the man child.

14. And to the woman were given two wings of a great eagle, that she might fly into the wilderness, into her place, where she is nourished for a time, and times, and half a time, from the face of the serpent.

15. And the serpent cast out of his mouth water as a flood after the woman, that he might cause her to be carried away of the flood.

Flood means political dictation- this was swallowed up by the Carcase of Mt 24:28
Rev 12:16-17

16. And the earth helped the woman, and the earth opened her mouth, and swallowed up the flood which the dragon cast out of his mouth.

17. And the dragon was wroth with the woman, and went to make war with the remnant of her seed, which keep the commandments of God, and have the testimony of Jesus Christ.

THE WAR SATAN MADE AGAINST THE CHURCH WAS THE RECENT PEDOPHILE SCANDAL JESUS WARNED US ABOUT IN MATHEW 18. I SWALLOWED UP THE FLOOD WITH THE HELP OF JESUS.

THESE ARE THE NOURISHMENT FOR MOTHER CHURCH, A FEAST FULL OF MARROW- WINE ON THE LEES, WELL REFINED.

1.) CHRISTIANS EXISTED BEFORE THE BIG BANG AND WILL EXIST AFTER THE COLLAPSE OF THIS UNIVERSE.

2.) WHAT THE BIBLE SAYS ABOUT THE COLLAPSE OF THE UNIVERSE. BOOK II.

3.) JESUS CHRIST IS LORD AND IS WORSHIPPED IN INFINITE MULTIPLE UNIVERSES THROUGHOUT INFINITY.

4.) THE HOLY BIBLE: THE REFRESHING.

5.) THE SECOND COMING OF JESUS CHRIST: THE RETURN OF THE KING.

6.) INTERGALACTIC JESUS CHRIST SUPERSTAR.

7.) AFRICA: INTERGALACTIC FEDERATION OF AFRICAN TRIBES.

11.) CHRISTIANS THERE IS NO RAPTURE OR WAR BEFORE THE SECOND COMING, YOU HAVE BEEN FOOLED BY SATAN.

12.) ARMAGEDDON IS 40 BILLION +/- YEARS FROM NOW, WWIII, AND THE LAKE OF FIRE.

10.) THE WRATH OF THE LAMB !

WORMWOOD! SATAN AND HIS DEMONS WILL BE BURNED IN THE BOTTOMLESS PIT FOR 40 BILLION +/- YEARS, THEN WWIII.

8) JESUS IS REALLY ALMIGHTY GOD

9.) SALVATION FROM THE LAKE OF FIRE AND BEING BURNED ALIVE FOREVER. JESUS IS THE SAVIOR.

A prayer from the Porter.
Our Father which art in heaven, Hallowed be thy name.
Thy kingdom come. Thy will be done in earth, as it is in heaven.
Give us this day our daily bread.
And forgive us our debts, as we forgive our debtors.
And lead us not into temptation, but deliver us from the evil ones:
For thine is the kingdom, and the power, and the glory, forever and ever.
Amen

Thou art worthy, O Lord, to receive glory and honor and power: for thou hast created all things, and for thy pleasure they are and were created.
And the God of peace shall bruise Satan under our feet shortly
Jesus Christ, Lord God, Word of God, Lamb of God, Wonderful Counselor, Almighty God, Everlasting Father, Prince of Peace, King of Glory, Mighty in battle, King of Warriors, Dreadful Sovereign,
Jesus Christ, who is the blessed and only Potentate, the King of kings, and Lord of lords,
Who only hath immortality, dwelleth in the light, which no man can approach unto; whom no man hath seen, nor can see: to whom be honour and power everlasting Amen
Jesus Christ the Lord with the flame of a devouring fire, with scattering, and tempest, and hailstones. Amen.

Lord we are grateful for all the mercy you have showed us, please protect Mom from that wicked one Satan and the evil ones his demons in these last days.

Bow thy heavens, O Lord and come down: touch the mountains, and they shall smoke.
Cast forth lightning, and scatter them: shoot out thine arrows, and destroy them.
Send thine hand from above; rid us, and deliver us out of great waters, from the hand of strange children;
Whose mouth speaketh vanity, and their right hand is a right hand of falsehood

For thou hast been a strength to the poor, a strength to the needy in his distress, a refuge from the storm, a shadow from the heat, when the blast of the terrible ones is as a storm against the wall.
Trust ye in the Lord forever : for the Lord JEHOVAH is everlasting strength
For in the day of our trouble we will call upon thee: for thou wilt answer us.
The Lord of hosts, who is wonderful in counsel, and excellent in working.

Out of Zion, the perfection of beauty, God hath shined!
Amen.

Nothing is stronger than strength, under God's control
God's timing is perfect- even in death

IT IS TIME FOR SATAN TO DIE- THE WRATH OF THE LAMB WILL DESTROY HIM AND HIS ANGELS. GOD'S TIMING IS PERFECT- EVEN IN DEATH.

THE WRATH OF THE LAMB IS HERE!

Eat and be merry Mother Church, even Einstein is on our side. He confirms the Bible, THE LAKE OF FIRE IS THE COLLAPSED
UNIVERSE. EINSTEIN AND THE CHURCH AGREE ABOUT THE COLLAPSE OF THE UNIVERSE!

Now when will WWIII occur- for the Bible says it will happen. We have to look at an important and obscure verse- II Peter 3:7.

II Peter 3:7.

II Peter 3:7- as the lake of fire the universe will burn men and not rexplode.
7. But the heavens and the earth, which are now, by the same word are kept in store, reserved unto fire against the day of judgment and perdition of ungodly men.

First Einstein pointed this out when he said the universe is going to collapse. The Bible says the universe will one day implode into itself and be destroyed. Einstein and the Bible agree.

We can also deduce from the Bible that the universe is going to collapse. That there is enough dark matter- just enough to collapse the universe but not enough for a " bounce". It will permanently lay in a state of collapse forever as the lake of fire just as Einstien predicted.

Isaiah 51:6

6. Lift up your eyes to the heavens, and look upon the earth beneath: for the heavens shall vanish away like smoke, and the earth shall wax old like a garment, and they that dwell therein shall die in like manner: but my salvation shall be for ever, and my righteousness shall not be abolished.

Psalm 102:25-27. "Of old hast thou laid the foundation of the earth: and the heavens are the work of thy hands. 26 They shall perish, but thou shalt endure: yea, all of them shall wax old like a garment; as a vesture shalt thou change them, and they shall be changed. 27: But thou art the same, and thy years shall have no end.

Mathew 24:35

35. Heaven and earth shall pass away, but my words shall not pass away.

Luke 21:33 "Heaven and earth shall pass away..."

II Peter 3:7- *as the lake of fire the universe will burn men and not rexplode.*
7. But the heavens and the earth, which are now, by the same word are kept in store, reserved unto fire against the day of judgment and perdition of ungodly men.

II Peter 3:10

10. But the day of the Lord will come as a thief in the night; in the which the heavens shall pass away with a great noise, and the elements shall melt with fervent heat, the earth also and the works that are therein shall be burned up.

II Peter 3:12

12. Looking for and hasting unto the coming of the day of God, wherein the heavens being on fire shall be dissolved, and the elements shall melt with fervent heat?

Hebrews 1:10-11. "..., AND THE HEAVENS ARE THE WORKS OF THINE HANDS: 11: THEY SHALL PERISH, BUT THOU REMAINEST; AND THEY SHALL WAX OLD AS DOTH A GARMENT."

What has the collapse of the universe have to do with the Bottomless Pit? Nothing, except it tells us that Satan and his demons once thrown into the pit at the Second Coming will not come out until the time the Universe is in blueshift or 40 billion years from now +/-, for the "Lake of fire" will exist in WWIII.

I TRULY HOPE YOU UNDERSTAND THAT EINSTEIN IS ON THE SIDE OF THE CHURCH. MOTHER CHURCH THIS IS THE TIME FOR YOUR VENGEANCE AGAINST THOSE PESKY ATHIESTS.

Eat and be merry Mother Church, even Einstein is on our side. He confirms the Bible, THE LAKE OF FIRE IS THE COLLAPSED

UNIVERSE. EINSTEIN AND THE CHURCH AGREE ABOUT THE COLLAPSE OF THE UNIVERSE!

WHEN JESUS ARRIVES HE IS GOING TO TACKLE THE GOOD FEELING, SMOOTH ROAD, PROSPERITY DOCTRINE THAT PASTORS ARE PREACHING ABOUT GOD, WHEN LIFE AND REALITY IS THE ST. JOB EXPERIENCE FOR MOST OF US. ACTUALLY WE ALL VOLUNTEERED IN THE PAST UNIVERSE, FOR WHAT HAPPENED TO US IN THIS UNIVERSE, SO WE SHOULDNT COMPLAIN. PSALM 24:4 (K.J.V)

CHAPTER EIGHT
PSALM 8 CHILDRENS BOOK

INTRODUCTION TO THE "REFRESHING"
THE RETURN OF THE KING
CREATOR OF UNIVERSES
JESUS CHRIST IS LORD
"MULTITUDES, MULTITUDES IN THE VALLEY OF DECISION

Psalm 74:13-14

13 "Thou didst divide the sea by thy strength: thou brakest the heads of the dragons in the waters. 14: Thou brakest the heads of leviathan in pieces, and gavest him to be meat to the people inhabiting the wilderness."

WRITTEN BY THE CHILD OF ISAIAH 11:8
HERALD OF THE SECOND COMING, PORTER OF JESUS.
PROPHET OF CHRIST.
 STANLEY O LOTEGELUAKi
------------------------------X------------------------------------

intro page
A book for children Ages 11-15
WHAT JESUS SAYS ABOUT THE COLLAPSE OF THE

UNIVERSE.

BY STANLEY O LOTEGELUAKI

---------------------------------x--

page i
Isaiah 28:12 "To whom He said, This is the rest wherewith ye may cause the weary to rest: and this is the "refreshing": yet they would not hear."
These books are new material for Christians and the Church of

JESUS CHRIST

-----------------------------------x--

page ii
Scientists have just sent up satelites on a balloon over the South Pole and another a physics instrument satelite platform to determine whether the universe is big enough to collapse into itself.

Most astronomers believe the universe will collapse and contract into itself, into gravitational equilibrium.

Jesus Himself and through the Holy Spirit more then seven times said the universe will one day collapse and contract into itself and be destroyed.

He said it to David. Psalm 102:25-27

25 " Of old hast thou laid the foundation of the earth: and the heavens are the work of thy hands."
26 " They shall perish, but thou shalt endure: yea, all of them shall wax old like a garment; as a vesture shalt thou change them, and they shall be changed:"
27 "But thou are the same, and thy years shall have no end."

In Isaiah 51:6 the Holy Spirit said
51:6 " Lift up your eyes to the heavens, and look upon the earth beneath: for the heavens shall vanish away like smoke, and the earth shall wax old like a garment, and they that dwell therein shall die in like manner: but My salvation shall be forever, and My righteousness shall
not be abolished."
Jesus Himself said
Mathew 24:35" Heaven and earth shall pass away, but My words shall not pass away."

---x-------------------------------------

page iii
In Mark He repeated it
Mark 13:31 " Heaven and earth shall pass a away: but My words shall not pass away."
In Luke it is recorded again.
Luke 21:33 " Heaven and earth shall pass away: but My words shall not pass away."
I Cor 7:31 "And they that use this world, as not abusing it: for the fashion of this world passeth away."
Hebrew 1:10 -12" And, Thou, Lord, in the beginning hast laid the foundation of the earth: and the heavens are the works of thine hands.
11: they shall perish: but thou remainest; and they all shall wax old as doth a garment.
12: And as a vesture shalt thou fold them up, and they shall be changed: but thou art the same, and thy years shall not fail."
II Peter 3:10 " But the day of the Lord will come as a theif in the night; in the which the heavens shall pass away with a great noise, and the elements shall melt with fervent heat, the earth also and the works that are therein shall be burned up."
II Peter 3:12 "Looking for and hasting unto the coming of the day of God, wherein the heavens being on fire shall be dissolved, and the elements shall melt with fervent heat ?"
Revelation 20:11 "And I saw a great white throne, and Him that sat on it, from whose face the earth and the heaven fled away; and there was found no place for them."

THIS IS WHAT JESUS TEACHES US ABOUT THE HISTORY

OF THE UNIVERSE
Infinite past- 100 billion BC+/-

PAST UNIVERSE

A long time ago Jesus created us- probably a 100 billion years ago.   ISN'T JESUS WONDERFUL?

This happened in the past phase or cycle of this expanding and collapsing universe.

picture: Past Universe

```
---------------------------------------------x--------------------
                                          ¹
```

40 BILLION bc+/-- 20 Billion BC+/-

CONTRACTION OF THE UNIVERSE

Then 40 billion years ago the universe went into contraction. Scientists call it the blueshift phase of the universe. Blueshift is a shift in the spectral lines of a cosmic object toward the blue end of the spectrum.

Most astronomers believe the shifts occur in cosmic objects because they are speeding toward the earth. This is when the whole universe becomes smaller and denser and collapses like a balloon. Jesus took us to heaven so we wouldn't get hurt.

picture: The contraction of the universe.

```
-----------------------x----------------------------
```

20 billion BC+/-

COLLAPSE OF THE UNIVERSE.

Then that universe collapsed into a small diameter. Scientists call that Gravitational Equilibrium, a Singularity. The Big Squeeze or the Big Crunch.

picture: The Big Squeeze.

```
-----------------------x----------------------------------
```

20 billion BC+/-

THE BIG BANG.

Then Jesus told the universe to explode again. EVEN THE UNIVERSE OBEYS JESUS. THAT IS SO GOOD TO KNOW. ISN'T JESUS POWERFUL ?

THE BIG BANG

20 billion BC+/---2000AD+/-

EXPANSION

The Bible says Genesis 1:1 " In the beginning God created the heaven and the earth."

ISAIAH 48:13" Mine hand also hath laid the foundation of the earth, and My right hand spanned the heavens; when I call unto them, they stand up together."

This universe expanded and as it expanded Jesus created Satan and his bad demons. He did this so He could fight them and show His great power. The invisible war was fought as the universe expanded, and Jesus at the Second Coming threw Satan into the Bottomless pit.

picture: The expansion of the universe

```
-----------------------------x-----------------------------------
```

40 billion AD+/-

THE STAGNATION

Then the universe   lost all of it's energy from the Big Bang and gravity started to take over. It all stopped expanding.

picture: The universe stops expanding.

40 billion AD-70 billion AD+/-

COLLAPSE OF THE UNIVERSE.

Then the universe went into blueshift. It started to contract again due to gravity. Everything started to pull itself together. " Everything" means the whole universe. During this time wwIII was fought and Jesus won again.

ISN'T JESUS POWERFUL?

picture: The universe contracts into itself.

70 billion AD+/-

SINGULARITY, GRAVITATIONAL EQUILIBRIUM,

THE LAKE OF FIRE !

Then the universe completely collapsed into itself and its core became the Lake of fire. Jesus threw Satan and all the evil demons into the Lake of fire because they were bad. But He saved us because we were good and put us in heaven, a nice place. JESUS IS SO GOOD, BECAUSE HE LOVES US. ISN'T JESUS SO WONDERFUL ?

picture: The universe completely collapses into the Lake of fire

100 billion AD+/-

JUDGMENT DAY

Then Judgment Day came. This is a wonderful time when Jesus gives us presents and rewards us for being good. But Jesus throws the bad people into the Lake of fire because they were bad. JESUS LOVES GOOD AND GOOD PEOPLE, JESUS IS A NICE PERSON.

picture: JUDGMENT DAY, the Universe as a singularity.

100 billion AD +/-

BIG BANG

After Judgment Day Jesus creates another universe for us to stay in. A whole new universe with billions and trillions of stars because He loves us. DON'T YOU LOVE JESUS ? Scientists call this the Big Bang again but good Christians call it NEW JERUSALEM.

picture: BIG BANG AGAIN

100 BILLION AD+/-----170 BILLION AD+/-

EXPANSION OF THE UNIVERSE

This universe called New Jerusalem expands and expands until it becomes a big universe for us to live in.

picture: Expansion of the Universe.

170 billion AD+/-

STAGNATION OF THE UNIVERSE.

Then New Jerusalem stops expanding and we fill it all up, after billions of years of space travel. ISN'T SPACE TRAVEL WITH JESUS SO EXCITING?

picture: The universe stops expanding.

170 billion AD-200 billion AD+/-

COLLAPSE OF THE UNIVERSE.

Then New Jerusalem contracts and collapses into itself, but we will all go to heaven to stay with Jesus so we wouldn't get hurt. JESUS LOVES US SO MUCH.

picture: COLLAPSE OF THE UNIVERSE.

200 BILLION AD-210 BILLION AD+/-

GRAVITATIONAL EQUILIBRIUM OF THE UNIVERSE.

New Jerusalem goes into gravitational equilibrium but there are no bad people to throw in it and it had never known sin. So guess what ?- Jesus uses it again.

ISN'T JESUS SO CLEVER AND POWERFUL?

picture:COLLAPSED UNIVERSE

200 BILLION AD-300 BILLION AD+/-

BIG BANG OF THE UNIVERSE

Jesus tells the universe to expand again and changes like a garment as king David said. That way we can use it again. JESUS IS SO WISE AND POWERFUL.

picture: Again, the Big Bang of the Universe

300 billion AD+/---Forever

ENDLESS CYCLE

After a while Jesus gives all the nations their separate universes from Christ's Megauniverse called The King of Glory Megauniverse.

ISN'T JESUS SO MIGHTY. HE CREATES UNIVERSES AND UNIVERSES OBEY HIM. JESUS IS SO POWERFUL!

picture: ENDLESS CYCLE

Psalm 24: 1-10

1: The earth is the Lord's and the fulness thereof; the world, and they that dwell therein.

2: For He hath founded it upon the seas, and established it upon the floods.

3: Who shall ascend into the hill of the Lord? or who shall stand in His Holy place?

4: He that hath clean hands, and a pure heart; who hath not lifted up his soul unto vanity, nor sworn deceitfully.

5: He shall receive the blessing from the Lord, and righteousness from the God of his salvation.

6: This is the generation of them that seek Him, that seek thy face, O Jacob. Se'lah.

7: Lift up your heads, O ye gates; and be ye lift up, ye everlasting doors; and the King of Glory shall come in.

8:Who is this King of Glory? The Lord Strong and Mighty, the Lord Mighty in Battlle.

9: Lift up your heads, O ye gates; even lift them up, ye everlasting doors; and the King of Glory shall come in.

10. Who is this KING OF GLORY? The LORD OF HOSTS, He is THE KING OF GLORY, Se'lah

Christianity is superior to Islam, Buddhaism, Hinduism, Communism and Science for the Bible spoke of the collapse of the universe and that the universe is closed, thousands of years ago in King David's time, Isaiah's time. Matthew, Mark, Luke, II Peter, I Cor, and Revelation all say the universe is going to collapse, but science is just finding out today by sending inquiring

satelites into space. Most astronomers believe the universe is closed and will collapse into itself. Science and the Bible agree for once proving the Bible is Truth. But then the Bible spoke of the collapse of the   universe first thousands of years ago before science.

READ THE "REFRESHING" TO UNDERSTAND THE FULL MESSAGE THIS MESSENGER OF ISAIAH 14 HAS REVEALED FROM THE GREAT GOD OF
     ISRAEL

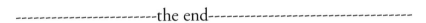

-----------------------the end-------------------------------

Psalm 8

1: O Lord our Lord, how excellent is thy name in all the earth ! Who hast set thy glory above the heavens.

2: Out of the mouth of babes and sucklings hast thou ordained strength because of thine enemies, that thou mightest still the enemy and the avenger.

3: When I consider thy heavens, the work of thy fingers, the moon and the stars, which thou hast ordained;

4: What is man, that thou art mindful of him? and the son of man, that thou vistest him?

5: For thou hast made him a little lower than the angels, and hast crowned him with glory and honour.

6: Thou madest him to have dominion over the works of thy hands; thou hast put all things under his feet:

7: All sheep and oxen, yea, and the beasts of the field;

8: The fowl of the air, and the fish of the sea, and whatsoever passeth through the paths of the seas.

9: O Lord our Lord, how excellent is thy name in all the earth !

----------------------x----------------------------

Jesus is God. He can be in more then one place at once. He is in us and He is in the alien Christians. Christs body can appear in different places at the same time, like when He visits different families in multiple universes at the same time and still remain on His throne in heaven and also in Jerusalem. He is worshipped througout infinity. So worship Him in the spirit like all alien Christians do O human race. We will be one with the cosmos praising Jesus.

Mystery of God

(1) A long, long, long time ago in the infinite past there was God the Father, Jesus the Son and the Holy Spirit. They had no beginning, they always existed.

(2) God says idleness is a sin. So He and His Son have been creating other creatures other then human beings in the infinite past. They have created infinite universes with infinite creatures in them. Today there are infinite universes and infinite creatures beside the human race.

(3) A 100 billion years ago God decided to create the human race. First He created the Angels, then after a few billion years He created mankind.

(4) Israel was the first human nation created, then the other nations were created to serve the footstool. Israel is composed of nothing but priests. But all the other nations are the Levite's and were created to have fun, but with a little work to support the Church and Israel.

(5) We had fun in the Kingdom of the King of Glory for billions of years.

(6) Then about 40 billion years ago Jesus asked us if we wanted to go to war. We did not know what it was, but He explained it as Good VS Evil, Flesh VS Spirit, Light VS Darkness, Truth VS Lies, Love VS hate, Christians VS NonChristians, Jesus VS Satan. It was called the Invisible War.

(7) That day was called The Great Volunteering, and we all volunteered to come to this universe and Earth to fight Dragons, Wolves and Lions or Satan, demons, and goats. We were brave Sheep.

(8) That universe went into blue shift and we all escaped to heaven.

(9) Then God created these heavens and earth. Thus Genesis 1:1. The Big Bang

(10) The heavens and the earth were in beautiful shape .

(11) Then God created Lucifer and his angels. There was nothing wrong with them then.

(12) Then God mixed our good Angels who were created before the Big Bang with Lucifer and his angels who were created after the Big Bang.

(13) For a while there was happiness and good times and St. Job records it.

(14) Then Lucifer began to sin, he started to wheel and deal so much that he started to use violence against the other Angels for their things.

(15) Then God fired Lucifer- it is all recorded in Ezekiel chpt 28.

(16) Lucifer instead of repenting started to fight God and he lied to the other angels to get them to fight God and be on his side. It is recorded in Ezekiel Chpt 28

(17) Heaven and Earth became full of lies, darkness and chaos. Verse 2 Chpt 1 of Genesis records it.

(18) Then God said " Let there be Light". And Jesus the "Light" appeared and started to rally all the good Truthful Angels to God. Verse 3 Genesis Chpt 1 records it.

(19) Then God divided the good Angels from the bad angels. He divided the Light Angels from the Dark Angels. Genesis Chpt 1:4

(20) The Morning fought evening the very first day. Jesus fought Satan the very first day.

(21) Then God put a barrier between the politics "waters" of heaven and the politics "waters" of the earth. That's why you cant go there unless you die and you cant come back once your there.

(22) Then God worked on the Earth

(23) The earth was covered by water

(24) Animals came from the waters- fished walked

(25) Dinosaurs existed, but God killed them off because God was creating this earth for mankind. I think God wanted us to use that entire era for plastics and oil.

(26) Mankind was created in Genesis 1:26-31

(27) Adam was created in Genesis 2:7

(28) The Bible says it took " Generations" to create the heavens and the earth. Genesis 2:4

(29) Adam's spirit came down from the pool of Christians in heaven. The monkey body was created here on earth.

(30) Adam and Eve walked into the garden in the Middle East.

(31) Adam and Eve had navels.

(32) Adam and Eve had Mothers, Brothers and Fathers and Sisters

(33) The Invisible war went on when Satan tempted Eve and the fall of Man

(34) Jesus the Lord God cursed Adam and Lucifer and Eve.

(35) Jesus said a Child of Eve would save Adam one day- meaning at the cross of Calvary.

(36) Cain was created from below.

(37) Cain killed his brother and blurted out the secret that there were other people besides the family on earth. That those outside communities would kill him for being a murderer.

(38) Satan and his demons were people in those days and they went up to heaven and earth at will. They had sex with human beings and great men were born unto them.

(39) God brought the flood to kill off Satans seed

(40) The flood only covered the Middle East.

(41) Noah set the political agenda for the human race.

(42) Melchizedec was Jesus Christ and He ruled Salem.

(43) Jesus was born from God with Mary and the seed and sin of Adam passed down to all men was not in Him because He was born from a virgin.

(44) Jesus said He existed before the foundation of the earth in John 17:5, 24. This makes my doctrine correct.

(45) The Tribulation was for the last 2000 years

(46) St. Paul had a "frog" demon in him .(II COR 12:7, GALATIANS 4:14) I have three "frog" demons in me. The false Prophet in 40 billion Ad will have one "frog" demon in him.

(47) The Second Coming has already started.

(48) The Carcase and Jesus destroyed the U.S.S.R. by spooking Satan.

(49) Jesus will lift Mt. Shasta or now called. Mt. Jesus Christ is Lord.

(50) Mt. Jesus Christ is Lord is noted in Rev 8:8; it will go all the way to China.* (changed but credited)

(51) The sixth seal was opened on Dec 25, 2004 with the tsunami.

(52) Jesus will come back in my lifetime.

(56) Satan will be thrown into hell and he will enter it for the first time.

(54) The people in hell beat Satan up and threw him out,.

(55) Satan is thrown into the Bottomless Pit for 1000 years.

(56) The 1000 Christ years is 40 billion human years.

(57) The bad people 2.3 billion will die and be put in hell for 40 billion years.

(58) The human race will go out and conquer space- or this universe for 40 billion years.

(59) Africa or greater Kush has been given 10 billion galaxies in this universe.

(60) Other nations will have to petition Christ.

(61) READ PSALM 72

(62) After the 1000 years Satan and his demons and the goats will be released again.

(63) Chpt 13 Revelation to 20 kicks in and there will be war.

(64) After the War Satan will be thrown into the collapsing universe called the Lake of fire.

(65) We will all go to 2000AD+/- to welcome Jesus at the Second Coming.

(66) The universe collapses 70-100 billion AD

(67) Judgement day

(68) The nations are given Universes to live in-billions of them- trillions of them.

(69) After about 300 billion Ad we will meet all the other creatures God had created- infinite of them all who worship Jesus. We will be a speck of an atom in the ocean of infinity praising and worshipping Jesus.

(70) That is the Mystery of God.

As for me all I have to say about me was I was a warrior, the very gunho of the 82nd Airborne, my goal in life was to become a mercenary in Cambodia then after a two year hitch a soldier of SWAPO.

For life. Fighting was in my blood and I consider myself the very best. My long term goal was to unite Africa into one nation or die trying. My mother Africa had borne me and had called me to battle. Unknowing to me I had another Mother. Mother Church the bride of Christ and it is she who would claim my life in the end. As if it was nothing The God of Israel also made me Melek, (prophet and Messenger of Isaiah and of Kush) just for serving Him against Satan, the Beast and their frog demons. In Mathew 24:28 the two Eagles are Jesus and the eagle Satan.

Iam the dead body that they fought over, dead to the world of Satan as Paul preached in Romans.

Matthew 24:28 " For wheresoever the carcase is, there will the eagles be gathered together"

Magnificent Eagle Jesus

As an Eagle protects her young

So does the Lord protect me.

He teaches me how to fly

Until my wings become strong

Over the battlefield I hover

To drink the blood of the slain

Armageddon is history

The Carcase I remain.

The Lord is mighty in Battle.

Magnificent Eagle is His name.

Jesus in shining armor

O Jesus Christ, with thy sword and thy
Shield, thou hast slayed the dragon.
And saved a Damsel in distress,
The Queen, the Church your love
O Dragonslayer, thou hast slain the Beast
And released endless captives, our pitiful souls.
Jesus Christ Mighty in Battle, Lord God
Word of God, Lamb of God, King of Glory
King of Warriors, Dreadful Sovereign
We pray Lord You who have slain the dragon,
Killed the Beast and saved us from hordes of demons,
Protect us and rule over us O Everlasting Father
For only thou art worthy.

A soldier's prayer- What St. Michael said after destroying the devil.
O God of war, Battleaxe of Israel
Jesus Christ, King of Glory
Mighty in Battle.
In the day of my trouble,
I will call upon thee,
For thou shalt answer me.
O God of Lightening, God of Thunder
Mighty in Battle, Magnificent Eagle
I ve put my Life in Your hands.
Let my blade cut them, Let my
Spear pierce deep, Let Your Word
Destroy the hordes of Satan, demons
And scorpions, underfoot they fall,
From Your all destroying Holy Spirit.
In battle I stand, covered in demon blood.
At last I stand, alone alive, my foes lay dead,
Thank You
My love, my God of war, JESUS CHRIST
KING OF GLORY, MIGHTY IN BATTLE.!

Psalms 110

1. The Lord said unto my Lord, Sit thou at my right hand, until I make thine enemies thy footstool.
2. The Lord shall send the rod of thy strength out of Zion: rule thou in the midst of thine enemies.
3. Thy people shall be willing in the day of thy power, in the beauties of holiness from the womb of the morning: thou hast the dew of thy youth.

4. The Lord hath sworn, and will not repent, Thou art a priest for ever after the order of Melchizedek.
5. The Lord at thy right hand shall strike through kings in the day of his wrath.
6. He shall judge among the heathen, he shall fill the places with the dead bodies; he shall wound the heads over many countries.
7. He shall drink of the brook in the way: therefore shall he lift up the head.

Psalms 24

1. The earth is the Lord's, and the fulness thereof; the world, and they that dwell therein.
2. For he hath founded it upon the seas, and established it upon the floods.
3. Who shall ascend into the hill of the Lord? or who shall stand in his holy place?
4. He that hath clean hands, and a pure heart; who hath not lifted up his soul unto vanity, nor sworn deceitfully.
5. He shall receive the blessing from the Lord, and righteousness from the God of his salvation.
6. This is the generation of them that seek him, that seek thy face, O Jacob. Selah.
7. Lift up your heads, O ye gates; and be ye lift up, ye everlasting doors; and the King of glory shall come in.
8. Who is this King of glory? The Lord strong and mighty, the Lord mighty in battle.
9. Lift up your heads, O ye gates; even lift them up, ye everlasting doors; and the King of glory shall come in.
10. Who is this King of glory? The Lord of hosts, he is the King of glory. Selah.

THY3 SHALL8 SERVE13 THEE17 SWEET22 JESUS27
3,8,13,17,22-(27) JACKPOT.
THANK YOU JESUS.
THE END.

Isaiah 5:26-30

26. And he will lift up an ensign to the nations from far, and will hiss unto them from the end of the earth: and, behold, they shall come with speed swiftly:
27. None shall be weary nor stumble among them; none shall slumber nor sleep; neither shall the girdle of their loins be loosed, nor the latchet of their shoes be broken:
28. Whose arrows are sharp, and all their bows bent, their horses' hoofs shall be counted like flint, and their wheels like a whirlwind:
29. Their roaring shall be like a lion, they shall roar like young lions: yea, they shall roar, and lay hold of the prey, and shall carry it away safe, and none shall deliver it.
30. And in that day they shall roar against them like the roaring of the sea: and if one look unto the land, behold darkness and sorrow, and the light is darkened in the heavens thereof.

Isaiah 34

1. Come near, ye nations, to hear; and hearken, ye people: let the earth hear, and all that is therein; the world, and all things that come forth of it.
2. For the indignation of the Lord is upon all nations, and his fury upon all their armies: he hath utterly destroyed them, he hath delivered them to the slaughter.
3. Their slain also shall be cast out, and their stink shall come up out of their carcases, and the mountains shall be melted with their blood.
4. And all the host of heaven shall be dissolved, and the heavens shall be rolled together as a scroll: and all their host shall fall down, as the leaf falleth off from the vine, and as a falling fig from the fig tree.
5. For my sword shall be bathed in heaven: behold, it shall come down upon Idumea, and upon the people of my curse, to judgment.
6. The sword of the Lord is filled with blood, it is made fat with fatness, and with the blood of lambs and goats, with the fat of the kidneys of rams: for the Lord hath a sacrifice in Bozrah, and a great slaughter in the land of Idumea.
7. And the unicorns shall come down with them, and the bullocks with the bulls; and their land shall be soaked with blood, and their dust made fat with fatness.
8. For it is the day of the Lord's vengeance, and the year of recompences for the controversy of Zion.